Separate Societies

IN THE SERIES

Conflicts in Urban and Regional Development
edited by John R. Logan and Todd Swanstrom

Separate Societies

Poverty and Inequality in U.S. Cities

William W. Goldsmith
and Edward J. Blakely

FOREWORD BY HARVEY GANTT

TEMPLE UNIVERSITY PRESS
Philadelphia

Temple University Press, Philadelphia 19122

Published 1992
Printed in the United States of America

The paper used in this publication meets the minimum requirements of American National Standard for Information Sciences—Permanence of Paper for Printed Library Materials, ANSI Z39.48-1984

Library of Congress Cataloging-in-Publication Data
Goldsmith, William W.
Separate societies : poverty and inequality in U.S. cities / William W. Goldsmith and Edward J. Blakely ; foreword by Harvey Gantt.
p. cm. — (Conflicts in urban and regional development)
Includes bibliographical references and index.
ISBN 0-87722-932-5 (alk. paper). — ISBN 0-87722-933-3 (pbk. : alk. paper)
1. Urban poor—United States. 2. Inner cities—United States. 3. Urban renewal—United States. 4. Regional planning—United States. 5. United States—Social policy—1980– .
I. Blakely, Edward James, 1938– . II. Title. III. Series.
HV4045.G65 1992
362.5'0973'091734–dc20 91-33128

TO OUR PARENTS

who told us our country should be fair

Contents

List of Figures and Tables

Figures

Tables

Foreword

BY HARVEY GANTT

I have always refused to believe that people can be confined to any permanent status in America. There is no permanent poverty, permanent joblessness, permanent hopelessness—not "in the land of the free and home of the brave." So to that end, I have pressed the limits. As a boy I participated in the great civil rights movement—and was arrested in a sit-in demonstration. My inclination toward a "nontraditional" career in architecture and insistence on being educated in my home state of South Carolina (even if it meant breaking down the racial barrier) was a reflection of these beliefs.

Beyond personal advancement these beliefs were manifested in a broader sense. The programs of the "New Frontier" and the "Great Society" intrigued me. I became involved as a city planner in housing programs in Roxbury, Massachusetts, jobs programs in Charlotte, new town building in rural eastern North Carolina—all part of working to make the promise of America real to average folks. Finally, that work led to elective office—curiously, at a time when government generosity toward urban and poor communities was beginning to dry up. And yet even in the lean Reagan years as mayor of Charlotte, I along with others sought to make a difference, scraping together funds to continue housing programs, to continue jobs programs, to continue community development.

Let us look at the present state of domestic affairs. As the compelling statistics presented by William W. Goldsmith and

Edward J. Blakely show, while perhaps 80 percent of us in America are doing fairly well and see some promise for the future, we must all be troubled by the other 20 percent of us who are beginning to show signs of having little hope that the promise of America can be made real.

And even among those 80 percent, most of whom are salt-of-the-earth working folk, many hold tenuously to jobs that may soon be shipped overseas, or fear rising health care cuts with diminishing health insurance benefits, or use a public education system that may not meet the needs of the job market in the year 2000.

The concern for those at the bottom has been waning, reflected in the neglectful public policy of the last eleven years at most levels of the government. The 1990 Census showed widening gaps between the rich and poor. Goldsmith and Blakely explain how that happened. And the Census showed that the growth in poverty has become even more substantial and intractable in urban America than in rural America.

The problems of ignorance, drugs, AIDS, crime, violence, and teenage pregnancy are beginning to manifest themselves in a kind of nihilistic destruction in the ghetto that is reflective of lost hope, low self-esteem, and the breakdown of family and community.

Somewhere along the line, we are all to blame for the state of things, even those of us who seem to "do good" by working as planners in the big urban centers, or in state and federal offices. We worked to build the great transportation networks that facilitated the explosion of suburbia and the resultant physical, social, and political isolation from central-city problems. We helped to facilitate the growth of new activity nodes and regional shopping malls in metropolitan areas that produced the ultimate decline in the quality of central business districts nationwide. We helped substantially with urban renewal clearance programs and public housing reservations that solidified the physical isolation of the poor. But probably most telling is that even when looking back on the "good" programs in the 1960s and 1970s—good housing programs, neighborhood programs, jobs programs—it is difficult for us to find the success stories today.

Two years ago I revisited one of my projects, one that I had worked on in Roxbury almost twenty years ago. I was disheartened at the lack of real progress. We have not come as far as we would like to think we have. And the truth is that with all the liberal and conservative efforts of the past twenty-five years, progress for minorities—and just plain average folk—has been small and discouraging.

So there are challenges that await those of us who are planners, activists, and social engineers, just as there are challenges for the nation. The immediate challenge is to join others to help focus the nation on a meaningful domestic agenda that will address the needs of the working American and the critical needs of urban America. Do not allow this agenda to be the domestic agenda of Jesse Helms or David Duke. Do not allow this agenda to be cluttered with false issues like reverse discrimination or racial quotas.

Support candidates in your communities who understand the importance of reducing racism and promoting education, community development, and job training. Get excited about educational policy and the restructuring of education to help poor youngsters. Early childhood education may be the key initiative that needs immediate attention.

As an intermediate challenge, I urge you to dedicate your professional skills, whatever they may be, toward ending the social and political isolation of urban centers. We have helped cities explode; now I believe we have to find ways to knit cities and suburbs back together. A declining tax base in the center city must be reversed. Somehow those in the suburbs and state legislatures must see this as a cancer that affects us all. What we need now are courageous, articulate leaders who see the bigger picture and want to define new relationships and new structures to deliver service. We need more spokespersons from the inner cities of America, running for public office on a larger political stage, building broader coalitions. Finally, I want to challenge minority professionals especially to engage in these struggles in the places where they grew up or in similar places where they now live. No matter what our professional careers are, we all need to go home to be role models and mentors to a lot of young people who have been victimized by the policies of the last twenty-five years.

Harvey Gantt ran for the U.S. Senate from North Carolina in 1990, making history as the first African-American Senate nominee from the Democratic party. He was mayor of Charlotte for two terms in the 1980s. He is an architect and city planner, holding degrees in architecture from Clemson University (their first African-American student) and in city planning from the Massachusetts Institute of Technology. A slightly modified version of this foreword was presented as a speech to the Division of Black Planners at the 1991 Convention of the American Planning Association.

Acknowledgments

This book was written in close collaboration with Lisa Bornstein, Elizabeth Mueller, and David Campt, who wrote early drafts of much of the book. The five of us spent 1988–89 discussing these matters, collecting information, analyzing statistics, and debating. Since then, the principal authors have rethought the book's arguments, debated them with others, rearranged chapters, collected new information, and redrafted. Our debt to the other three is very great, as will become apparent as their own work appears in print over the years.

We thank three other groups of people. In the first group are scholars who have laid the foundations. Among the many excellent studies that told about urban poverty in the 1980s, five defined the high ground: Bennett Harrison and Barry Bluestone's *Great U-Turn,* Thomas Boston's *Race, Class, and Conservatism,* David Ellwood's *Poor Support,* Michael Katz's *Undeserving Poor,* and William Julius Wilson's *Truly Disadvantaged.* Of the many studies that focus on progressive city politics, three have been particularly helpful: John Mollenkopf's *Contested City,* Pierre Clavel's *Progressive City,* and John Logan and Todd Swanstrom's *Beyond the City Limits.* The many others who have compiled statistics, undertaken studies, and written about poverty and urban affairs cannot be acknowledged here, but dozens who deserve our thanks appear in the notes and the bibliography.

Second, we thank colleagues who have directly helped our thinking. A group of people debated these ideas in a seminar in Berkeley in 1989. Without their arguments, as well as their written works, this book would be very different. We are grateful to Angela Blackwell, Ed Church, Pierre Clavel, Robert Giloth, Eugene Grigsby, Marie Kennedy, Norman Krumholz, Jackie Leavitt, Robert Mier, Julia Quiroz, Derek Shearer, and Margaret Wilder. The idea for this book grew from discussions with James Gibson and Erol Ricketts. Several colleagues read drafts and made suggestions: Pierre Clavel on the central themes; Damaris Rose on Chapters 1 and 2; and Susan Christopherson, Matthew Drennan, and Thomas Vietorisz on Chapters 3 and 4. John Forester suggested collecting new information for Chapter 5. We thank all these people very much, but we are sure not all their good ideas have survived our drafts.

Third, we thank those who helped with the data collection, bibliography, analysis, and production. In addition to the work done by Bornstein, Campt, and Mueller, at Berkeley Susan Sullivan helped with research and George Washington prepared figures. At Cornell Gwen Urey collected and analyzed data, proofread and edited, and prepared all the final figures; she and Eveline Ferretti prepared the final bibliography; Kathy Seeburger conducted telephone interviews, and for brief periods Robert Letcher, Sharon Lord, and Marayam Muhammad assisted. Gwen Urey prepared the index. Reference librarians at Cornell's Olin Library were extremely helpful. David Van Arnam, Demetra Dentes, Cathy Girardeau, Nancy Hutter, and Arleda Martinez helped with typing and copying.

The Rockefeller Foundation's Equal Opportunity Division provided generous financial support.

Separate Societies

Chapter 1

Separate Status: Top-Down Economics and Bottom-Up Politics

Everyone knows something about concentrated urban poverty. A new mini-industry advertises it. Television programs, news items, editorials, and magazine articles display its ravages. Scholars write of "persistent" poverty, the "underclass," or the "new" poor, trying to understand why poverty is so severe in the ghetto and the barrio. Although these labels have served us well by helping to awaken a new interest in the problems of the urban poor, we fear they are too easy to misunderstand and misuse. We have learned a great deal from the new generation of studies that accompanied the growth of urban poverty in the 1980s. Now, we want to go in a slightly different direction, to focus on a set of unsolved and unanswered questions.

We take a broader view, observing that national industry, the domestic economy, and politics are entangled in a new and debilitating international web. Global-scale social and technical transitions are combining with new domestic politics to reverse long-term national trends. For nearly 50 years the nation committed itself to reduce poverty, equalize resource distribution, and augment the middle class. These improvements, incomplete though they were, have been reversed. Economic and political forces no longer combat poverty—they generate poverty!

From this broader perspective we see a poverty with several dimensions, which we try to capture in a single word: *separation*. Separation encompasses ideas of social segmentation, economic inequality, and sharp geographic isolation. We see separation not just as a matter of degree, but of kind, a process like the melting pot in reverse. It is like phase transition or symmetry-breaking in physics. Much change can be absorbed before alteration of form. As water gets colder, it changes only its temperature. Suddenly, the homogeneous substance gets too cold, and some of the water turns into ice. American society is like water just above the freezing point, dangerously close to dissociating into separate parts.

We find it unsettling how often Americans (and we include ourselves) unconsciously allow the use of segmentation, inequality, and isolation to hide poor people, objectify them, and rationalize their condition. As the poor are separated, they become more distant from the nonpoor. This distance itself naturally makes inequality more palatable to those who are better off, and the separation increases.

Perhaps more than ever before, in the last decades of the twentieth century Americans have found this separation to be pushed on them by the force of events. As their leaders attempt to promote competition in an ever more globalized economy, they find it convenient to ignore at least this one set of domestic concerns. New separation and political use of differences in race, social background, and place become the unavoidable consequences of new competition. In turn, these practices then build upon discrimination against the poor and minority persons in offers of employment, the assignment of status, and the distribution of income. They also encourage discriminatory provision of housing, public services, and neighborhood quality. These various inequalities then further extend the separations. As Cleveland mayor Michael White suggests, the majority in America want to leave the city behind: "Big cities are becoming a code name for a lot of things:

for minorities, for crumbling neighborhoods, for crime, for everything that America has moved away from."[1]

In his antiutopian novel *Player Piano*, Kurt Vonnegut imagines an America divided. At the top, a tiny group of managers, engineers, and technocrats use their brains and positions to guide the future and protect their country club privileges. At the bottom, a repressive army accompanies the underclass of Reeks and Wrecks who do the dirty, dull, and unskilled work, or just hang around, unemployed, drinking, miserable. H. G. Wells predicted an even sharper class division in *The Time Machine*, with the underground vestiges of the English working class devouring the above-ground vestiges of their rulers. Is it possible that exaggerated inequalities be a prominent component of our future? Is America beginning to retreat, to divide in two? Are we eroding the middle-class gains of a half-century, tearing up the foundations of the future? Evidence about the depth of division rending the middle class is worrisome. At the bottom of the social class structure the evidence of debilitating poverty and isolation is conclusive.

We see dichotomies everywhere in American society. Corporations build magnificent office towers where they manage worldwide networks of factories, offices, and high finance. These global headquarters rise above the latest "public" squares, the enclosed, air-conditioned, privately owned atriums. In adjacent neighborhoods, there are families in welfare hotels and homeless people on the streets. In 1988, top officers of the largest corporations took home paychecks averaging $2 million, up 14 percent from the year before. The best paid manager, who sat atop Disney Enterprises, "earned" about $40 million.[2] Meanwhile, the average wage paid to working Americans continued to fall. Even global corporations pay low salaries to many of their American workers. Both inside and outside the corporate sector are problems of unemployment, low-wage work, and dependency that afflict people who live in poor, minority neighborhoods.

Against the temporary advantages, such as the ability to better manage global economic matters by ignoring domestic needs, the long-run costs of these separations are enormous. We believe these costs are already reflected in the lack of capacity to build agreement for dealing with a series of important national issues. In fact, high rates of poverty and increasing separation are themselves becoming drags on American competitiveness. To see why, we first need to understand the origins of poverty.

Theories of Poverty

Poverty in modern societies is a complex phenomenon. Thus it can be discussed most advantageously after some agreement on meanings.[3] We find it useful to distinguish among three usually competing, sometimes overlapping concepts of poverty. These concepts focus attention on the behavior of the poor, or liberal public policy, or economic structure. In other words, they call attention to an individual's personal problems, or temporary circumstances that may be corrected by public assistance, or flaws in basic structure and politics.

Poverty as Pathology

Some theorists view poverty as pathology. Poor people are said to suffer from the defects of their own (pathological) activity.[4] Policymakers and others who subscribe to this behavioral view concentrate on psychological and motivational inadequacies. They sometimes argue that poverty is increasing because a permissive welfare state has generated a large group of nonparticipants, marginal people, bums. The original, often more generous and sympathetic conceptualization of these ideas referred to a "culture of poverty." Originating in anthropology, the notion was aimed at the complexities of modernization and urbanization in the Third World. Social scientists claimed that family poverty was persistent because wrong values and attitudes were passed on by parents and communities to new generations.[5] Although subsequent researchers refuted these ideas, they have been reused recently by more conservative policy analysts in advanced industrial countries in superficial ways, disconnecting the plight of the poor not only from the responsibilities of others, but also from the impediments of their situation. At worst, these ideas can be used to justify expressions of racism, sexism, and individualism, offering little to counteract the ethnocentric, reactionary logic of the street: "Lower-class blacks lacked industry, lived for momentary erotic pleasure, and, in their mystique of soul, glorified the fashions of a high-stepping street life."[6]

The notion of the culture of poverty and its suggestion that the poor are irrational (and therefore to blame for their own problems) have been outmoded by excellent formal studies and criticism. Here there are convincing arguments that put the blame for poverty on social structure, situation, and lack of opportunity.[7] A tradition in fiction testifies to the obstacles imposed on rational and well-organized poor people by those who subscribe to demeaning stereotypes. James Baldwin, for example, leads us to imagine how New York's police and courts entrap and then condemn an innocent young sculptor. Fony's dilemma in *If Beale Street Could Talk* is that in spite of his talent, honesty, and enterprise he cannot escape the punishment inflicted by those who adopt the negative stereotype of the young black man. We find the story repeated over and over by perceptive writers, and we find it verified by research.

One of the obstacles to undoing these stereotypes is that oppressed or unfortunate people positioned at the bottom, where society itself is most unfair, will sometimes behave in ways that appear to be self-destructive because they have no other choice. In the extreme, as Jonathan Kozol argues in *Rachel and Her Children*, many of them (the homeless in this case) begin to believe they are worthless because that is how they are treated. The underlying reality is very different. They are not worthless, and most often their behavior is reasonable, given the limited range of accessible options, their restricted backgrounds and skills, and the dangers inherent in experimentation, such as seeking new and distant jobs.[8]

Elements associated with this notion of a culture of poverty do still play a role, of course, in theory as well as reality. Assistance must be provided; people whose "adaptive" behavior increases their (and others') difficulties need help to move into the mainstream. Drug addiction and alcoholism, for example, cannot be controlled without behavior modification (but these problems are not confined to the poor). Whatever its utility in particular cases, however, this sort of behavioral approach is not a fruitful path for discussion. As we argue below, it will be more useful for us to examine ways to change the situation, not to change people's attitudes. We agree with William Julius Wilson that we should not "postulate that ghetto-specific practices become internalized, take on a life of their own, and therefore continue to influence behavior even if opportunities for mobility improve." We believe that more equal access to better jobs and other improvements in the structure of equality would cut down on counterproductive behaviors and "would also make their transmission by precept less efficient."[9] Lawrence Mead addresses the suspicion that poor people are lazy:

> The poor accept work along with other mainstream social norms. . . . [T]hey do not contest work in principle. They are not radicals seeking social change. There is simply a larger gap between their professed norms and actual behavior than there is for most people. The inclination to avoid demeaning labor is hardly confined to the disadvantaged.[10]

Poverty as Incident or Accident

The second view of poverty, also quite common, is to understand poverty as incident or accident. Those who hold this view think the growing problems of the poor are caused largely by cutbacks in national and local resources devoted to the promotion of social equity.

Throughout much U.S. history, certainly from the end of World War II until the 1970s, it was not unreasonable to envision rising tides, lifted boats, and an ample supply of lifesavers or safety nets to rescue those "accidentally" thrown overboard—those with very poor skills, those disabled because of illness or accident, those in declining rural areas, and a few in inner-city neighborhoods. Optimism and increasing affluence were accompanied by a social and political sense of responsibility, kept current by the demands of the struggling poor, unions, neighborhoods, and, sometimes, by aggrieved victims of racial and ethnic discrimination. In a continuation of the tendency toward social democracy from the 1930s, interrupted only temporarily by the reactionary anticommunism of the late 1940s and 1950s, what is often called the American social contract provided transfer payments, gradual expansion of entitlements, and the elaboration of public services and protections. These programs were generally effective in dealing with the problems of the elderly or of married couples or families who were socially or physically isolated. They limited (but did not eliminate) poverty, led to expectations of further improvement, and were even accompanied by some caps on extravagance, such as progressive taxation. Poverty still existed, but it was less onerous and was perceived as temporary. The opportunity structure was seen to be strong enough to allow all those who tried, to move into decent, rewarding life conditions.

Exponents of this view tend to think poverty is easily, rather mechanically remedied, by means of public programs that provide short-term relief. In the 1980s, sad to say, the evidence supporting this view has been mostly negative, in good part because of the political difficulties of funding and maintaining such programs. As the economy has restructured and the nature of public policy has changed to fit global challenges, public transfer programs have worked less well. For example, New York State's Work Incentive program (WIN), aimed at welfare mothers, has helped very few women move into stable employment.[11] There are hardly any examples of successful programs, other than disability payments or unemployment benefits, and even these are now under threat. The chief illustration of success is the long-term, large-scale reduction in poverty among the elderly that has resulted from Social Security pensions and Medicare benefits.

No doubt this liberal, macrosocial view must be taken into account, in which poverty simply reflects temporary weakness in the economy, to be corrected by (also temporary) public generosity. It is based on the correct observation that a strong demand for labor, to create numerous and well-paid jobs, is a necessary basic factor in any fight against poverty. It recognizes the importance of generous unemployment insurance and health and retirement benefits. Unfortunately, many factors in the U.S. industrial response to a globalized economy mitigate against full American economic recovery and a persistent and strong demand for labor. This problem leads us to advocate a contemporary battle to be waged simultaneously for a better economic policy and against poverty and the growing isolation of impoverished communities.

Poverty as Structure

In the third and most comprehensive view, observers see poverty as structure.[12] In this view, to which we subscribe (with important reservations to be explained below), certain patterns of large-scale socioeconomic arrangements, as well as change, create poverty and prevent its alleviation. Some arrangements create more poverty than others, and developments in the United States have moved in this direction. Students of the international economy mark the beginnings of a new era for the United States with the advent of an intensified global capitalism, beginning as early as the mid- to late 1960s. The most generally accepted date for marking the change is 1973 or 1974, after the first global oil price shock—when a new world economic pattern took hold. The effects of these changes were unmistakable by the late 1970s, as global difficulties led the Carter administration to cut back on urban aid.

Perhaps the most striking feature in the minds of many Americans is the fact that since then the federal government has been unwilling to exercise clear and independent influence over the domestic economy. Part of this reluctance stems from difficulty. For example, it has become more difficult for the Treasury and Federal Reserve to use Keynesian fiscal and monetary tools to control inflation, unemployment, and interest rates simultaneously. The old relationships no longer hold—largely because the United States is now much more integrated into a global economy, with numerous powerful nations therefore participating indirectly in the domestic economy. By remote control foreign corporations or central banks can manipulate U.S. economic forces in much the same way (although with much less influence) that U.S. multinational corporations, the Treasury, and the Federal Reserve System have for many years manipulated Third-World economies. Part of the balance of power now lies with foreign markets, corporations, banks, and governments, as well as U.S.-based corporations themselves operating overseas.

This globalization of the American economy has forced massive changes in the industrial structure of U.S. cities, reinforced by federal policy and only weakly resisted by local politics. Patterns of international migration have changed, and so have labor markets. With few exceptions, minority populations in central cities are now more than ever victims of poverty, marginalized and exploited, pushed aside or employed at low wages. Rising credentialism excludes those without formal education and training from good jobs. An uneven and undependable labor demand has always threatened the poor, but the global changes of recent years have made the market even less forgiving.[13]

In today's difficult world, poverty is defined in terms of a growing group of racially distinct Americans who are socially disconnected from the greater society, educationally handicapped, and institutionally victimized not only by labor markets but by the social-welfare and penal systems. Severe poverty is seen to be built into the economic and political structure, generated by three inter-related forces. The first is a set of long-term, intergenerational disconnections from the mainstream society, mainly through lack of employment, which result in physical, social, and political isolation. The second force arises from educational and social handicaps that prevent the poor and nearly poor from entering the transformed high-tech, high-touch workforce, where skills and personal presentation are both important. The third force is institutional hostility of the welfare systems, penal institutions, and related bureaucracies that make the poor the victims and dependents of public charity rather than participants in generating resources for themselves or their families. All three forces are reinforced by changes in national policies in response to international economic pressures. In these changed circumstances of a rising and desperate poverty, residual assistance has become insufficient and inappropriate.

Local Institutions

These pessimistic, structuralist views can be painted into the background only if we can justify a positive, more optimistic option, which is why we have written this book. Even though separation and rising poverty now lead to political incapacity, they also signify a positive potential. We see pressures to reduce separation, inequality, and poverty as key parts of a new vision and strategy to deal with rising global competition. In this view, policies to restructure the economy and policies to reduce poverty should work hand in hand.

We believe, in fact, that the recent upsurge in urban poverty has been generated not simply by transformations in the structure of the global and domestic economies, but by a particular set of American political responses, which have also helped guide these transformations. These responses are not always conscious, but neither are they inevitable, forced by autonomous events. They are rooted in history, economics, and politics, to be sure, but they are choices nonetheless.

When the squeeze came from the global economy, public institutions were unprepared to relieve the inevitable difficulties confronting the poor. Corporate redeployment and government economizing insured that city labor markets would shrink, especially for basic jobs. The federal government cut funds for cities and poor people, and reduced guarantees for benefits and services. The budget reductions hit public jobs and services in central cities the hardest. The tax revolt was managed by a new politics that coalesced after thirty-five years of white, middle-class suburbanization. In the scramble to survive lowered incomes and the neighborhood decay that came after shutdowns, contractions, layoffs, and budget cuts, those with enough money or power tried to get out of the city and get ahead. Those with less were left behind and increasingly separated physically, occupationally, and socially from the main society.

It is our argument that politics and economics can be reshaped, not only to respond more positively to worldwide events, but simultaneously to attack problems of domestic urban poverty. Such reshaping, we believe, will begin when the pressures resulting from urban segmentation, inequality, and isolation force community-level influentials and politicians to respond. We believe that as local institutions change, they will be strengthened, restructured, and redirected. We mean to include small businesses and neighborhood organizations, union locals and branch plants, civil rights associations and school reform groups, and many others. Multilocal coalitions, as we will argue, should be formed to press for reallocation of federal resources in favor of domestic needs and for redirection of the national economy in favor of workers and common citizens. Only then can a successful attack begin to undo the problems of severe urban poverty.

We contend that reshaping the city into a new vehicle for national human and physical resource development is the best course for national economic revitalization. At the national level, action to reduce poverty will unleash new human capacity. At the local level, human resources can be reformed. Because problems of poverty are deep, apparent, and threatening, local authorities, local political institutions, and community organizations can be turned seriously to the task of dealing with poverty. As central-city officials know, regardless of their politics or color, on their own they cannot succeed; but through cooperation with state and national coalitions and by means of other influences on national politics, local politics can move toward success. New policies should be directed toward strengthening such possibilities. This is our thesis.

We advance our arguments in the chapters that follow. In Chapter 2 we document the appalling conditions of poor and minority people in central cities, examining these conditions in relation to inequalities in the national distributions of income and wealth. In Chapter 3 we analyze the connections between the structure and movement of the new global economy and the dilemma of the poorest Americans. There we examine widely dispersed, globalized markets and production arrangements that are managed by the tightly centralized control systems of major corporations. In Chapter 4 we extend the arguments and see how changing industrial patterns have harmed most American cities and workers. Simultaneous dispersal of jobs and centralization of management have removed good jobs from cities and left behind minorities and women and their children. With limited social contact outside their embattled neighborhoods and with weakened social contracts tying them to the larger community, these people have fallen into a persistent poverty with few routes for escape.

Then, in Chapter 5, we first lay out options for better federal policies. Next we search for sources of political support. Finally, we focus on new roles for local government and community-based organizations, finding what is innovative about them and what constrains them. There we argue that only through local reconstruction and a new organization of politics involving grass-roots and neighborhood groups will new initiatives emerge for the required transformation of national political economics. That transformation, in fact, will rechannel resources toward this domestic crisis. In the end, democratic participation and politics will have to give direction to the economy, or the nation will be divided politically and immobilized, unable to compete. The sources for change are to be found in coalitions formed from below.

We advise the reader that there is a tension throughout this study. We are faced with a conflict between two findings. On the one hand, powerful global economic forces play a major role in determining the life chances of American citizens. On the other hand, the situation of the poor can be radically improved only through a staged process of local empowerment, the formation of new political coalitions, and the consequent reformulation of a national agenda. The reader may find, concerning the first view, that the arguments in Chapters 3 and 4 appear to be top-down and accepting of the force of structural arrangements like competitive markets, and too despairing of the potential good influence of human agency through social movements, political action, and the like. The arguments in these chapters display our deep concern that global economic forces be better understood by the nation's policymakers. Global contributions to severe poverty in American cities can be traced to corporate behavior in a newly expanded, more competitive, and highly integrated world market. We also hope to influence people active in social movements—those organizing to alleviate the handicaps of poverty, improve neighborhoods, and repair severed social connections. With a clear grasp of the structural impediments to their programs, they will better be able to use moral arguments and to keep sight of what, in the long run, they intend.[14]

At the other extreme, the reader may find that the tasks we set in Chapter 5 for changed local governments and coalitions of local forces are too demanding; the possibility of challenging and improving federal policy may seem remote. After all, how can we imagine violating the structural integrity of these global economic and political arrangements? Not easily, to be sure. But as Peter Marris has written, small changes in thinking sometimes lead to large changes in institutions. Collective resistance has enormous potential for causing change in the system:

> Despite the enormous concentrations of economic power; despite the remoteness of the decisions which determine the fate of a factory or a neighborhood; despite the subservience of political institutions to the requirements of capital; despite the ideological manipulation embodied in control over newspapers and television—despite all this, it only works because most people, most of the time, choose to go along with it.[15]

We ask the reader to examine both sides of the question. The problems of urban poverty in the United States today are immense. Their resolution will require complex solutions and far-reaching changes. The energy for change must come from below, but its target must be very broad. It is a time to act locally, because we need global change.

Chapter 2

Separate Assets: Race, Gender, and Other Dimensions of Poverty

The American Century is over. The great postwar boom has collapsed, and international events have transformed the nation's economy and politics. Traditions of social relations are disintegrating. In the mid-twentieth century there was a common belief that all Americans shared an economic destiny. The wealth of the nation would flow to all citizens who displayed diligence and thrift. This belief lasted perhaps forty years. After four decades of progress, the basic social contract that connects people and opportunities has begun to break. Whereas in the earlier period citizens generally (and accurately) expected economic improvement, now most cannot. In cities especially, poverty has been increasing.

In recent years poverty has been made much worse in periods of uneven economic decline but barely relieved during episodes of improvement in the general performance of the national economy. Neither economic growth nor public subsidy has solved the problems of poor people. The failures are perhaps best revealed by the severe inequalities in the distributions of income and wealth. We will use a series of basic facts about these distributions to construct a platform from which we can view the middle class, the poor, and, most important, those who are very poor and thrown together in inner cities. Only after framing this evidence can we interpret their problems. In this chapter, as background for subsequent chapters, we thus display the statistical dimensions of poverty.

The evidence of severe poverty is overwhelming. Thirteen percent of Americans are poor, even by conservative definitions. The poor are disproportionately African-American and Latino, and they have become highly concentrated in large central cities. Very poor people and their neighborhoods face truly severe problems. Some of the problems, like low incomes, lack of resources, and inadequate public services, are general, requiring pervasive remedies; some, like homelessness and poor housing, crowded or poorly run schools, and inadequate police protection, are specific, perhaps subject to focused solutions.

Serious as this poverty is, it wags at the tail end of monumental inequalities in access to opportunity that affect many Americans who are not poor. The increasing and more persistent poverty that pervades central cities is thus closely connected to changes in the entire distribution of income, which have also greatly extended the distance between the upper and the middle classes.

Two public questions about income in the late 1980s served to raise distributional issues in an unusual way, relating them to our argument about separation. The questions revealed and defined the concerns of two distinct social groups, with distant viewpoints. The first question had to do with judges' salaries (Is the bench underpaid?). The second had to do with hourly pay, minimum wages, and welfare (How low must incomes be to keep American workers competitive?). These questions illustrate the myopia identified by John Kenneth Galbraith: a conservative White House argues that higher incomes should be offered to the rich, lower wages to the poor, in both cases as incentives to work.[1]

Among America's opinionmakers there was only one answer to the first question, and very little debate: we must make up the 30 percent that federal district judges have lost to inflation in the last twenty years. In early 1989, the chief justice of the Supreme Court made the extraordinary move of holding a press conference to call for higher judicial salaries.[2] Even Congress, politically unable at the time to raise its own salaries, made it clear that judges' salaries should be higher. The case is readily made by columnist Anthony Lewis: "In the metropolitan areas where most federal judges sit, it is difficult to provide good housing for a family and to put children through college on $89,500 a year. And by the standards of the legal profession, the figure is extremely modest."[3] Some worried that the independence of the judiciary was threatened by low salaries. According to economists and other observers, judges were deeply disadvantaged compared to other attorneys, whose salaries were much higher.

In fact, only a tiny percentage of American households, most of them with two people working, earn as much as federal judges. For the majority, the debate over relative compensation among well-to-do Americans focused public attention on the wrong issues. Most Americans earn not just less, but much less. Counting income from all earners, only one in twenty households can equal the judicial figure. More to the point, half the households in the country take home only one-quarter as much money as a judge.[4] By that standard, either the judges are doing extraordinarily well, or many people are doing very badly.

The second question, about less elevated wage levels, reveals conflict between employers' concerns that wages be kept low enough to assure international competitiveness, and workers' concerns that wages be high enough to keep individuals and families above the poverty level. How much can we afford to pay workers without losing out to international competitors? Who are the working poor? What happens when displaced factory workers must hire on at hamburger stands for much lower pay? Why when husbands and wives both work to earn wages do so many of their households barely survive? Debates over these kinds of issues reveal an America different from that inhabited by the federal judiciary and members of Congress.[5] According to the "low-budget" definition of the Bureau of Labor Statistics (BLS), more than a third of American families have incomes that are too low to help them maintain "a sense of self-respect and social participation."[6] The range of poverty is quite broad, and it falls very low.

At the very bottom, one of every seven American families earned less than $12,500 in 1990, and more than a quarter of those poor families earned less than $5,000.[7] For whites and minorities alike, men's inability to get well-paid work is the most common proximate cause of family poverty, but the effects of poverty fall most visibly on women and children, especially on women bringing up children alone. The problem is most concentrated in the cities, where minority people are packed in segregated quarters and suffer from severe discrimination. This is manifested by the continued and persistent concentration of African Americans and other minority persons in inner-city census tracts.[8]

If it is difficult for federal judges to provide good homes and educations for their families, then it must be nearly impossible for people who are very poor. In fact, this is the case. More and more families came to live on the streets and in shelters throughout the 1980s, and millions of others then and now live in neighborhoods and buildings that discourage self-respect and social participation. Still others make livings from drugs and crime, are in jail, or do not survive. Their children are born underweight and often drug-dependent, have poor medical care, do not get good schooling, and play on unsafe streets. Very often young parents (especially young, single parents) cannot provide supervision, young men and women cannot get jobs, and community social institutions provide little help. In central-city communities, minority families are isolated more than ever before, and in some districts there is a situation of near hopelessness. In 1989 New York City's commissioner of human resources estimated that "[o]ne-third of the nearly half-million children on public assistance [live] . . . in isolated pockets of such intense poverty that they are cut off from the world of work and independence."[9]

To display the situation of these children and their parents, at the bottom of American society, we discuss four topics in this chapter. The first two—the distribution of income and wealth and indexes of poverty—we treat at length. The second two—the problem of low wages and underemployment and the fact of geographic isolation—we merely introduce, because they will be treated in more detail in Chapters 3 and 4. In each case we raise special questions of race, gender, and age.

The Distribution of Income and Wealth

Poverty and wealth are more closely related than is commonly understood. Income is mostly from salary and wages, which depend on employment; employment and income rise and fall with the economy. Wealth is the accumulation of unspent previous income, including inheritance. People with no wealth, low wages, or no wages tend to be at the bottom of the distribution, with only some of them helped by redistributive public programs.

There are many ways to measure the relative well-being of segments of the population. Even standard measurements of the distribution of income (the most common and perhaps the most practical and dependable measure) come in a variety of forms, compiled from different sources, aggregated in different ways. But they tend to tell the same story: in broad contours, things are bad and getting worse.

What is perhaps most striking overall—but too rarely discussed—is the fact that in the United States, compared to other industrial nations, income shares have been highly unequal throughout the postwar period. Economic growth and redistributive policies masked differences and led to improvements for about twenty-five years, but in spite of growth since the mid-1970s, there has been distributional regression. Accurate measures have been available since the end of the Second World War. Look first at the long run. In 1947, the average household in the top income quintile (that is, those in the top 20 percent of households ranked by income) received thirteen times as much as the average household in the bottom quintile. Two decades later, by 1979, inequality had diminished somewhat, but incomes of the top group still averaged eleven times those of the bottom group. In another ten years, by 1989, the top group had risen again, so that its average income was more than twelve times that of a typical household at the bottom.[10] As the Center on Budget and Policy Priorities reports,

> The growth in the incomes of the richest one percent of Americans has been so large that just the *increase* between 1980 and 1990 in the after-tax income of this group equals the *total* income of the poorest 20 percent of the population. . . . In fact, Congressional Budget Office figures show that in 1990, *the top fifth will receive as much after-tax income as the other 80 percent of the population combined.*[11]

A snapshot of the 1989 income distribution appears in Figure 2.1, which highlights the disparities. The largest share goes to the top quintile, the smallest to the bottom. Evidence presented later in this chapter shows that specific disparities by race, ethnicity, and gender are even larger.[12]

We now look more closely at recent changes. The share of aggregate family income earned by the poorest fifth of families fell by 16 percent between 1973 and 1989, and income shares of the next three-fifths also fell. Altogether, that is, relative incomes fell for 80 percent of all families in the 1980s, while they rose for 20 percent. The top one percent of families gained the most.[13]

The distribution of real disposable family income (that is, income after taxes are deducted and transfer payments are

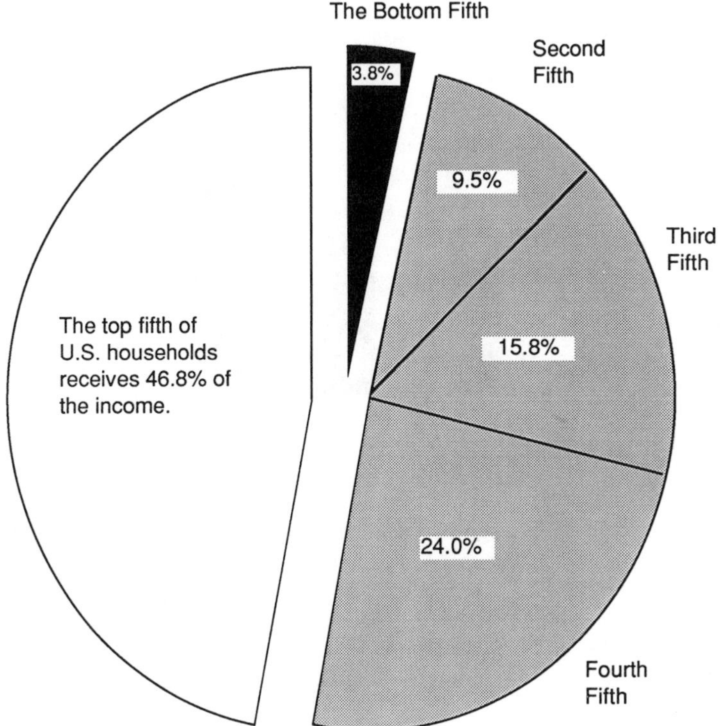

Figure 2.1. Income Shares by Household, Quintiles, 1989. *Source:* Bureau of the Census, *Money Income and Poverty Status in the United States, 1989* (Washington, D.C.: U.S. Government Printing Office, 1989), Series P-60, No. 168, Table 6.

added) worsened even more dramatically between 1977 and 1990.[14] Figure 2.2 shows how the income of each quintile grew (or declined) from 1973 to 1979, then to 1989. Two generalizations are possible: poorer families grew relatively poorer; and the disparities increased more rapidly in the most recent period. Of particular note, a 1991 report from the Congress shows that the real value of family incomes (that is, their purchasing power after removing the effects of inflation) actually declined for the poorest half of all families from 1979 to 1989.[15]

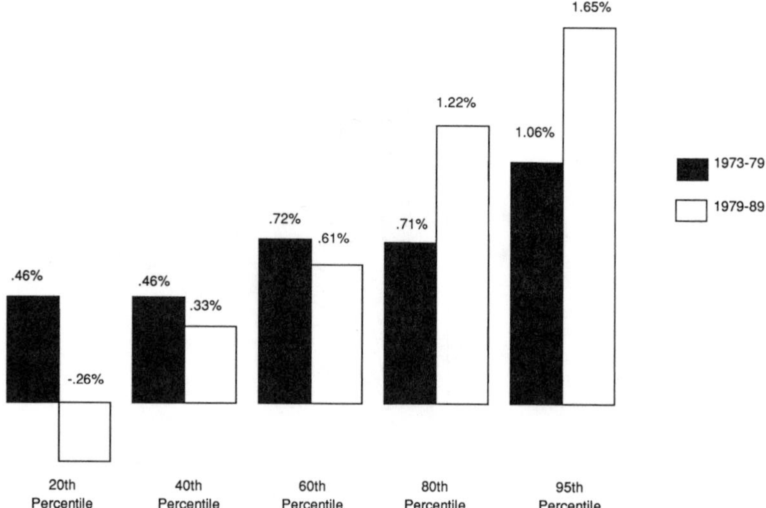

Figure 2.2. Rate of Change in Family Real Income, Quintiles, 1973–89. *Source:* Bureau of the Census, *Money Income and Poverty Status in the United States* (Washington, D.C.: U.S. Government Printing Office, 1989), Series P-60, No. 168, Table 5; No. 129, Table 14; No. 97, Table 22; and Gary Burtless, "Trends in the Distribution of Earnings and Family Income," testimony before the Senate Budget Committee, Feb. 22, 1991.

The ownership of wealth is even more highly concentrated than income. "Wealth" is the term used by economists to refer to stocks, bonds, cash, and real property, including factories, shops, offices, and equipment.[16] Here the statistics indicate marked social division. The 2.6 million households at the rarefied upper end had an average net worth of nearly $1 million in 1988; together they constituted less than 3 percent of all households, but owned more than one-quarter of the national wealth.[17] The group next to the top, another 6 percent of the households, owned on average a net wealth of $340,000; combined they owned a second quarter of all the nation's wealth. In contrast, the remaining 90 percent of the households taken together owned just half of the nation's wealth, most of that in owner-occupied housing.[18] Continuing the downward trends

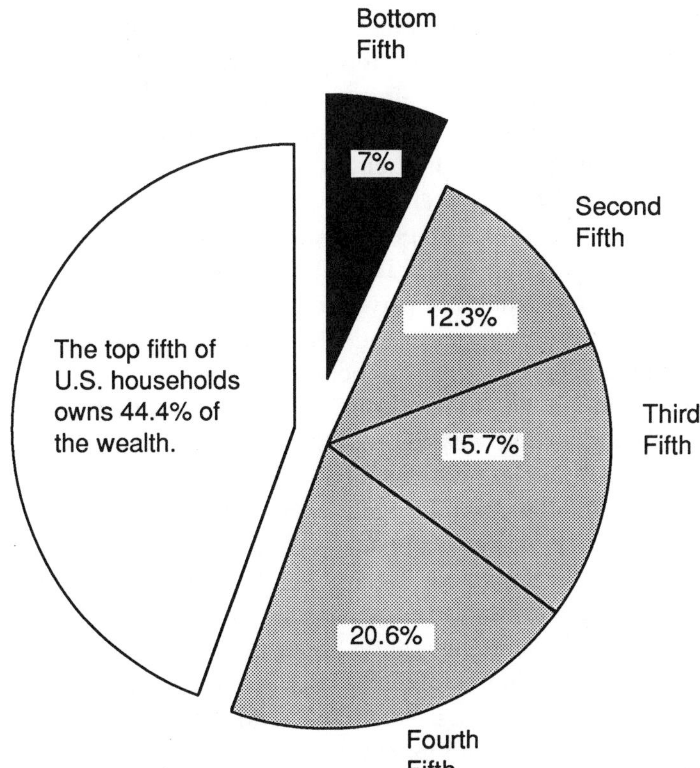

Figure 2.3. Household Wealth Distribution, 1988. *Source:* Judith Eargle, *Household Wealth and Asset Ownership, 1988* (Washington, D.C.: U.S. Department of Commerce, Bureau of the Census, 1990), Series P-70, No. 22, Table B.

found in surveys in 1962 and 1983, and paralleling our findings on income, the already miniscule wealth of the majority (including the poor) declined further to 1988. In fact, median wealth holdings for all but the highest income quintile declined in absolute values after adjustment for inflation.[19] Figure 2.3 shows the extreme inequality of average wealth holdings and relative shares in 1988.

When equity in vehicles and homes is excluded, the remaining categories in the economist's measure of wealth are "productive assets." In 1988, the top group, the wealthiest 3 percent of households, held almost two-fifths of these assets—approximately fourteen times its proportionate share. The next 6 percent of households held another one-quarter of the wealth. Thirty-four percent held very modest amounts of wealth, and the bottom 57 percent of households held virtually no productive wealth at all. This productive wealth, of course, results in income that is a privilege of ownership, in the form of dividends, interest, and rent. The return on assets is called "unearned income," in distinction to wages and salaries. As the numbers show, unearned income accrues with huge disproportion to a tiny, wealthy minority.

Aggregate, single-indicator measures of inequality are used to interpret the data by telling how far the distributions deviate from uniformity, or perfect equality. Reliable, detailed distributions are not available for wealth holdings, so we must rely again on figures available for income. In the period since World War II, family-income inequality—measured here by the standard statistic, the Gini coefficient—has risen and fallen several times, even though, as we have said, overall inequality throughout remains high in comparison to other advanced, industrialized nations. The distribution improved until 1955, after which inequality sharply increased, peaking in 1960.[20] Between 1960 and 1966, the distribution improved again, but since 1968 inequality has worsened fairly steadily, most dramatically after 1980. Figure 2.4 shows the steady increase in inequality from 1968 to 1989.

As this collection of statistics begins to suggest, even the notion of the American middle class turns out to be not well supported by the historical data. In 1967, for example, 55 percent of *full-time* workers did not earn enough to meet a lower-middle-class living standard. According to the Bureau of Labor Statistics, a family of four, with worker, housekeeper, and

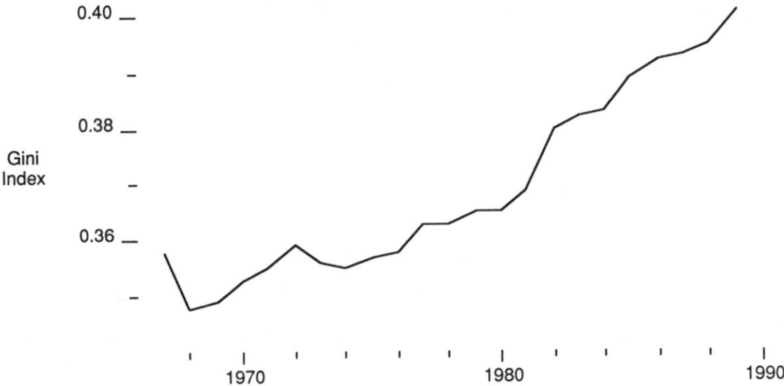

Figure 2.4. Family Income Inequality, Gini Coefficient, 1967–89. *Source:* Bureau of the Census, *Money Income and Poverty Status in the United States, 1989* (Washington, D.C.: U.S. Government Printing Office, 1989), Series P-60, No. 168, Table 6.

young children, then needed at least $6,400 ($21,000 in 1986 dollars) to purchase the "lower-middle" consumer basket of goods and services; half of the country's full-time workers still earned too little to buy this much, without supplementary income from a working spouse. Using more recent data for African-American men we find that 58 percent of those with full-time jobs in 1989 fell below the minimal middle-class standard.[21]

Many workers live in households with two earners, as more women have taken jobs outside the home, thus allowing a few more families to squeeze into the middle class. Nonetheless, many workers and their households, limited by low wages or the vagaries of temporary or part-time employment, fall far below even these minimal standards.

All these inequalities of income and wealth are heightened by racial and ethnic distinctions. Throughout this book, when we speak of differences by ethnicity and race, we will most often contrast African Americans and whites, frequently adding information about Latinos (or Hispanics).[22] For the most part, we are constrained by available statistics, which give fairly complete and historical information about African Americans and whites, less about Hispanics, and still less about other minority persons, such as Native Americans or recent immigrants from Asia, the Caribbean, or Central America. While we are troubled by this lack of information and eager that more comprehensive statistics be collected, two factors provide compensatory relief. First, the problems of African-American poverty are so serious and manifold that any examination of the ample statistics is likely to uncover issues pertinent to other groups. Such a focus will not, to be sure, identify the other groups' problems with precision, but it is likely to encompass most of them. Second, we believe that for various historical reasons anticolor racism, applied with increasing intensity to those with darker skins, is most readily revealed in the United States by studying of the situation of African Americans. We do *not* claim that racism is absent in the experiences of other minorities in America—all to the contrary. Nor do we claim that their experiences with racism are the same as those of African Americans. What we *do* claim is that it is enlightening to explore the (more readily available) information about African Americans and (to a lesser extent) Latinos, and that this information should be used to corroborate and augment other, more detailed studies.

Income distribution figures for the population as a whole, unequal as they are, obscure the large gaps that divide racial and ethnic groups. African-American relative to white incomes have diminished (with fluctuations) from 1970 to 1990. The dashed regression line fitted to the data in Figure 2.5 shows a pronounced twenty-year tendency toward relatively lower incomes for African Americans. At lower income levels, the gap is widest: in 1989 incomes of the poorest 20 percent of African-American families were only 44 percent of the incomes of their poor white counterparts (these details are not shown in Figure

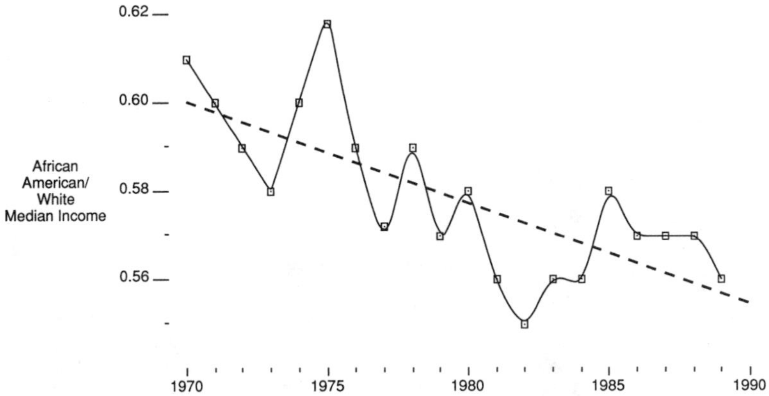

Figure 2.5. Ratio of African-American to White Median Family Income, 1970–89. *Source:* Council of Economic Advisors, *Report of the President, 1991*, Table B–30.

2.5). At the center of the two distributions, we find that in 1989 the median African-American family earned $20,000, versus $36,000 for whites and $24,000 for Hispanics.[23]

Poor families are disproportionately headed by women. This is compounded by the fact that African American families overall are more likely to be headed by women. Figure 2.6 shows, for example, that of all non-white families with incomes up to $10,000, 75 percent are headed by women. In the group of white families with no income, 58 percent are headed by women.

Income inequality *among* African Americans and among Hispanics is also greater than it is among whites. It has worsened (since 1975) for all three groups, but most dramatically among African Americans, marked by a tendency toward separation into middle class and poor that has been much commented on in the literature.

Measures of wealth holdings reveal still larger gaps between whites, on the one hand, and African Americans and Hispanics, on the other. Holdings of stocks, bonds, cash, and real

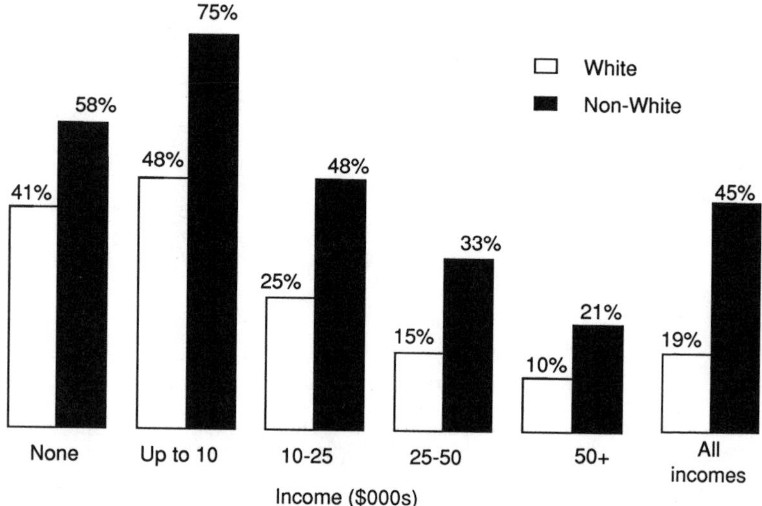

Figure 2.6. Percentage of Families in Each Income Group That Are Female-Headed, by Race 1990. *Source:* Bureau of the Census, *Current Population Survey*, computer tape, 1991.

property, including houses, appliances, and automobiles, are drastically skewed. There appears to be an unbridgeable chasm by race and ethnicity. The difference is especially marked at the lower levels of the national income distribution, which includes most African-American and Hispanic households. For those households in the lowest U.S. income quintile, for example, median African-American and Hispanic wealth is infinitesimal. More than one-third of all African-American households have no productive or personal assets; that is, their net wealth in 1988 was zero or lower. Median household wealth for the poorest one-quarter of the Hispanic households (all of whom are in the lowest U.S. income quintile) was only $377 in 1988. The comparable figure for white households (13.7 percent are in the lowest all-race quintile) is $8,839. For all income groups together, median net worth in 1988 for white households was

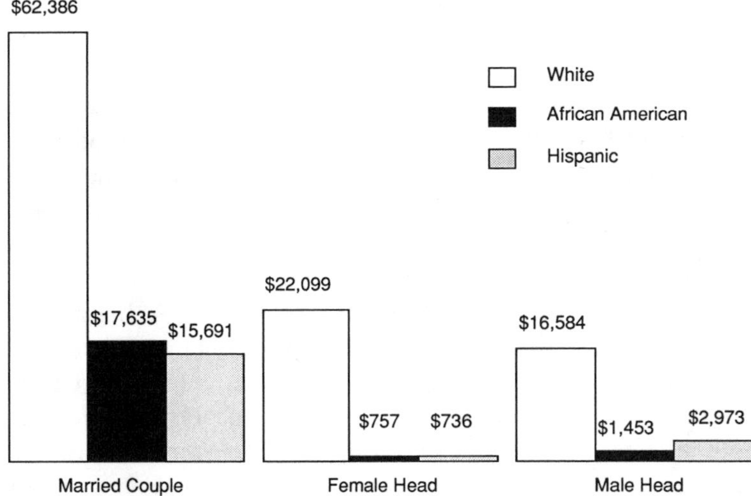

Figure 2.7. Median Household Wealth, by Race and Household Type, 1988. *Source:* Judith Eargle, *Household Wealth and Asset Ownership, 1988* (Washington, D.C.: U.S. Department of Commerce, Bureau of the Census, 1990), Series P-70, No. 22, Table B.

$43,270, eight to ten times as high as for African-Americans ($4,160) or Hispanics ($5,524).[24] The wealth gap ratio is widest between female-headed white and African-American households. Figure 2.7 illustrates these drastic differences.

Indexes of Poverty

Since 1973, as the statistics on income distribution suggest, the total number of poor people has risen, even as the economy has grown. Although poverty has been and is disproportionately concentrated among households headed by women and minority persons, the recent increase has affected many white male citizens as well.

The official "poverty line" is defined by the Social Security Administration (SSA) in terms of the amount of money needed to purchase the goods and services their statisticians deem necessary for survival, calculated (for lack of a simple statistical alternative) to be three times the minimum cost of food for a family. With the other two-thirds of their money, families must pay for rent, utilities, clothing, medicine, and all other costs. The food budget is calculated by a group of dieticians who put together menus that meet all the essential nutritional requirements and that are the best buys for the money. Although this figure is adjusted annually to reflect price changes, it is nevertheless inadequate because food prices are higher in poor neighborhoods, nutritional information and practices are suboptimal, and poor families typically need to spend more than one-third of their income to get enough food. In 1990, this SSA line was set at an annual income of $6,451 for one person, $12,575 for four people, and ranging from $23,973 to $27,596 for a family of nine.[25] There are alternative definitions. As we have noted, the Bureau of Labor Statistics once defined a "low budget" line below which families could not realize "a sense of self-respect and social participation." When the SSA poverty line was invented, it was set 40 percent *below* the original BLS low budget line, thereby excluding many (previously included) poor families and individuals from the new official count.[26] *The official poverty line now in use (SSA) is thus a stringent standard that underestimates considerably what most Americans would judge to be the income needed for a family to escape poverty.*[27]

The number of impoverished people, even as underestimated by this stringent SSA line, has increased substantially in the last fifteen years. In 1960, there were about 40 million poor people. The number fell to 24 million in 1969, staying almost level for 8 years (it stood at 25 million in 1977). Then it rose. By 1983 the number had risen to above 35 million—15.2 percent of the population. Since then, the number at first decreased moderately, but by 1986 it had stabilized. In 1990, 32 million people

Figure 2.8. The Number of Poor People, 1959–90. *Source:* Bureau of the Census, *Money Income and Poverty Status in the United States, 1989* (Washington, D.C.: U.S. Government Printing Office, 1989), Series P-60, No. 168, Table 19.

fell below the SSA line—12.9 percent of the population. Perhaps as a symbolic end to the decade, from 1989 to 1990, the U.S. population grew by 200,000, while at the same time the number of poor people grew by 199,000. Borrowing a term from Bennett Harrison and Barry Bluestone, we note that there was a "great U-turn" in poverty from 1959 to 1990 (see Figure 2.8).

For families (that is, excluding households composed of single or unrelated people), the situation has changed in similar ways. After declining for many years, poverty again rose until 1983, when 12.3 percent of all families had fallen below the SSA line—a higher percentage in poverty than at any time since the early 1960s. As Figure 2.9 indicates, three groups of roughly equal size comprise 84 percent of all families in poverty—those headed by white women, by white married couples, and by African-American women. The majority of all American families (71 percent in 1989) are headed by white married couples, so it should be no surprise that among them

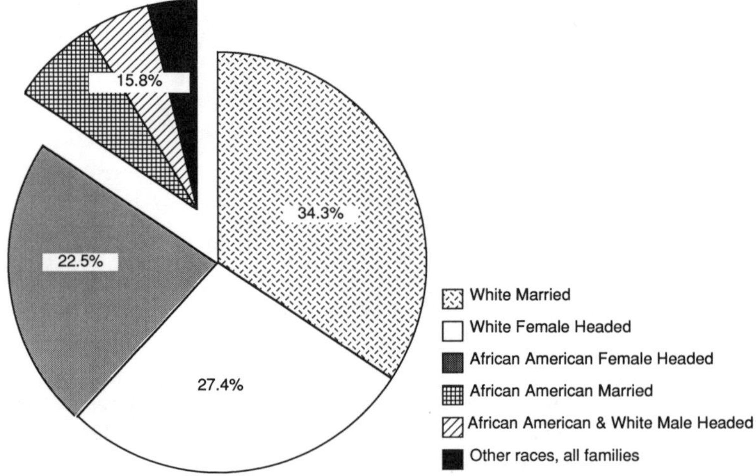

Figure 2.9. Proportion of Poor Families, by Race and Family Status, 1989. *Source:* Bureau of the Census, *Money Income and Poverty Status in the United States, 1989* (Washington, D.C.: U.S. Government Printing Office, 1989), Series P-60, No. 168, Table 23.

are more than one-third of all families in poverty. The next largest number of poor families, just over one-quarter, are headed by white women. Families headed by African-American women are the third most numerous category.[28]

The alternative view of American poverty is revealed by flipping these coins to their other sides. Consider women and poverty. Nearly one in every three families that were headed by a woman in 1989 was poor, whereas the rate was only one in eight for families headed by single males, and one in eighteen for married-couple families.

All of these groups—whites, minorities, women, and families with children—followed the historical pattern of change for families as a whole, the numbers in poverty increasing through the late 1970s and early 1980s, until about 1983, and then stabilizing, at rates higher than any since the early 1960s. Families with children under 18 years old are more likely to be poor than others.[29] Female-headed households with children fare the worst: half are poor.[30] One in five American children lives in poverty.[31] Such extensive poverty, with all its personal agony and potential social dangers, had not occurred since the early 1960s.

As poverty has become more widespread, it has also become more invisible through segregation, workplace segmentation, and geographic isolation. In an odd turn, however, the extremities of poverty have become more visible, as ghetto violence increasingly makes the headlines, illiteracy and hunger generate incompetence and disease, and beggars and homeless people become a common feature of the urban landscape. Because of the difficulties of collecting data (and the inattention of federal authorities) there exist no reliable counts of the homeless. A report by the National Academy of Sciences estimates that 1.3 to 2 million people are homeless for one or more nights in the course of a year. Children form the fastest-growing group among the homeless: 100,000 children under age 18, excluding runaways, are homeless each night.[32]

Information on hunger is probably no more precise, but it is equally damning. Estimates from a nationwide survey indicate that more than 5 million children under age 12 in the United States—one of every eight children in the country—suffer from substantial food shortages because of poverty. Another 6 million children are close to the margin, either hungry or risking hunger.[33]

The effects of poverty on health are devastating, as we know from figures on infant mortality and life expectancy. The 11.5 million children who risk being hungry, whose families comprise 40 percent of all families with small children, are more likely than others to suffer from fatigue, irritability, headaches, and related health problems. More serious still, according to the U.S. Public Health Service, infant mortality in the United States is the highest in the First World. America ranks twenty-fourth among industrial countries.[34] Depending on the measures used, the U.S. rate is 50 to 100 percent worse than that of

Japan. The high rate results from poverty-related problems, such as maternal malnutrition and inadequate prenatal care. Public agencies do not publish health status statistics by income group, but by race and ethnicity. Racial classifications as surrogates for defining the poor are, as data earlier in this chapter suggest, very crude, but we at least can use the race-based statistics as a lower limit for estimating the magnitude of health problems of the poor. Babies born poor (in this case, African-American and Puerto Rican compared to white babies) are about twice as likely to be underweight.[35] Infant mortality rates are about twice as high for poor babies (in this case, African Americans and Native Americans) as for babies of the nonpoor.[36] Between 1984 and 1988, according to the Public Health Service, the disparities grew by 10 percent: "the difference in life expectancy between the white and black populations . . . increased from 6.2 to 7.4 years for males and from 5.0 to 5.5 years for females."[37]

When broken down by race and ethnicity, the already ominous figures on poverty become even more troubling. For a long time, very high proportions of African Americans and Latinos have been below the poverty line. Minority households have rates of poverty two to three times as high as whites. Overall, because there is a much higher proportion of African-American than white households with female heads, the income disparity is even greater: 27.8 percent of all African-American families were poor in 1989, compared to 7.8 percent of white families. Hispanic families headed by women were the most likely to be poor, with the families of African-American women running a close second. More than a quarter of white families headed by women were poor. For all groups, extremely high percentages of female-headed families with children under eighteen are poor, as Table 2.1 shows.

When we consider the elderly, we find a dramatic difference. The incomes of the elderly have improved as a direct result of Social Security retirement benefits, mainly the payment of monthly income to retired persons and the reimburse-

TABLE 2.1
Poverty Rates, by Selected Household Status and Race, Percentages, 1989

Household Status	White	African-American	Hispanic	Other
Married couples (all)	5.2	11.8	16.2	10.0
Married couples (with children)	6.5	13.3	19.6	12.1
Female-headed (all)	25.4	46.5	47.5	39.5
Female-headed (with children)	36.1	53.9	57.9	53.6
Unrelated women	16.9	35.3	31.0	22.3

Source: Bureau of the Census, *Current Population Survey, Money Income and Poverty Status in the United States, 1990*, P-60, Tables 23 and 24.

ment of health care costs. According to the Census Bureau, the rate of poverty fell drastically in just thirty years, from more than a third of all elderly people in 1959 to just over a tenth in 1989. This decline in poverty demonstrates that specific and well-targeted national policies can make a difference. Social Security benefits were an initial budget-cutting target of the Reagan administration, but highly organized resistance by Grey Power advocates forced a retreat. There remain great disparities, nonetheless. Elderly African Americans remain three times more likely to be poor than elderly whites, and poverty rates for elderly Hispanics still fluctuate greatly with the business cycle, because many do not receive Social Security and are thus dependent on employment, often at part-time, low wages. Some of this disparity reflects the difficulty of access by relatively recent immigrants to the Social Security system.[38]

Low Wages and Underemployment

Earning Poverty: The Wage-Earning Poor and the Feminization of Poverty

Remarkably, the increase in American poverty happened even in periods when unemployment rates did not rise. Much poverty, it is now generally agreed, resulted from an increasing

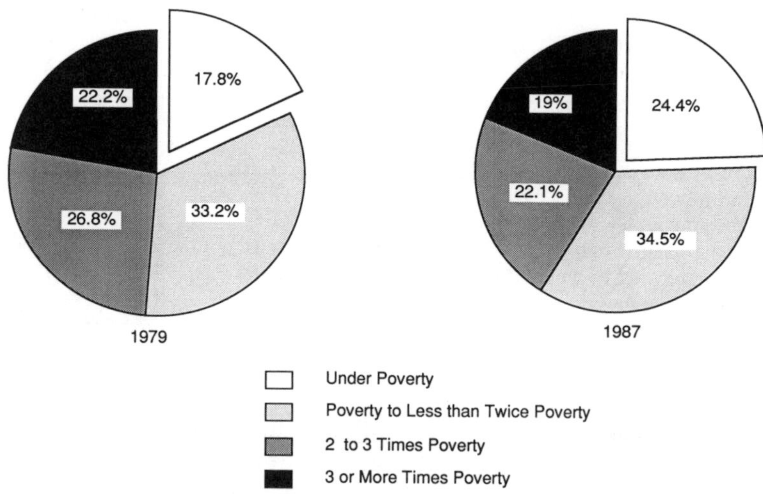

Figure 2.10. Hourly Earnings for Men, 1979 and 1987. *Source:* Bennett Harrison and Lucy Gorham, "What Happened to Black Wages in the 1980s: Family Incomes, Individual Earnings, and the Growth of the African American Middle Class," working paper no. 90-1, Carnegie Mellon University School of Urban and Public Affairs, Pittsburgh, Pa., 1990.

proportion of poorly paid job-holders. As shown in a whole series of research reports that began with studies by Barry Bluestone and Bennett Harrison, the increase in poverty among those with jobs, whatever their race, results from an increase in low-wage jobs, the falling purchasing power of those low wages, and the intermittent and part-time nature of much work. After a dramatic improvement from the early 1960s, ever since 1973 the employed poor have grown steadily as a proportion of the workforce.[39] Figure 2.10 shows that low-wage jobs for all men grew much faster than middle- and high-wage jobs through the 1980s. For African-American men aged 25 to 34, the proportion earning poverty-level wages rose even more sharply—up 151 percent from 1979 to 1989.[40]

The number of employed poor people, mostly part-timers, rose from over a third of the poor population in 1967, to 41 percent in 1989. Looking for the moment at just one segment of the workforce, factory production workers, we see ample reasons for part of the wage U-turn and the increase in poverty. As Gary Burtless, a researcher at the Brookings Institution, writes: "In the two and a half decades from 1947 through 1973, the inflation-adjusted hourly earnings of an average production worker in private employment rose more than 70 percent, or about 2.1 percent a year. During the next fourteen years, from 1973 through 1987, average real hourly earnings *fell* 5.4 percent, or about 0.4 percent a year."[41] The wage-earning poor, even more than the poor in general, tend to be white. Most low earners fall in the prime working years. Those impoverished adults who are employed full-time tend even more to be white, male, and of prime working age.[42]

According to calculations made by the Census Bureau, a higher proportion of workers took part-time jobs in the 1980s than earlier, many of them not by choice. At the same time, low-wage employment grew as a component of full-time, year-round work as well, increasing from about 15 percent in the 1970s, to more than 17 percent in 1986. The purchasing value of low wages, as measured by the real value of the minimum wage, has fallen considerably in recent years, declining steadily since 1978. Families of three or four with one bread-winner earning the minimum wage were no longer able to stand above the poverty line after 1981. By 1989 the minimum wage had fallen so far that its buying power was at the same level it had been in 1956.[43] As Burtless writes, "If the real value of the minimum wage had remained constant over the 1980s, the minimum wage rate in 1988 would have been $4.34 an hour. The actual minimum was $3.35, or about 23 percent lower."[44]

A large part of the story of the increase in the working poor has to do with the increase in the number of female-headed households. Women have historically earned less than men, and this difference has pushed many families headed by women into poverty. In 1989, the median annual income of full-time employed women was $18,780, two-thirds that of men.

An increasing number of households are headed by employed women. Labor-force participation rates for white women rose from 43 to 58 percent between 1972 and 1991. Rates for African-American women were already 51 percent in 1972. By 1985, 63 percent of the African American women over 20 years old were in the labor force.[45] Women in their child-rearing years now have paid jobs much more often than they used to. At the same time, participation rates for men of all races and ages have fallen since 1972.

Figures 2.11 and 2.12, which diagram U.S. Census data for 1989, provide a summary view. Figure 2.11 is organized initially by gender, Figure 2.12, by race and ethnicity. Together they show that the burden of poverty falls disproportionately on women with children, especially on African-American women with children. Women head 10.9 million families, 7.4 million with children (see Figure 2.11). Of these families, 43 percent (3.2 million) are poor; just over half of these poor, female-headed families are white, just under half are minority. There are about 7.5 million African-American families in the United States (see Figure 2.12). Of those families, 28 percent (2 million) are poor. Proceeding down the chart, 86 percent of those poor African-American families have children, and 80 percent of those families with children are headed by women. These figures show who is poor, and the preceding arguments showed that most poor family heads are in the labor force. In the next section, we explore in more detail the problem of low earnings.

Underemployment and Earnings Differentials

Underemployment is the principal cause of poverty. If we add together workers who have part-time or short-term jobs involuntarily, those who are unemployed and want jobs, and those

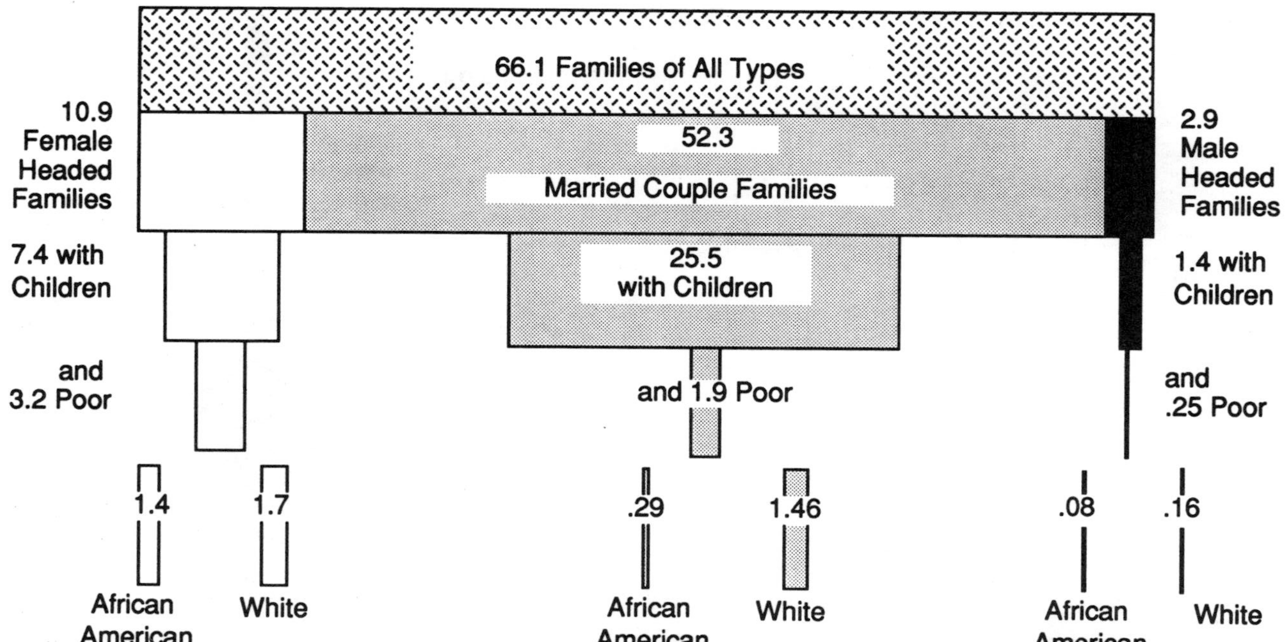

Figure 2.11. Family Poverty Tree, by Family Type, 1989. *Source:* Bureau of the Census, *Money Income and Poverty Status in the United States, 1989* (Washington, D.C.: U.S. Government Printing Office, 1989), Series P-60, No. 168, Table 21.

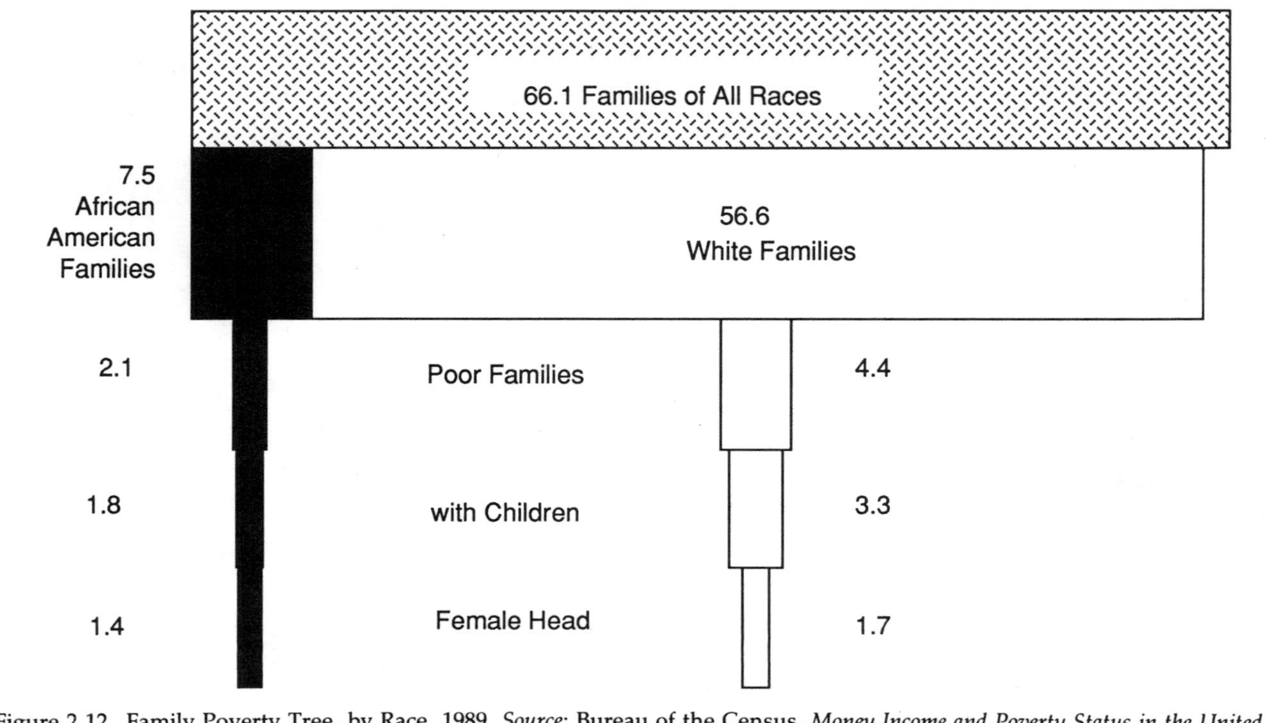

Figure 2.12. Family Poverty Tree, by Race, 1989. *Source*: Bureau of the Census, *Money Income and Poverty Status in the United States, 1989* (Washington, D.C.: U.S. Government Printing Office, 1989), Series P-60, No. 168, Table 21.

who are too discouraged to look for jobs, we get a useful bottom-line measure (although still an underestimate) of those unable to earn adequate incomes.[46] An even broader measure is the labor-force nonparticipation rate, which (while including some potential workers who do not want or need to work) also counts those who are prevented from working by physical or personal reasons. By no means does the behavior of labor markets explain all poverty, but as we will see in subsequent chapters, we cannot understand poverty unless we know who are unable to get well-paid work.

Analysis of the nonparticipation rates of central-city residents by race, region, and age shows that for every region and age group, African-American men fare worse than white men. (Throughout this section, once again, reference is made mainly to the experience of African Americans and whites, because the census category of "Hispanics," which overlaps both these groups, is treated less fully by the statistics, and information for other groups is unavailable.) Labor-force nonparticipation for both African-American and white men rose substantially between 1969 and 1982, but African-American rates were considerably higher in all regions, especially in the Northeast and North-Central states.[47] For white men, unemployment rates increased from 1974 to 1980, and then again to 1988. Rates for those without college "roughly *doubled* between 1974 and 1988," while the rates for college graduates stayed the same.[48]

Underemployment as a proportion of the overall labor force has been rising nationally for twenty years. The highest concentrations are among youth, women, and minorities.[49] In 1970, 7.7 percent of white workers were thus marginalized, nearly doubling by 1982 to 15.3 percent. Then only adult white males had underemployment rates below 15 percent. Even at these relatively low rates, underemployment is a major cause of severe poverty. The rate for African-American workers was already at a much higher level in 1970 (14.6 percent), and by 1982 it had risen to 27 percent, a true Depression-level indicator. Underemployment rates for African-American and Hispanic women are particularly high, ranging between 35 and 42 percent. Overall rates are over 20 percent for all minority and female groups.

Measures of formal unemployment, the subcategory of nonparticipants most often reported and discussed, vary in similar ways. In 1982, central-city African-American men had a 23.4 percent unemployment rate, while the comparable rate for central-city whites was 9.5 percent. Moreover, central-city African-American men, aged 16 to 64, had unemployment rates more than twice as high as those of white men with comparable levels of education. African-American men who had completed at least one year of college had unemployment rates more than 3.5 times higher than their white counterparts. Throughout the 1980s, as sociologist John Kasarda has shown, rates of joblessness for African-American men with little education stayed at astonishingly high levels, especially in central cities.[50] Table 2.2 shows, for example, that in 1982 and 1987 half of the uneducated respondents in central cities were neither in school nor at work.

Intermittent work, the most frequent reason for low annual earnings, was most concentrated among minority women and young African-American men, reflecting the higher unemployment rates of younger workers and their greater difficulty in obtaining full-time work at any wage. In contrast, older women and older minority persons were more likely to have full-time, full-year work, although still at low wages.

TABLE 2.2
Percentage Not at Work, African-American Men Aged 16–62, Less Than High School Education, 1969–87

Part of Metropolis	1969	1977	1982	1987
Central city	18.8	38.3	49.5	49.5
Suburban ring	16.3	31.4	38.2	33.4

Source: John D. Kasarda, "Urban Industrial Transition and the Underclass," *Annals of the American Academy of Political and Social Science* 501 (Jan. 1989): Table 8, p. 42.

Young, single mothers are particularly vulnerable. Among single mothers who work, 53 percent are unable to earn above poverty-level incomes, generally because their work is intermittent or their wages are low. Married women were the least likely to be underemployed, but still had an underemployment rate of over 20 percent in the mid-1980s.[51]

Although some economists argue that racial discrimination today plays a small role in the labor market, there is ample evidence that considerable bias still exists. As Thomas Boston argues, race-related earnings differentials result from discrimination at three stages of the labor market. At the final stage, where most research focuses, minority workers on average still get less pay for the same jobs. Even after accounting for differences in age, education, region, job experience, family size, and other factors, and in spite of much improvement as a result of civil rights and equal pay legislation, wages in many occupations for African Americans are still lower than for whites.[52] One stage earlier, and of more consequence, discrimination unfairly reduces incomes by limiting access of minority workers to preferred lines of industry, where jobs are better and pay higher.

Worse yet, at the first stage of labor allocation, African-American workers "are disproportionately concentrated among low-paying occupations," even after controlling "for job-related attributes, age and other demographic differences."[53] In each sector of the economy, white adult wages are on average at least 20 percent higher than African-American wages. In advanced corporate services, a sector where employment has grown dynamically, wages for white adult men average $10.33 per hour, while African-American wages are only $6.85 per hour. Hispanic workers also earn less per hour than white workers.[54] In traditional manufacturing, African Americans and women are extremely likely to have unskilled and poorly paid work. In services both African Americans and women are more likely to obtain relatively higher-level jobs. In high-technology industries, the few African-American men with jobs are likely to find their occupational categories enhanced, but women have continued to be funneled into traditional operative and clerical work, and analysts predict more of the same.[55]

Occupational segregation by race and gender has a powerful effect on income. As Table 2.3 shows, an African-American man has less than 40 percent the chance of a white man for obtaining a high-paying occupation (that is, above $700 per week [March 1991]). For low-paying occupations (below $400 per week) the tables are turned—Afrian-American men are much more likely to hold these positions (64% more likely than white men). For women, the wage structure is much lower, but the race difference is reproduced. The best paid women—managers and professionals, for example—earn at the median from two-thirds to three-quarters the salaries of men. Few African-American women can get access to even these salaries. Although 28 percent of white women are at this level ($500–550), only 14 percent of African-American women are.

Supplementary national statistics show that most women's employment continues to be traditional. Women are relegated to administrative and clerical-support occupations (women hold 78 percent of these jobs) and general-service positions (61 percent). African-American employees are most heavily concentrated in four occupational categories: services; handlers, equipment cleaners, helpers, and laborers; transportation; and machine operators, fabricators, and laborers. Hispanic employees are most heavily concentrated in similar occupations. These occupations tend to be the lowest-paying.[56]

These and other data suggest that industrial and occupational changes resulting from restructuring, international competition, and corporate reorganization have combined to reinforce already segmented labor markets, leading to increased unemployment, underemployment, nonparticipation, and, ultimately, lower earnings. Past and current discrimination against minorities and women in labor markets concentrate the hardship. White men face considerably better structures of op-

TABLE 2.3

Good Jobs versus Bad Jobs: Employment by Major Occupation, Race, and Gender, March 1991

	Men			Women		
Occupation	Median Weekly Wage	White	African-American	Median Weekly Wage	White	African-American
Professional	$737	12.7%	7.0%	$542	16.5%	11.1%
Executive, administrative, & managerial	776	14.9	7.4	498	11.9	7.0
Technicians & related support	564	3.2	2.4	448	3.5	3.3
Protective services	519	2.6	4.5	376	0.5	1.4
Administrative support, incl. clerical	467	5.4	8.9	344	28.3	27.2
Precision production & crafts	494	19.5	16.0	339	2.0	2.4
Sales	522	12.2	5.6	314	13.0	9.0
Operators, fabricators, & laborers	391	18.8	30.9	269	7.4	12.6
Services other than protection & private household	286	6.5	14.5	244	14.6	23.6
Agriculture	268	4.1	2.6	242	1.1	0.2
Private household		0.0	0.2	172	1.2	2.6
Totals		100	100		100	100

Source: Bureau of Labor Statistics, U.S. Dept. of Labor, *Employment and Earnings 38*, no. 4 (April 1991), Tables A75 and A23.

portunity than any other group, but corporate reorganization has disrupted the lives and incomes of many white males as well. Nevertheless, in an attempt to enhance flexibility, companies are increasingly parceling out abuse to others, those most at risk in society. People of color, especially women and youth, remain the most vulnerable groups in the labor market. It is hardly surprising that whatever improvement in wages of African Americans and Hispanics that occurred from 1973 to 1979 was virtually dissipated in the 1980s.

One of the most striking effects of this social regression is growing inequality from region to region and especially from city to suburb. Later, in Chapter 4, we will analyze these issues in detail. Now we turn our focus to the high incidence of poverty in central cities.

The Geographic Concentration of Poverty

In 1959, most poor people (56 percent) were in rural areas and small towns; 27 percent were in the central cities, and 17 percent were in suburbs. By 1985, the distribution had reversed itself, with the bulk of the poor now found in the central cities (43 percent) and suburbs (28 percent), often in crowded neighborhoods in close proximity to one another.

Urban poverty is centered in the nation's largest cities, especially those with the largest minority populations. Between 1970 and 1980, the poor population of the fifty largest cities grew nearly 12 percent, while the overall population of those cities fell by more than 5 percent. Twenty percent or more of the populations were categorized as poor in 1980 in New York, Chicago, Philadelphia, Detroit, Baltimore, San Antonio, Memphis, Cleveland, Boston, New Orleans, St. Louis, El Paso, and Atlanta.[57] Poverty rates in central cities and metropolitan areas as well increased from the early 1970s until the early or mid-1980s.[58]

TABLE 2.4
Percentage of Area Population That Is Poor, by Race, 1975–89

	Central Cities			Central Poverty Areas		
	All	White	African-American	All	White	African-American
1975	10.7	7.0	18.2	15.0	10.8	29.1
1980	17.2	12.1	32.3	38.1	30.9	43.8
1985	19.0	14.9	32.1	37.5	34.2	41.2
1989	18.1	14.9	32.1	37.3	31.7	42.8

Source: Bureau of the Census, *Current Population Survey, Money Income and Poverty Status in the United States, 1989,* Series P-60, various years.

Poverty is concentrated in particular neighborhoods. Table 2.4 shows that there has been a significant increase in the prevalence of poverty in central cities and central-city "poverty areas." (Poverty areas are neighborhoods in which at least one of five households is officially poor.) In 1989, for example, although the metropolitan poverty rate stood at 12 percent, close to the national average, more than 37 percent of those living in poverty areas were poor.

Metropolitan areas with the highest rates of poverty tend to have larger proportions of poor people crowded into "high-poverty" census tracts. (High-poverty areas are neighborhoods in which at least two of five households are classified as poor.) Cities with the greatest concentration of poor people in such isolated districts include New York, Chicago, and Philadelphia: each had more than 100,000 poor people in high-poverty tracts in 1980. While these three cities, together with Newark and Detroit, had the largest increases in concentrated poverty, the phenomenon was widespread throughout the country's big cities. In Cleveland, looking back from 1987, Edward Hill and Thomas Bier find that poverty rose in "poverty tracts" in the 1980s:

> Those areas with large portions of their work force employed in lower-skilled occupations associated with factory work were the

spawning grounds for poverty at the end of the 1980s. This strongly suggests that change in the structure of the regional economy had a direct impact on the neighborhoods of the city and on sections of its close-in suburbs.[59]

Given high poverty rates among African Americans, it is particularly significant that still in 1990, high proportions of African Americans lived in overwhelmingly segregated neighborhoods; in some cities segregation even increased from 1980 to 1990. As Table 2.4 also shows, throughout the 1980s, one-third of the African Americans living in central cities were poor, and more than two-fifths of those living in central-city poverty areas were poor.

Table 2.5 further documents the greater concentration of poor African Americans relative to other poor Americans. Whereas 40 percent of the nation's poor whites who live in central-city areas were concentrated in poverty neighborhoods in 1989, 71 percent of African Americans were. In the suburbs the concentrations decline, but the gap between the poverty rate for African Americans and the overall poverty rate in the tract increases: poor African-American suburbanites are three times as likely as poor whites to live crowded together in poverty neighborhoods (40.1 percent compared to 13.0 percent).[60]

Racial segregation in American cities is intense. Although statistics show change from year to year, apparent improve-

TABLE 2.5
Percentage of Poor People Concentrated in Poverty Areas, by Race, 1975–89

	1975		1980		1985		1989	
Poor Population	White	African-American	White	African-American	White	African-American	White	African-American
Central city	32.1	70.1	25.4	58.8	42.8	74.9	40.0	71.0
Suburbs	10.2	39.3	13.3	44.1	14.0	45.4	13.0	40.1

Source: Bureau of the Census, *Current Population Survey, Money Income and Poverty Status in the United States*, Series P-60, various years.

ments generally reflect the temporary statistical effects of migration, rather than true integration. (For example, as a Los Angeles neighborhood "tips" from all-white to all-Latino as a consequence of immigration, the Census might measure 50 percent white and 50 percent Latino. This census snapshot would give a very partial picture. A movie, showing the changes from year to year—and the totally segregated endpoints—would more accurately reflect the social reality.) As Douglas Massey and Nancy Denton point out,

> not only are blacks in our largest cities disproportionately likely to share tracts with other blacks, they are very unlikely to share a tract with any whites at all. Moreover, if they go to the adjacent neighborhood, or to the neighborhood adjacent to that, they are still unlikely to encounter a white resident. These agglomerations of monoracial tracts are densely settled and geographically restricted, comprising a small portion of the urban environment closely packed around the center city.[61]

Table 2.6 shows how segregated the largest metropolitan areas really are. In Los Angeles, for example, 79 percent of the African-American population would have had to move to a whiter census tract to even out the racial population distributions. Half the African Americans in the San Francisco Bay Area lived in tracts where at least half the population was African American and less than 42 percent was white.

Updating these numbers to 1990, from preliminary census estimates for the country's ten largest central cities, provides little relief. In Chicago, 71 percent of all African-American residents live in virtually one-race census areas, where at least 90 percent of their neighbors are also African-American. In Detroit, 61 percent live in such totally segregated areas, in Philadelphia, 53 percent. In Atlanta, Washington, D.C., New York, Houston, and Dallas, very high proportions of the residents are similarly isolated, from 43 percent to 29 percent. In Boston this measure of extreme segregation is lower, but it is still 19

TABLE 2.6
Residential Segregation, Ten Largest Metropolises, 1980

Metropolis	Population Size (1988) (thousands)	Percent Black	Index of Racial Segregation	Racial Composition of Tract of Typical Black	
				Percent Black	Percent White
New York	17,053	15	78	64	28
Los Angeles	13,920	8	79	61	30
Chicago	7,396	21	88	84	14
San Francisco	4,950	8	71	51	42
Philadelphia	4,904	17	78	70	28
Detroit	4,434	20	88	80	20
Washington, D.C.	3,849	14	71	69	30
Dallas	3,513	28	78	67	30
Houston	3,306	16	74	66	31
Miami	3,212	20	79	68	30

Source: Reynolds Farley and Steven Schechterman, "The Social and Economic Status of Blacks: Does It Vary by Size of Metropolis?" Table 6 from photostat, Population Studies Center, University of Michigan, Ann Arbor, June 1990.

percent. Even in Los Angeles, 7 percent of the African-American population is totally segregated. In Detroit, Philadelphia, and New York from 1980 to 1990 the degree of segregation actually worsened![62]

Severe residential segregation is not restricted to the largest cities, however. Although segregation does decline somewhat with city size, it remains considerable across the size spectrum. The index of racial segregation (see Table 2.7) is still at a high level, 57 percent, even for metropolitan areas with fewer than 100,000 people.[63] Even in cities not usually included on the "race-problem" agenda, isolation can be severe.[64] As Milwaukee city alderman Michael McGee tells us, the 1980s produced not only wealth but despair. The upscale buildings, restaurants, and museums of downtown "look beautiful. The other world is living good." But given manufacturing job

TABLE 2.7
Residential Segregation, 203 Metropolitan Areas, by Population Size, 1980

Population Size	Number of SMSAs[1]	Index of Racial Segregation	Racial Composition of Tract of Typical Black: Percent Black	Racial Composition of Tract of Typical Black: Percent White
2,000,000+	15	78	66	31
1,000,000 to 1,999,999	17	74	57	41
500,000 to 999,999	33	71	57	41
325,000 to 499,999	29	66	47	51
250,000 to 324,999	22	64	43	56
150,000 to 249,999	38	64	47	51
100,000 to 149,999	40	59	44	55
Under 100,000	10	57	34	63

Source: Robert J. Wilger, "Black-White Residential Segregation in 1980" (Ph.D. diss., University of Michigan, Ann Arbor, 1988), Table 3.3. Printed in Reynolds Farley and Steven Schechterman, "The Social and Economic Status of Blacks: Does It Vary by Size of Metropolis?" photostat, Population Studies Center, University of Michigan, Ann Arbor, June 1990.

[1]Standard Metropolitan Statistical Areas.

losses, ghetto unemployment, welfare increases, and isolation, just "go a few blocks and it changes before your eyes."[65]

These statistics on geographic segregation by income and race are telling, but in many ways they underestimate isolation. Segregation of smaller neighborhoods is higher, reflecting block-by-block separation, especially by race and ethnicity. Segregation in social insitutions—schools, churches, small recreational facilities—is extremely high. More important for our investigation, poor people living in the poorest central-city neighborhoods are increasingly disconnected from local labor markets. Most adults living in high-poverty areas do not have jobs. Close to three-quarters of these adults were out of the labor force altogether in 1980. Another 8 percent of all the adults were officially unemployed (yielding an unemployment rate of 29.6 percent), leaving only 20 percent actually holding jobs. Contrast this 80 percent "high-poverty area" jobless rate with the rates for African Americans in central cities (50 percent) and suburban rings (33 percent), shown above in Table 2.2. Only 38.1 percent of families in these high-poverty areas had earnings; 61.1 percent received public assistance.[66]

Not only are poor African Americans (and Latinos) themselves very highly concentrated in these "poverty" and "high-poverty" areas, but they comprise very large proportions of the poor. In 1989 poor African Americans made up 42 percent of all the poor in central cities and 56 percent of the poor in central-city poverty areas.[67] This concentration of poor people by race increased for many years, along with associated cultural, social, and political isolation, and there is little reason to expect it to decrease in the absence of major political changes. The number of poor African Americans in "high-poverty" areas grew 58.6 percent between 1970 and 1980, while poor white people in those areas increased by only 1.6 percent during the same period.[67] The numbers of households headed by women also are higher in neighborhoods where the poverty concentration is high. Very high percentages of children are poor in female-headed households in poor neighborhoods.[68] Camilo Jose Vergara speaks of "new ghettos" in the worst areas, where

> group homes for children and battered women share buildings with homeless families; drug treatment centers, methadone clinics, shelters, soup kitchens and correctional institutions are also springing up. . . . [T]he new ghettos are defined by what they lack. . . . [P]eople . . . are too disconnected to have formed effective organizations. The transient character of the majority of the residents leaves such urban areas unclaimed, and thus politically powerless.[69]

The Persistence of Today's Poverty

Of the many people who pass through poverty, a smaller number remain poor for long periods of time, but the number is by no means insignificant. One in twenty in the entire U.S. population was officially poor at least 80 percent of the time between 1974 and 1983—double the rate for the period 1969 to 1978.[70] Partial evidence suggests no improvement during the latter half of the 1980s. By this rather strict eight-out-of-ten-years definition, and using the official poverty line, the long-term poor were concentrated in the highest proportions in Southern cities (Atlanta, New Orleans, Memphis) and depressed rustbelt cities (Cleveland and Detroit), but their greatest numbers were in the biggest cities. In six cities alone—New York, Chicago, Los Angeles, Philadelphia, Houston, and Detroit—there were estimated to be more than 1.6 million persistently poor people in 1980.

Within cities, these long-term poor people were most often located in "poor" tracts (20 percent poverty). More than three-quarters of persistently poor African-American persons lived in those areas, a proportion similar to poor African Americans overall. In contrast, although poor whites are not so crowded together (only a quarter of them lived in "poor" census tracts), 61 percent of *persistently* poor whites were crowded in poverty tracts.[71]

Although they are by no means in the majority, taken together a considerable number of people who fall persistently below the poverty line lived in households with intact families, or where the householder was disabled or elderly, or where the householder worked a substantial part of the year. In three-fifths of the persistently poor households in 1980 the head of household was either married and living with a spouse, disabled, elderly, or was usually employed. Thus 60 percent of the long-term poor look like the "deserving" poor.

On the other hand, the remaining two-fifths of the persistently poor often have problems that come closer to pejorative stereotypes, such as welfare-dependence, unemployment, or high rates of dropout from high school. In addition, because African-American families are over-represented among the persistently poor, misuse of the data allows racist stereotyping of the country's poorest people. In fact, most poor African-American families, including those who have been poor over the long term, are poor for the same reasons that white families are—lack of well-paid work with only one employee in the family (often a woman, with little education—close to half have dropped out of school before completing the eighth grade). Children are also highly over-represented among the persistently poor of all races, and most of these are under age 6. We address the structure of employment in the next chapter.

The economic chasm that divides Americans is deepening. The bad situation of the persistently poor in inner-city neighborhoods has hardened into a self-perpetuating form. Barriers of race, ethnicity, and income are eroding the social fabric of our cities and undermining our national economic well-being.

Once we account for race and ethnicity, household demographics, and physical isolation, we have the basis for "explaining" most of the inequality of income that the statistics show. Large numbers of Americans are poorly educated and underskilled, suffer from discrimination, and are hampered by low self-esteem. African Americans are increasingly isolated from mainstream American jobs, education, culture, and economic life, as are Puerto Ricans, Chicanos, Central Americans, women who manage families alone, and slum dwellers. These groups form the base for the evolution of new patterns of urban poverty.

These social, economic, and geographic separations mirror and catastrophically extend the divisions that have been deepening even among better-off Americans, as the middle class has been disintegrating into a more and more affluent portion at the top, and a harder-struggling group of workers and unemployed adults at the bottom.

Sophisticated and experienced observers from the Third World are shocked as they now see in the United States scenes that display familiar sorts of distinctions. The gap between well-off and very poor confronts these visitors when they see beggars outside elegant city shops and restaurants, or when they hear of neighborhoods that are dangerous to visit. These observers have learned to live with, but not to notice such distinctions in the big cities of Asia, Africa, and Latin America. The present danger in the United States is that we are creating a bottom level, like that taken for granted by some in the Third World, with no access to the top. As the next two chapters show, our social institutions now guarantee this result. This is not what America should be about.

Chapter 3

Separate Opportunities: The International Dimensions of American Poverty

In the previous chapter, we identified the driving forces of poverty as underemployment, falling real wages, and a badly skewed income distribution. In this chapter we look at pressures in the global economy that are overwhelming the domestic economy and creating the context for this transformation. In essence, U.S. policy has moved to include the domestic labor pool inside the world workforce. This change not only weakens domestic labor, but prevents it from finding a new perch in the American economy, given labor's isolation from those who control American politics.

In the first two sections, we observe that in the game of industrial restructuring, the bad cards have been dealt to labor. U.S. industry has responded to reorganized global markets by reducing wages as a short-term measure to meet competition. They have worsened working conditions, increased unemployment, and raised poverty. Minorities and others trying to get on the bottom rung of this economic ladder have discovered that the rung has been sawed off and shipped overseas. In the third section we explore the relocation of industrial activity. As industrial composition has shifted and places of employment have moved, labor has been stranded and workers and their families have been impoverished. In the fourth section, we briefly examine components of international economic reorganization, focusing on international trade and saturated domestic markets. Financial and corporate changes have cut into the profits of U.S. firms, which in turn have moved to downgrade labor. Finally, we look at how the globalization of finance and regulatory systems has led to instability, rising speculation, and high levels of debt. Each of these not only generates poverty but erodes the capacity for the sound domestic policy that is required to fight poverty.

Although real wages grew continuously from the end of the Second World War until 1973, they declined precipitously in the 1980s. As we have shown, real wages in 1991 are still far below the levels of the early 1970s. Worse yet, many workers are unable to find full-time or steady work, or any work at all. Minority persons and women suffer additionally from discrimination. It is our argument that these worsened conditions result from inappropriate public policy in the face of the restructuring of industry, shifts in labor demand, and weakness of workers against employers. Sharp shifts in worldwide patterns of economics and politics laid the basis for rising poverty, and layoffs and low wages then combined with untimely and ill-designed political shifts and fiscal withdrawal to cause the recent growth of poverty.

The competition that accompanies increased "openness" of national economies, with less restricted trade, labor, and capital flows, has placed pressure on governments and firms to restructure their operations according to international (rather than national) technological, commercial, and regulatory conditions. New technologies and practices have played a critical role in the restructuring of the global economy and in the reorganization of occupational patterns, urban economies, and whole regions.[1] This, in turn, has led to the reshuffling of national priorities so that low-skilled labor has become far less valuable to the economy, except at bargain-basement low wages. Perhaps the most astonishing result of all is that the explosion of poverty in recent years took place in spite of a period of heralded national economic recovery, as business entered competitive markets on international terms, but without any national strategy.

Under these circumstances, policymakers ought no longer think that poverty problems issue solely from local, or even national, pressures. "Just as a city is not a sufficient unit of analysis of an urban economy, neither is a nation."[2] Although we do not agree with Hazel Henderson that "What's happening in Washington is less important than the globalization processes" or that "the [White House] is as much being buffeted around as the government of any other country," we do think poverty grows in part because of failure to respond properly to international economic pressures. We do agree that, "The inability of governments to manage domestic economies because of the enormous capital flows, along with these globalization processes, is one of the key" causes of our problems.[3]

Whereas once the United States was highly insulated from international economics and politics at least during peacetime, by the beginning of the 1990s it had become merely one (even if still the *leading* one) among equals in the industrial world. And where once the United States could manage the Third World with gunboat diplomacy, even seizing foreign customs offices so as to collect payments on the dock, it now suffers penalties when bankrupt nations fail to pay their debts.[4] The U.S. economy is still mainly domestic, and it need not fear three ultimate financial indignities—it has not suffered hyperinflation, it has not declared bankruptcy or suffered insolvency, and it has not been forced to accept formal instructions from the International Monetary Fund. Nevertheless the country now endures grave economic problems that derive in large part from mismanagement of international finance. Many of these difficulties result in increasing poverty at home.

Three features dominate the current situation: America is less influential in worldwide economic affairs; the international economy itself is less stable; and the landscape of domestic industry has been transformed. In these circumstances, and given the more complete interpenetration of U.S. and world markets, it would be almost impossible to eradicate poverty by relying on the usual domestic economic policies, employment and training programs, or efforts that focus on jobs alone. Policies have not faced up to America's new place in the world.

As we will see, corporate strategies to meet international competition have resulted in disinvestment, deskilling, relocation abroad, and retreat into financial rather than productive activities. These changes, undertaken in part to deal with the pressures of globalization, are only temporary responses to longer-term, more ominous global economic trends.[5] The changes are private, uncoordinated, conflictive, and unsuccessful. The strategies themselves have generated new difficulties, like fiscal crises for particular places and massive unemployment for certain social groups within the United States. Not least among these problems is the pushing out of large numbers of people from the labor market, the victims of the previous chapter, who find fewer and fewer opportunities for good jobs.

Industrial managers and union officials have broken their mutual admiration contracts, and the high wages of organized factory workers and many other employees have been hacked away. After years of progress with technical innovation, product development, advertising, and big assembly lines, American industry contemplates decline. Many industries reached the top of the curve of mass consumption and production and the peak of their technological superiority in the 1970s, which they then followed with cutbacks, shutdowns, job loss, and capital flight. The superprofits that reward technological leadership and fatten domestic wages now belong to industries in other countries.[6]

The transformation began as the steam ran out of U.S. postwar hegemony. Briefly stated, after the full force of the still-limited American welfare state, with its Keynesianism, high wages, supportive labor legislation, and extensive public services, rising expenditures began to outstrip tax resources.[7] Services could not be provided without huge public deficits on top of higher taxes. The Treasury financed the Vietnam war with deficits, and inflation kept moving up and up. To stem inflation, conservatives began to snip the threads of the social safety net; then they cut wholesale. Reactionary politics attacked liberalism. In California in 1977 there was Proposition 13, which drastically limited property taxes and therefore undermined the financial basis for education, public services, and a multitude of locally supported public programs. In Massachusetts, Proposition 2½, passed in 1979, similarly strangled municipal efforts to deliver expected services. In New York City corporate officers who directed the Municipal Assistance Corporation temporarily resolved the city's bankruptcy. They installed an austerity program similar to those approved by international lenders to balance the books of insolvent Third-World countries.

Except in comparatively wealthy suburbs, schools, public services, and maintenance of facilities were neglected, budgets stagnating or reduced. Ronald Reagan, Margaret Thatcher, and other ideologues led an almost global reaction against using public resources to meet domestic human needs, as political leaders, corporate managers, and other well-paid people fought for increased wealth by lower taxes as the path to economic recovery. In the United States the people who could least afford the dismantling of an already weak welfare state were required to bear the burden of a drastic economic overhaul.

The details of the U.S. industrial adaptation to globalization bears examination. We begin by observing how the labor force has been demoted, later turning to changes in industrial organization, trade, and finance.

Restructuring for Whom?

The collapse of the international regulatory system, increased competition, rapid technological change, and the emergence of new patterns and higher volumes of trade in the last decades have meant that U.S. firms are less insulated from international market pressures than they were prior to the 1970s. Given the rise of new competitors, increasing import penetration, and market saturation, relocation can at best be a partial response to international changes. The alternative is internal corporate restructuring, designed to enhance flexibility, increase profits, cut costs, reduce risks, and gain markets. Numerous business texts, self-help management books, and the business press have commented on the process. The restructuring of an industry may include the reorganization of corporate ownership, changes in organizational structure and style, and alteration of occupational and employment relations. There are several consequences of restructuring most pertinent to our study of poverty in American cities. Jobs are lost, wages are cut, and occupational changes are implemented in order to reduce payroll size. There are changes in the way profits are made and consequently the way investments occur. Public policies reinforce and echo industrial restructuring efforts. New employment relations, uncharacteristic of the post–Second World War period, become dominant. (This last consequence of restructuring is discussed below, in the section on labor segmentation.)

Changes in the composition of industries directly affect employment opportunities. New types of jobs and the decline of traditional industrial employment have caused dramatic shifts in occupational categories, wages and benefits, and promotional ladders. Mixed with segmentation of the labor market by race, gender, and age, these shifts lead to marked deficiencies in the structures of opportunity. As we will see in Chapter 4, these deficiencies operate locally to harm city dwellers. Two trends—the shift from manufacturing to service jobs and the disappearance of middle-income jobs—have expanded structures of disadvantage and reduced job opportunities.

The relative decline of manufacturing and rise of services have dramatically worsened the opportunities available to blue-collar workers. Manufacturing work in relatively large firms in many sectors (such as steel, rubber, plastics) and many occupational lines has been historically more secure and better paid than comparable work in service industries.[8] Moreover, these manufacturing industries have traditionally had internal labor markets, with some upper-level jobs generally filled by current employees moving up in the firm. Once employed, even in an unskilled, "entry-level" job, a worker had good opportunities for raises and some chance for promotion; foremen were recruited from the assembly line. Service industries, in contrast, have lower wages and a radically different entry structure. In 1983, various services paid less than manufacturing: wholesale trade paid wages only 56 percent of manufacturing wages, finance—84 percent, social community services—57 percent, and private services—67 percent.[9] Service industries also have more bifurcated occupational distributions, with many barriers between low-wage, low-skill jobs at the bottom, and high-paid, professional, and managerial jobs at the top. Internal labor markets and promotional ladders are uncommon, and union pay scales, with cost-of-living increases, are almost unheard of. Bus "boys" do not become assistant managers; nor do they organize to demand higher wages.

Thus we find that the distributions of occupations in the two sectors differ greatly. Manufacturing workers are heavily concentrated in one middle-income occupational category: operations and maintenance. This is a result of many years of successful negotiations, strikes, and related union struggles in the most highly developed sector of the economy. Service occupations are more widely distributed, but also more heavily concentrated in lower-paying jobs.

These differences in occupational distributions between manufacturing and services generate different patterns of income inequality. The growth of manufacturing employment in the 1950s, 1960s, and 1970s, with reduced inequality in earnings for men, led to reduced inequality of family income. With a few exceptions, cities with higher proportions of manufacturing jobs had lower levels of inequality for both men's wages and family incomes.[10] One explanation for the subsequent severe inequalities and the worsening income distributions noted in Chapter 2 is that the decline of manufacturing and the concentration of service-sector employment in two highly separated wage groups—well-paid and poorly paid—result directly in a bifurcated earnings pattern and more inequality.[11] Additional trouble comes from a new source: manufacturing itself. As part of global restructuring, the manufacturing sector has developed more separated employment pools, leading to growing internal polarization. This results from such changes as the downgrading of manufacturing processes and the development of two-tier wage systems, allowed by deregulation and weakened unions in response to competition from cheaper labor—and more efficient operations—overseas. All this contributes to growing inequality.[12] Much of this inequality is manifested in urban industrial areas with large out-of-work African-American labor forces.

Employment growth has been concentrated in low-wage occupations, and we may expect a continuation of this trend. As we saw in Chapter 2, several groups get low pay: many workers in year-round, full-year positions; and most women, part-time workers, and temporary workers. Estimates for the future are bleak. Table 3.1 presents projections for employment growth until the year 2000. The Bureau of Labor Statistics predicts a 15 percent increase overall, but expects much higher growth in six of thirty-three discrete occupational categories. Five of the six are now dominated by workers with college educations, as the first two columns in the table show. These jobs will not provide general employment relief to the unemployed, the unskilled, or the poor. As the two right-hand columns show, African-American and Latino workers are now under-represented in most of these same growth categories, the exceptions being health services and (for African Americans only) health technology. In these sectors they are over-represented, but in these sectors as well, much smaller percentages of the workers have more than a high school education.

During what may turn out to be the peak years of restructur-

TABLE 3.1
High-Growth Occupations, 1988–2000

Occupation	Percent Growth, 1988–2000	Percent Held by Workers with College Education, 1988		Representation Relative to Representation in Workforce, 1988	
		1–3 Years	More than 4 Years	African-American	Hispanic
All	15%	21%	23%	10%	7%
High technology	52	38	64	70	43
Health assessment	38	35	56	80	43
Law	30	2	95	20	29
Health technology	84	40	22	140	57
Other technology, excluding science and engineering	39	27	54	70	57
Health services	34	22	5	280	86

Source: Gary Silvestri and John Lukasiewicz, "Projections of Occupational Employment, 1988–2000," *Monthly Labor Review* 112, 11 (Nov. 1988): Tables 10–11, pp. 42–65.

ing, in the shift from manufacturing to services between 1979 and 1984, 11.5 million American workers lost their jobs.[13] Of these 11.5 million workers, 5.1 million had held their jobs for at least three years and thus were counted as displaced by the U.S. Bureau of Labor Statistics (BLS) because "their plants or businesses closed down or moved, their positions or shifts were abolished, or not enough work was available for them to do."[14] Another 4.3 million workers were displaced from 1985 through 1989. As BLS analyst Diane E. Herz has written: "Worker displacement is often considered a symptom of poor economic times. While large job losses are expected during recessionary periods, far fewer are expected during expansionary ones." It is with some surprise, then, that Herz continues by pointing out that "Data for the 1980s show . . . displacements . . . were not uncommon even during years of rapid economic growth."[15]

In January 1990, more than six hundred thousand workers displaced in the post-1985 period were still either officially unemployed or had dropped out of the labor force after not finding new jobs. These high levels of unemployment pit workers against one another. More than 40 percent of the displaced workers who did find jobs took substantial cuts in earnings. When we consider transition costs, and then add those who remain unemployed, this means that more than 57 percent of the millions of regular employees who lost their jobs (after three or more years of steady work for the same employer) suffered huge financial losses.

Job losses are directly and indirectly attributable to internalization of the economy. Calculations by the U.S. Office of Technology Assessment (OTA) for 1984 suggest that increases in imports and decreases in exports exercise a tremendous negative effect on employment, the losses running as high as 25 percent in some industrial sectors.[16] Absolute net losses are estimated to be approximately 26,500 jobs for every $1 billion of direct, private U.S. investment that goes overseas.[17] The loss or gain of jobs in sectors that export or compete with imports is particularly important since these jobs tend to be higher paid than those in the rest of the economy. OTA estimates for 1984 were 1.5 million jobs lost in low-wage manufacturing, 2.3 million in medium-wage industries, and 1.6 million in high-wage manufacturing, plus more than 2 million in businesses that supply these manufacturers with materials and services.[18] Workers who lose these jobs are among those either unemployed or forced into lower-paying jobs, inducing a decline in the average real wages in manufacturing and the overall economy.[19] Those who aspire to these jobs find the ladder to employment cut off.

Although most analysts correctly relate domestic employment loss to rising imports and falling exports, the relationship is sometimes obscure. For example, most employment loss comes from gradual reductions, not from complete physical factory shutdowns. Also, the slowdown in U.S. manufacturing growth between 1973 and 1980 looks less severe when compared to still slower rates in other major industrial countries.[20] In addition, as we shall see in the next chapter, the severity of dislocation is much greater in highly specialized places, especially in old manufacturing areas in central cities, the Northeast, and the Upper Midwest. Conversely, the situation is not so bad in suburbs, the Southwest, and areas like Florida, where service industries are more developed.[21] Finally, as we have noted, employment growth in nonmanufacturing provides partial compensation everywhere for the losses in manufacturing, so that a focus on the imbalance of imported and exported merchandise will overstate the job loss, since it ignores any positive trade balance in services. A further complicating factor is that the shift to low-income employment reflects to some degree the entry of a large number of young workers—the baby-boomers—into the labor market.

Unfortunately, none of these factors either provides a strong alternative explanation or mitigates the severity of the manufacturing employment drop. Service employment is growing, but many service occupations are unstable and, as we have seen, often pay less. Service jobs also require different skills than blue-collar work, so that displaced manufacturing workers find the transition to comparable employment difficult. As a result, factory workers are likely to be unemployed for prolonged periods, losing their skills, their influence as role models, and their ability to support households. Moreover, service jobs require more public contact, which encourages more social (and racial) discrimination than the old manufacturing employment structure. Furthermore, in spite of the fact that some regions have been very hard hit, "the problem [of decline in manufacturing employment] has been national in scope."[22]

Overall, then, ignoring special cases like New York, San Francisco, and Boston, service job expansion has not compensated for manufacturing job loss. The transition is difficult and costly for the individual worker and society, and it is unfairly biased. Manufacturing jobs, for example, have traditionally provided better opportunities for African-American men to gain middle-income earnings than have other occupations; the decline in these jobs in particular has disproportionately hurt their employment opportunities.[23] In essence, entrance into the labor market is increasingly difficult and frustrating for the least qualified workers.

The drop in real wages discussed in Chapter 2 has been one consequence of the shift to lower-paid service jobs, of union concessions forced by corporate threats of relocation, shrinkage, or shutdown, and of declining industrial sectors. Real wages grew continuously from the end of World War II until 1973. As Figure 3.1 shows, from 1979 to 1989 wages declined precipitously; as late as 1990 they remained below the levels of the late 1970s. In manufacturing, the real weekly wage fell by 4.3 percent, and for all sectors it fell 3.9 percent between 1973 and 1985. During the same period, real average hourly earnings in all nonagricultural establishments fell 5 percent.

At first view, changing demographics also seem to cloud the connection between declining wages and the growth of low-income jobs. From 1979 to 1984 workers under 35 years of age accounted for 58 percent of the increase in low-annual-income jobs, while only making up 32 percent of the increase in all jobs.[24] An increase in the number and proportion of young workers, who have little work experience, would according to labor market theory be expected to drive wages down and shift the overall distribution of jobs to the low end.[25] As it turns out, this is not the case. G. W. Loveman and Chris Tilly have confirmed this: "The decrease in average earnings [for the entire labor force] is not attributable to the increasing fraction of young workers but to a significant decline in the earnings of

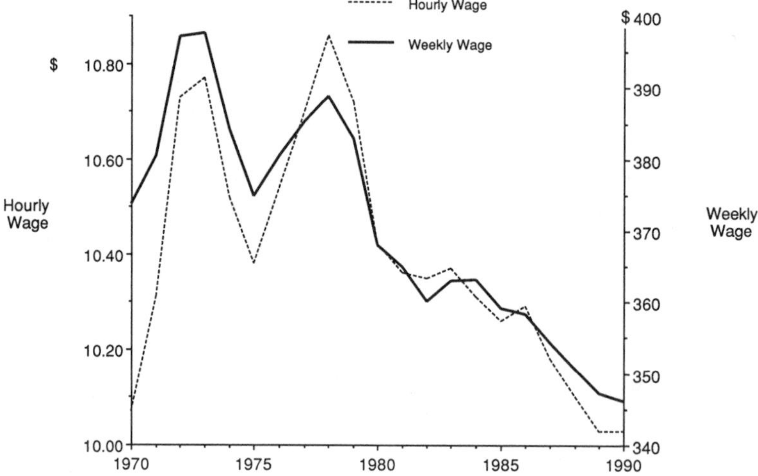

Figure 3.1. Change in Average Real Hourly and Weekly Wages, 1970–90 (in Constant 1990 Dollars). *Source:* U.S. Congress, House Committee on Ways and Means, *Overview of Entitlement Programs: Green Book, 1991*, Appendix F, Table 34.

young workers (both in absolute terms and compared to older workers) from 1967 levels, and even from 1979 levels."[26]

Stated more directly, entry-level jobs are even worse than before, paying less and offering fewer options and opportunities to workers. As we saw in Chapter 2, men of all ages suffered drastic wage reductions between 1979 and 1989. The specific data for *young* men leave little doubt. The disappointing comparisons between 1979 and 1987 appear in Figure 3.2. The situation was considerably worse for young African-American men. By 1987 one-third of all their jobs paid poverty-level wages.[27] The consequences are obvious: no honest, well-paid, male work in the private sector, disintegrating families, alcoholism, crime, and disillusionment.

In many respects, the growth of the service sector is a consequence not so much of a decline as of a changed industrial

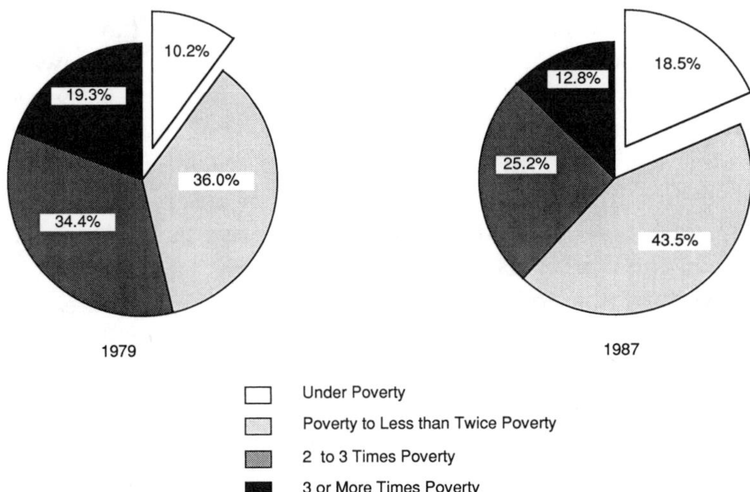

Figure 3.2. Distribution of Earnings for Men Aged 24–35, 1979 and 1987. *Source:* Bennett Harrison and Lucy Gorham, "What Happened to Black Wages in the 1980s: Family Incomes, Individual Earnings, and the Growth of the African American Middle Class," working paper no. 90-1, Carnegie Mellon University School of Urban and Public Affairs, Pittsburgh, Pa., 1990.

order.[28] The connection between services and the goods-producing sector means that the growth of services represents a fundamental transformation in the way production occurs. "Indirect" labor increases while "hands-on" labor decreases; a more complex industrial society emerges instead of a postindustrial one. Those who do physical labor are not only disadvantaged, but also positively discriminated against.[29]

Beating Labor to Pay for Bad Management: New Patterns of Work

As we have observed earlier, what has emerged is a bifurcated labor force—a two-tiered wage structure with many workers poorly paid in unstable, dead-end jobs and others (fewer) employed in jobs with either stability, opportunities for upward mobility, or high pay.[30] And of course the bifurcation is layered on top of racism and sexism that freeze out minorities and women even from the less-desirable jobs. We will see in Chapter 4 how these cleavages are arranged by neighborhood and city zone. Indeed, the discrimination that plays such a large part in housing markets is often matched in urban labor markets.[31]

We turn now to look directly at jobs and how they are allocated. Although macro-economists normally deny or gloss over sharp labor market discontinuities, in fact labor markets have always been broken down into segments arranged on the basis of race, gender, and other ascribed characteristics.[32] In line with changes in the global economy and U.S. adaptations to it, we find that new kinds of labor segmentation are emerging, including deepened divisions by race and gender. The automation of white-collar industry appears to be encouraging resegregation up and down the occupational hierarchy, with women and minorities once again restricted from access to top- and middle-management positions.[33]

Privatization, deregulation, and the growing use of nonunion subcontractors for government work have resulted in new forms of labor segmentation and increased competition among workers within segments.[34] In some cases existing patterns of segmentation—where they protected workers' rights—have been reduced. The use of nonunion labor has risen, with lower wages, benefits, and security, and the undermining of civil-service wage standards. Two distinct labor markets have been created within the public sector, a realm of employment in which minorities and women had in the past achieved substantial gains.

Corporations have pursued four strategies to counter the declining profits that have resulted from increasing competition: reduction of the number of workers on the payroll; increase in financial profits through speculation and investments; intensification of pressure on governments to support the restructuring of industry through more favorable monetary, fiscal, and regulatory policies; and reorganization of production to create new terms of employment. These last two strategies are less well studied than job displacement and financial speculation, which we will treat in subsequent sections. They are, nevertheless, particularly important to the geography of U.S. poverty, since emerging patterns of work tend to move labor disputes outside the traditional range of union activities.

In addition to the relocation of plants to nonunion areas, corporations have benefited from the government's reluctance—even refusal—to enforce social legislation designed to protect workers. In the 1980s we saw such federal antiunion activities as Ronald Reagan's dismissal of the air controllers and the destruction of their union, the Professional Air Traffic Controllers Organization (PATCO); the reversal of earlier prolabor findings by new appointees, so that the National Labor Relations Board (NLRB) restricted industrial organizing; and a five-year lag in NLRB action on complaints by unions that managers had used unfair labor practices, despite increased complaints registered with the board.

Individual firms increase their flexibility to respond to intense competition by engaging in new patterns of work. Patterns have been found to differ among manufacturing oligopolies whose operations are capital-intensive, oligopolies that are labor-intensive, and service firms that are competitive. In each industry type, as Susan Christopherson has shown, firms have worked out special strategies to increase what is now euphemistically called "labor flexibility." This flexibility reduces the opportunity structure for the worker, while increasing the options for the firm.

Capital-intensive oligopolies—generally large manufacturing firms with extensive work sites—have created relatively small cores of full-time workers and a larger set of part-time employees and subcontractors. The full-time workers are covered by benefit plans, offered job security, and expected to remain with the firm. Part-time workers receive lower wages and few benefits, if any. Similarly, the firm has no responsibility for workers employed by subcontractors and therefore need not provide either competitive wages and benefits or secure terms of employment. Union concessions regarding two-tiered wage scales reflect this corporate strategy and structure.

Labor-intensive oligopolies tend to be large firms with small work sites that operate primarily in sales, health care, and finance. Many of these industries have recently been deregulated or subject to changing federal regulations (e.g., deregulation of banking, or federal medical payment policies) that have forced them to become more cost-conscious. Like the capital-intensive firms, these companies create a bifurcated labor force. There is a core of full-time workers, often restricted by direct or institutional discrimination against minorities and women,[35] providing the base for essential activities. As Christopherson says, other workers "constitute an ever-changing ring" of part-time employees, with perhaps one-third of the workers in a firm hired on a part-time basis. Wages polarize along similar lines.

Among competitive service firms, there are two clear strategies for increasing flexibility through employment patterns. These firms are usually small, producing specialized goods or services. Some (industries such as publishing, advertising, and entertainment) require highly skilled labor and offer services on short-term contracts. These industries increase flexibility through well-paid independent contractors, such as professional consultants, who can provide the needed service or technical skill. Low-skill, competitive industries seek flexibility through the intensification of labor. Thus, in apparel and textiles, employees work at home and in sweatshops, with piecework wage rates. Even in clerical work, home-based employment has expanded.

These strategies have heightened the flexibility of businesses. They allow firms easily to reduce labor costs, for example, during short-term downturns in demand—but at the cost of increased unemployment and poverty, imposed through polarized patterns of work and distribution of working time.[36] Instead of the traditional forty-hour work week, both longer and shorter work weeks are becoming more common, this bifurcation being another employment strategy firms use to increase flexibility, reduce fixed costs, and improve profits.[37] Fully employed people in relatively good jobs are working longer hours and taking less leisure, either to make stretched ends meet or to keep their jobs in more competitive labor markets. Nearly one-quarter of all full-time workers were on the job forty-nine hours or more each week in 1989—up from about 18 percent in 1970. In 1989, more than 44 percent of male executives worked long weeks.[38]

At the other end of the spectrum, an increasing number of employees are part-time, temporary, or self-employed, offering what has been euphemistically called "contracted" labor. This strategy has resulted in the expansion of the new group of poor that figure so prominently in the statistics of Chapter 2—underemployed workers. Part-time jobs account for one-sixth of all jobs and in the 1980s grew faster than full-time jobs. One-quarter of the first 10 million jobs created after 1980 were part-time. Part-time workers can be divided into two groups—those who choose to work part-time and those who cannot obtain full-time work. Of the more than 19 million part-time workers, at least 5.6 million want to work more. To these should be added the many workers classified as voluntary part-time employees who, due to child-care or transportation costs, cannot afford to work full-time. Of those workers with such outside obligations (child care, education, and so on), 60 percent are married women over 25.[39]

Although part-time work has increased slowly as a percentage of total work (from 16 percent in the 1950s to about 19 percent in 1990), as the proportion that is voluntary has increased, part-time work overall (which can be measured) has become more sensitive to business cycles. Historically, voluntary part-time employment has increased with total employment growth and has been concentrated in the manufacture of nondurable goods and services. The involuntary part-time labor force—those who would prefer full-time jobs—is growing faster than the voluntary force. Reflecting the decreasing demand for labor, most involuntary part-time work is in manufacturing. Over half the part-time workers in manufacturing want full-time work.[40]

Temporary work has also expanded rapidly. Some 3 million people work at "temporary" positions, engaged in work which can last weeks, months, or years. In 1985, 944,000 "temps" were employed, and a projected growth of 6 percent to 1995 suggests a restructuring of the labor force, using a permanent "temporary" force for certain jobs. Of temporary workers, 64 percent are female, with one-third between 16 and 24 years of age. In January 1985, the Office of Management and Budget issued a circular permitting the employment of so-called temporary workers by the federal government; these workers could be hired for up to four years without benefits (except Social Security). The federal government in the late 1980s employed over three hundred thousand temporary workers in the executive branch alone. In this respect, the deficit, fueled by military spending and trade deficits, and forcing austerity, has a direct effect on the living standards and impoverishment of particular people.

Self-employed, independent "contractors" have also been increasing in the labor force since 1970. From 1950 to 1970, there was a steady decrease in the number of workers who were self-employed, a drop led by reductions in small retail operations. Reasons for increasing self-employment since then vary from personal to structural. Among structural causes for increased proportions of self-employed in the labor force are the deregulation of manufacturing, transportation, and service industries. For example, with deregulation, many previously unionized drivers, working in fleets or directly for shippers, were forced to become independent, self-employed truckers. Salaries also vary widely; in aggregate, self-employed women made less than half as much as men, averaging $7,900 per year as compared to $17,000.

Ignoring for the moment the long-term unemployed and those out of the labor market altogether, among the employed population it is thus displaced workers, temporary workers, and full-time, full-year, low-wage earners who fall most often into poverty. By comparison, part-time work was only a minor cause of below-poverty-level earnings. Some of these groups are temporary or self-employed workers, but the groups are not coterminous and comparisons are difficult. There are few studies of annual earnings, distribution of working hours, job benefits, and job security for these new forms of employment. The conditions of employment of these workers, especially involuntary part-time and temporary workers, make them likely targets for poverty.

From what do these worsened labor market situations arise? Can we connect the status of the domestic labor market to the global economy? We believe the answer is "yes," and we begin by looking at worldwide processes of industrial location.

Industrial Relocation in the International Economy

Contradictory territorial and institutional trends have long been essential in the organization and dynamic reorganization of capitalism. On the one hand, there is centralization of control over capital; and on the other, the spread of trade, production, and markets. Since the 1960s, an increase in overseas investment and manufacturing by U.S. corporations has brought about a dramatic geographic spreading of industrial operations. Concurrently, one of the fastest-growing sectors of the economy, corporate services, has concentrated in the industrial world's largest cities, generating employment, attracting foreign investment, and reshaping the geography of economic relations.

One of the earliest, simplest, and clearest models to depict these changes in the structure of the international economy is the New International Division of Labor (NIDL). From the NIDL perspective, when ownership and control are centralized and activity is dispersed, there are important economic, political, and spatial implications. To draw out these implications, we may conveniently divide multidivision industrial corporations into three groups:[41] headquarters' operations encompass innovation and finance, organization, and engineering activities such as product design; plant-level manufacturing requires complex machinery and skilled workers; assembly and other unskilled operations "in principle [require] no qualifications" for the workforce.[42] There is also a residual, of course—underemployment and unemployment for those left behind when industry moves.

These three kinds of activities in the international economy have different locational requirements. The tasks of finance and communication require corporate executives to have access to centralized network nodes. In contrast, simple assembly production may be relocated to remote areas, insuring easy access to cheap and unorganized labor. Head offices therefore prosper most in a few centers (often called "world cities" or "global cities"). But at the opposite end, businesses locate their assembly and processing plants in peripheral locations in the Third World to facilitate access to unskilled labor. As later writers using variants of the NIDL perspective pointed out, this pattern of industrial location also leads to increased operating flexibility and domination over labor. For example, firms use arrangements such as multiple sourcing of factory inputs and parallel production of the same products in identical factories in more than one country so as to give credibility to threats of factory shutdowns against striking unions.[43] Firms that spread their factory and assembly sites also gain ready access to foreign markets. The resulting allocation of tasks—the spatial division of labor—reflects internal organization of firms and the dispersal of their functions over a varied regional and national terrain. It is, we repeat, played out in the distribution of work, wages, unemployment, and poverty. To some degree there is even a hierarchy of countries, their ranks corresponding to their functions in the corporate organizational structure.[44]

As corporations adjust to the changing international order, they also initiate changes of significance for America. As they relocate manufacturing and assembly to other nations, they place unskilled and skilled workers in the United States in direct competition with Third-World labor markets.[45] Multinational corporations abuse their dominance and mobility to undermine national political power.[46] Finally, in a counterbalance as manufacturing moves to the periphery, corporate control activity creates world cities in the industrialized countries, which become the centers of growth and power, where skilled white-collar jobs of control and management are concentrated.[47]

Recent evidence and analyses have highlighted strengths and shortcomings of this NIDL approach. Although the interdependence of national economies has increased, it is based far less on the relocation of manufacturing activities to the Third World than on the relocation of production plants inside and among the heavily industrialized core countries of Western Europe, Japan, and the United States.[48] Plant shrinkages and shutdowns have debilitated old industrial areas, those places where poverty has grown so rapidly; industrial growth and startups, however, have tended to be in overseas economic giants (like South Korea, Japan, and Germany) rather than in the Third World. Additionally, because the specific needs of some manufacturing operations can be pinpointed—such as the need for skilled labor, advanced technology, massive capital, raw materials, and quickly responsive markets—the limited availability of these inputs restricts activity to highly specific regions of the world. The focused success of high-technology manufacturing in a very few locations in the advanced industrial countries may reflect such specific needs,[49] although it also reflects historical accident, or what location theorists refer to as "the momentum of an early start," like the inertia exerted by the concentration of high finance in New York. Within the NIDL's undifferentiated Third World there thus ends up very little highly sophisticated manufacturing; among some one hundred nations, advanced industry prospers only in a few so-called newly industrialized countries (NICs), such as South Korea, Taiwan, Singapore, Hong Kong, Mexico, and Brazil.[50]

Furthermore, as is now evident, these internationally inspired occupational structures and wage rates generate not only wealth from high-level jobs, but also poverty in American and other Western cities. The loss of high-wage manufacturing is one problem. The growth of the service sector itself leads to an increase in inequality by generating at the top a large number of well-paying managerial and professional jobs, very few new middle-income jobs, and masses of unstable, low-wage jobs. In an ironic reversal, even low-wage, low-technology manufacturing activities now prosper in the First World, as manufacturing growth depends on sweatshop conditions and cheap immigrant labor.[51] For routine assembly work, firms certainly do seek overseas labor, because it is cheap, especially in the Third World, but as workers willing to accept low wages have arrived in the new immigration, they have been put to work in American cities, too. A new internal labor market thus reflects Third-World patterns, with more unemployment and lower wages, fewer benefits, and reduced stability of employment.[52] The critical magnets for plants appear to be cheap, unorganized labor, usually workers inexperienced with industrial production.[53] Such locations in America even include suburbs with large reserves of underemployed women, as well as big-city immigrant and minority ghettos, enclaves just across the Mexican border, and small towns and rural areas that lie outside the manufacturing belt and are not unionized.[54]

Other perspectives on the international economy delineate hierarchical models that are slightly different, providing other clues for analysis. One vision is of a postindustrial society: the shift to services represents a move to an advanced stage of economic activity, following in an evolutionary form after agriculture and industry.[55] A functional hierarchy is based on the role of each country in the global economy, but now with service-based, postindustrial countries at the apex. According to this perspective, the growth of services should be encouraged and hardship (such as poverty) viewed as a temporary cost of transition.

Postindustrialists thus emphasize the importance of education and accommodation to technical progress as crucially important (and missing) elements of a good response to changing global conditions. They and others observe that the transformation alters the demands for labor, greatly reducing the need for people in manufacturing. More precisely, what has declined is demand for labor in the directly productive process, but without any parallel reduction of manufacturing (or agricultural) output.[56] As a result, it is the human, not the capital dimension of the equation that is altered.

Technological change results in the reorganization of production: the value of industrial products declines as automation cuts costs, allowing for an increased volume of nonindustrial activity, including personal services.[57] A few studies of unemployment within this perspective focus on the reduction in the amount of labor required in each successive stage of technological development—"the tendency for smaller increments of employment to be associated with each new 'vintage' of machinery and plant."[58] The fear is that, in the context of international competition, levels of capital investment using high-productivity machinery are not sufficient to reach full employment. "An increasingly large section of the population will continue to be expelled, or at least marginalized, from the sphere of economic activities."[59]

Some theorists argue that these changes in structure and hierarchy result from more fundamental shifts in the organization of society, based not only on the emergence of new technologies but on social systems associated with particular technological regimes.[60] Corresponding to the new wave of technology there will be new core cities and regions, with a corresponding reorganization of national power in the international economy. The United States will not remain the wealthiest country or the generator of new forms of social organization.

The global economy is changing in complex ways. Manufacturing continues to be important, but in transformed ways and in new locations. For example, modern steel production in Fujan, South Korea, in plants imported from Belgium, has brought buoyant growth and optimism to a former fishing village. In contrast, the collapse of old steel plants has virtually destroyed Gary, Indiana, turning it into one of the poorest and most depressed cities in America.[61] What few observers have noticed, however, is that steel is still produced in Gary, with equipment superior to that in Fujan. In fact, production takes place in Gary in one of the most modern and efficient plants in the world. But this does not solve the problem. The problem for the municipality of Gary—its residents, social institutions, and the former employees of the steel plant, their dependents, and those who worked in the "downstream" local economy—is that the new steel plant employs only a small portion of workers from the old plants. As in Fujan and Gary, the shape of things to come in most places will be greatly influenced not only by technology, but also by the way it is applied, and where. That is, many important events will respond to the internationalization of production and the centralization of control. All these changes, if they are not to destroy those unlucky enough to be at the bottom of American society, will require new policies to thwart harmful effects of dislocation, dehumanization, and marginalization of low-income people. In the fol-

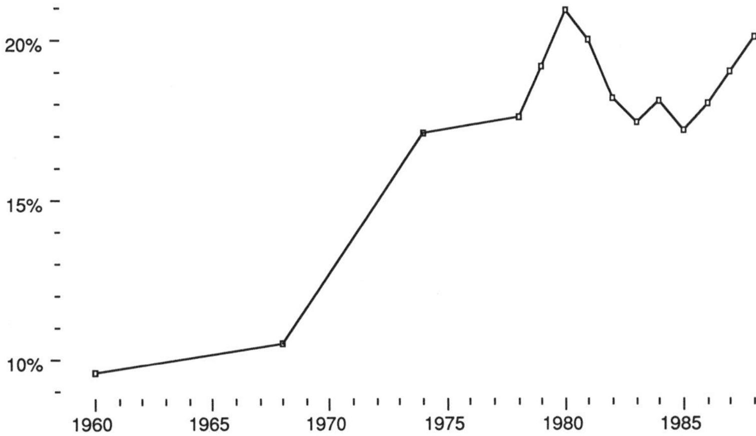

Figure 3.3. U.S. Trade as a Percentage of GDP, 1960–88. *Source:* Organisation for Economic Co-operation and Development, *OECD Economic Outlook: Historical Statistics, 1960–1988* (Paris: OECD, 1989), Tables 6.12 and 6.13.

lowing sections we explore more abstract facets of globalization, with the aim of identifying more focused issues of particular importance to understanding the sources of U.S. poverty.

Trade Flows, Market Saturation, and Corporate Profits

The growing internationalization of capital, commodity, and labor flows is a well documented trend. Evidence of growing international interdependence is revealed through the most cursory examination of data. Figure 3.3 reveals that total trade (imports plus exports) to and from the U.S. market has surged as a share of total economic activity. Until the late 1960s, trade played a relatively small role; imports were never more than 6 percent of GNP. By 1990, imports had grown more than two and a half times in relative terms, to 16 percent of GNP.[62] Do-

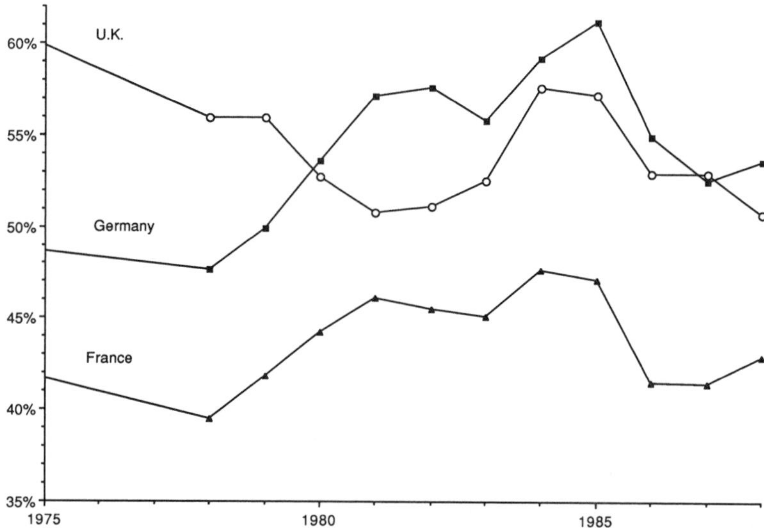

Figure 3.4. Trade as a Percentage of GDP in France, Germany, and the United Kingdom, 1975–88. *Source:* Organisation for Economic Co-operation and Development, *OECD Economic Outlook: Historical Statistics, 1960–1988* (Paris: OECD, 1989), Tables 6.12 and 6.13.

mestic manufacturing suffered the most. By 1986, almost 45 percent (by value) of manufactured products purchased in the United States were imported from abroad.[63]

In other advanced industrial countries, the role of imports and exports in national growth rose as well. There was a rise in the foreign trade of many countries beginning in 1965 and accelerating until 1985. Figure 3.4 documents recent changes for France, Germany, and Great Britain. As Harrison and Bluestone have demonstrated, the most rapid increases in commodity flows have occurred among old industrial partners themselves as well as with a few newly industrialized countries (NICs), each seeking to sell similar goods.[64] "All of the major industrialized countries (as well as the NICs) were producing very much the same collection of products and . . . trading back and forth . . . essentially the same products."[65]

This interpenetration of mass markets led to excess capacity in mass-production industries, as manufacturers in each country attempted to supply the demands of both their own and their neighbors' markets.[66] As competition increased for domestic and foreign markets, corporations operated their plants well below full capacity, thus eroding productivity and raising the unit cost of production.[67] The resulting cutbacks led to a lowering of demand for the domestic labor force in the United States and Western Europe. NIC labor was competing for precisely the same type of work, but receiving much lower wages and fewer social benefits in exchange. This placed domestic labor in competition with overseas labor and put lower-skilled domestic workers in the United States in competition with both overseas labor and one another. In this circumstance, the politically weakest labor groups, namely, African-American and Latino workers, were the losers, and poverty thus rose.

After at least seventy years of American leadership, productivity grew more slowly in U.S. industries than in those of competing nations throughout the 1950s, 1960s, and 1970s. Over those thirty years the growth rate of Gross Domestic Product (GDP) per worker in the United States was barely half the average of fifteen other major industrial countries.[68] Among the large industrial countries, Germany, France, and Japan in particular have increased productivity more rapidly than the United States, typically with two to three times the growth rate. In the United States there was a steep decline from the mid-1980s to the early 1990s.[69] Figure 3.5 shows one estimate of postwar decline in productivity in the United States. Whatever the ultimate judgment on American productivity growth in the 1980s and 1990s, pressure will continue to mount from producers in other nations with more steeply rising productivity. Slower American productivity gains are translated into relatively higher unit costs of production, which cannot easily be passed on to consumers, since markets are increasingly saturated and competitors have also cut costs. Selection among workers for remaining jobs thus becomes tighter, allowing em-

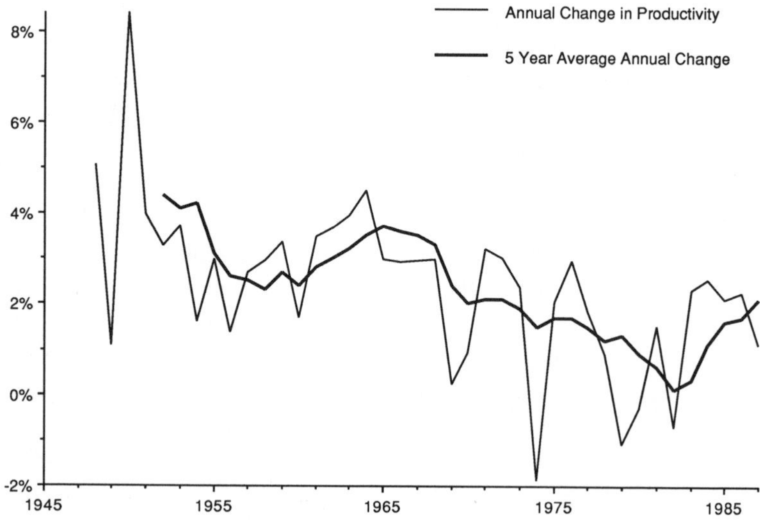

Figure 3.5. Percent Change in Productivity, 1948–90. *Source:* Council of Economic Advisors, *Economic Report of the President, 1991* (Washington, D.C.: U.S. Government Printing Office, 1991), Table B-46.

ployers to insist upon higher qualifications and more rigid screening for positions.[70] As the pressure rises, industry adjusts further. In its adjustment it has dealt out lower wages and more layoffs, reducing the supply of good jobs and indirectly adding to poverty.

By the mid-1970s, markets for consumer durables such as automobiles, washing machines, and radios slowed their expansion. As Piore and Sabel point out:

> This saturation was especially true in the U.S., where in 1979 there was one car for every two residents, compared with one for every four in the early 1950s. Ninety-nine percent of American households had television sets in 1970, compared with 47 percent in 1953. Similarly, more than 99 percent of households had refrigerators, radios, and electric irons, and more than 90 percent had automatic clothes washers, toasters, and vacuum cleaners.[71]

The problem of market saturation was compounded by the entrance of new competitors into the international market for consumer goods. Many Third-World countries pursued policies to encourage the growth of domestic industries. Some, such as the "Four Tigers" (Hong Kong, Singapore, South Korea, and Taiwan), focused on the development of an export base of mass-produced consumer durables. Others, such as Brazil, Mexico, and Argentina, concentrated on the creation of domestically oriented, mass-production industries. One clear consequence was the introduction of competition into markets once well-protected for the corporations headquartered in the industrialized countries. These pressures downward did not affect headquarters, but branch plants and subsidiaries. Similarly, lower-level workers were harmed much more than their white-collar contemporaries. Minority workers more than whites were pushed out of the labor force and into poverty.

The combination of relatively lower productivity in domestic production and increased competition for sales in U.S. and foreign markets translated into declines in the profits of U.S. corporations. From a high of 7.9 percent in 1965, the net after-tax profit ratio of U.S. corporations dropped unevenly by 1990, to only 3.9 percent, as depicted in Figure 3.6. Profits in manufacturing declined even more drastically from the mid-1970s on.[72]

In addition to increases in competition for markets and an increased volume of trade, new patterns of trade emerged in the early 1980s. Reflecting the relocation of production facilities abroad, intrafirm trade (that is, foreign trade between branches of one company) began to boom. In 1982, for example, 27 percent of all U.S. exports went from companies to their subsidiaries, and an enormous 56 percent of imports came from affiliates. The increases in intrafirm trade were reflected in changes in the geographical patterns of U.S. trade; here we see the beginning of growth in imports and exports directed to and from the Third-World locations of subsidiaries and affiliates. Many of the exports actually came back to the United States slightly

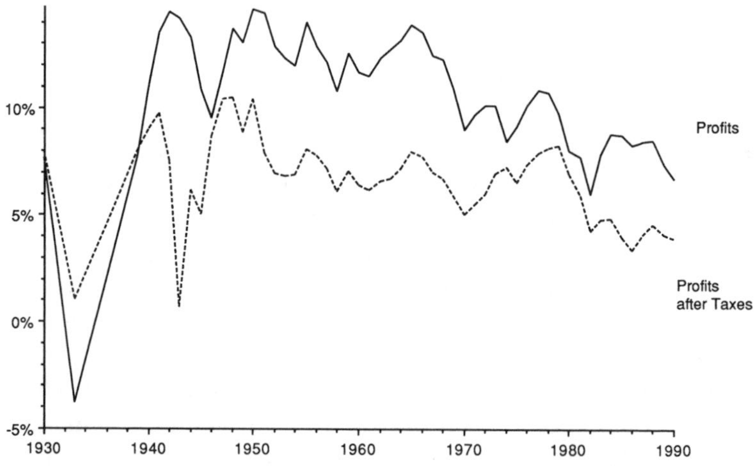

Figure 3.6. Profits as a Percentage of National Income, 1929–90. *Source:* Council of Economic Advisors, *Economic Report of the President, 1991* (Washington, D.C.: U.S. Government Printing Office, 1991), Table B-24.

modified as imports; between 1983 and 1985, one-third of the increase in U.S.-manufactured exports were components of goods later imported, after assembly or other work done mostly in Third-World "export platforms," such as the Mexican border *maquiladora* plants.[73] In essence, as we said in introducing this chapter, a world workforce replaced a domestic labor pool. The U.S. workforce has been unable to retain its privileged position in the world marketplace. They have joined with less fortunate workers in a global pool, isolated from political power.

Internationalization of Finance and Regulation: Instability, Speculation, and Debt

As international commodity flows changed, international financial markets were reorganized. As they reorganized,. they created additional pressures of increasing competition, uncertainty, and instability on firms, communities, and families. The globalization of finance has weakened the control any one country has over capital circulation. Simultaneously, however, increased capital flows, reduced financial regulations, and more developed communication technologies have increased the possibilities for speculative gain and thus opened new ways for firms to make money. These transformations have had an effect on the strategies that U.S. businesses use to increase profits. These strategies have exacerbated poverty in American cities by placing the fate of American workers and firms in the hands of foreign capital markets.

The internationalization of finance further weakened U.S. control over international exchange and investment. The introduction of the floating dollar, as a way to stabilize the international monetary system, proved to be destabilizing to trade and economic policy. Fluctuations in currency values influence the national economy by affecting capital flows, competitiveness, trade, employment, profits, and debt.[74]

High interest rates within the United States, and the low value of the dollar, did help to attract foreign investors. As U.S. investment abroad increased, so did foreign direct investment in America.[75] Between 1976 and 1980, foreign investors financed 196 plants in New York, 161 in California, 94 in North Carolina, and 87 in Texas.[76] Much of this investment, however, consisted of the purchase of existing plants and buildings rather than the construction of new ones.[77] Attracted by the declining value of the dollar, investors improved their access to the U.S. market, avoided import and tariff restrictions, found an available labor supply, and were blessed by intense recruitment by local government. In spite of this minor relief, investment slacked in the areas that traditionally absorbed low-skilled and underskilled workers, causing great difficulty for people at the low end of the economy.

Other sources of destabilization include the rise in oil prices under OPEC, followed by the huge increase in petro- and Euro-dollars entering the global economy. Forecasts of input prices are essential to the accurate planning of industrial production targets and market strategies; thus, the OPEC-manipulated price increases for petroleum, beyond the relative price effect, proved to be an unanticipated factor that greatly harmed some industries, such as autos and tires.[78] The magnitude of money flowing from the core oil-importing countries to the OPEC countries after 1973 has, as we have suggested earlier, several direct implications regarding poverty as well. First, as capital flowed out of the United States to be invested in industry in other nations, part of the U.S. labor force was idled. Second, the capital available for financing both domestic production and taxes for government services diminished.[79] Finally, the domestic agenda became hostage to congressional and presidential concern about foreign economic affairs for the first time in American history. Put more simply, after 1979, U.S. poor people had to compete for attention with Saudi Arabia's needs and interests. By 1991, the Persian Gulf war took precedence over domestic responsibility.

As finance was internationalized, U.S. economic growth in the 1980s was bought at great social costs—declining average living standards, growing inequality, and increasing poverty. Moreover, as Harrison and Bluestone point out, this growth, whatever its skewed benefits, was "achieved almost entirely by two manifestly undesirable means." First was the joint explosion of military budgets and the federal deficit, driven by both global political competition and global financial change. The federal government spent $1.3 trillion more than it collected in taxes and government receipts from 1981 to 1989.[80] Consumer and business indebtedness also increased.[81] The domestic debt is in good part a response to worsening domestic economic conditions. These growing debts have become a double burden on the poor. Government services have been reduced to balance the budget, and government programs aimed at correcting economic inequality have been abandoned. The second undesirable source of growth was distortion and underfunding of civilian research and development.[82] Thus, as the nation failed to renew its industries and underfunded innovation, enormous debts were poured like diluted cement into failure-prone foundations of the future.

These changes in the structure of world trade and finance have created additional pressures of increasing competition, uncertainty, and instability on companies, cities, workers, and their families. The nation is dividing itself economically and committing economic cannibalism among communities and classes. Corporations have relocated production activities, reoriented investment priorities away from production, and, as technologies and government regulations permit, reorganized production itself. In spite of these efforts, corporations have been only partially successful at fighting overseas competition. American shares of world trade have dropped; profitability and productivity rates have declined; and U.S. firms have failed to remain competitive in such manufacturing industries as steel, autos, television and videocassette recorders, and semiconductors. These problems all suggest a long-term decline in competitiveness of some American industries, with corresponding losses of the jobs upon which some American communities and large segments of the most vulnerable members of the labor pool depend.[83]

Financial Restructuring at Home: Instability and Speculation

As financial institutions have globalized, domestic financial markets (if it still makes sense to call them that) have been transformed. The volumes of stocks and futures traded increased fourfold from 1977 to 1987. The use of debt to finance mergers and acquisitions, the creation of junk bonds in the early 1980s, and the increase in mutual funds all attest to the aggressive competition to make profits, even if only on paper. Between 1983 and 1986, approximately 12,200 companies changed hands. In 1986, mergers, acquisitions, and takeovers amounted to nearly one-fifth of the market value of all traded stock.[84] As Harrison and Bluestone have noted, already by the early 1970s "the return on nonfinancial assets had fallen so low in the 'mature' industrial sectors—such as steel, auto, machine tools, apparel, and textiles—that the financial officers who came to dominate the firms in these industries chose to divert their available cash to activities other than manufacturing."[85]

As is widely appreciated by now, hostile takeovers have costs in other ways. Many corporate raids are initiated to produce profits without any intention of taking over or even restructuring a firm. Yet these transactions, and the "greenmail" money paid to hostile corporate raiders to forestall takeovers, result in reduced funds for reinvestment in productive capacity—the so-called hollowing of the American corporation. Many corporate leaders are troubled by this trend. In *Business Week* we read that "corporate managers are so busy trying to preserve themselves that the entire focus of business has turned to short-term payoffs. They're too busy fighting Wall Street to fight Japan. How can anyone concentrate on doing what is needed for long-term competitiveness—spending for plant and equipment, R&D, and job training—when they're so busy battling for survival."[86]

The emphasis on short-term profits means laying off workers, sacrificing research or capital investment, and selling off assets to gain a profit rather than investing in new products. These changes have dramatic implications for the American standard of living and income inequality. Acquisitions, takeovers, and mergers weed out some unproductive firms to insure economic efficiency, but they also do damage. In 1986, for example, Borg Warner, Goodyear, Holiday, and Potlatch were all targets of corporate raids despite reasonable market performance. In order to pay off junk bonds, otherwise profitable plants are sold and workers lose jobs. Fears of takeovers also prompt corporate restructuring. Union Carbide Corporation, following an unsuccessful raid, doubled its debt (to $5.5

billion), sold several profitable businesses, and cut 20 percent from its U.S. payroll.[87] Similarly, Goodyear and USX underwent corporate restructuring, including the sale of assets, plant closures, and employee dismissals, to improve stock performance and ward off future takeover attempts. As Unical Corporation chairman Fred Hartley said about the high costs of debt, "Every day we open the door we spend $2 million for interest. Think what that would have done for the U.S. if it had been put into job creation."[88]

The trend away from production and toward financial manipulations involves a parallel rise in the number of services required to conduct business, with occupational implications similar to those discussed in the previous section. Also, the focus on finance and quick profits has led to increasing instability. The earlier, much publicized failures of Continental Illinois Bank, Executive Life Insurance, and others were the edge of a crevice. Since then it has been an avalanche: savings-and-loan defaults amount to a half-trillion-dollar debt, many insurance companies are in trouble, and bank failures are mounting. These debts reduce the economy's capacity to produce both new wealth and new jobs.

Deregulation and Other Government Intervention: Aiding and Echoing Corporate Restructuring

Federal tax laws have long favored restructuring and speculative strategies, the very strategies that result in decreased productive investment, increased risk of financial collapse, and employee layoffs. Corporations can make money by closing plants and writing off the estimated value of closed plants against profits made in other units of the corporation. Union Carbide earned $620 million in tax savings by closing chemical plants. United Technologies received $424 million for closing down its computer-equipment subsidiary. For halting domestic production of some aircraft components, TRW was able to write off $142 million in tax liabilities.[89] Each of these transactions had enormous consequences on the workforce and in the nation. Other companies have used these tactics to reduce the size of their workforce and to stall unionization or collective action by workers.

Government tax laws also help corporations and traders to shift from productive investments to quick paper profits by treating interest on debt as a tax deduction while taxing the return on equity twice.[90] Acquiring debt to finance takeovers, stock buybacks, or pay "greenmail" is a less expensive form of financing than equity since, under current tax laws, interest costs are deductible but dividend payments are not.[91]

Federal policies have also promoted restructuring by allowing heightened competitive pressures to bear on firms operating in the United States. Industries that have been deregulated include communications, banking, insurance, stock-market transactions, and airlines in the 1970s, and trucking, railroads, oil, cable television, intercity buses, and AT&T in the 1980s. As a consequence of deregulation, many changes—some good and many bad—have occurred. Firms have changed product lines, markets, production organization, and production techniques. In the insurance and banking industries, for example, deregulation resulted in increased diffusion of new technologies, as firms rushed to introduce information technologies driven by the extremely competitive environment into which they were suddenly thrust. Worst of all, deregulation leaves the country without a rudder for steering through international waters. As we saw earlier in this chapter, most of the restructuring in response to deregulation puts enormous pressure on firms to reduce employment, cut wages, and intensify work.

Deregulation of these industries also changed the economics of doing business in various market segments, reducing the profitability of the mass market and standardized product offerings. This drove firms upmarket to corporate and wealthy consumers, and it led firms into serious market segmentation strategies. For instance, high-priced products such as so-called personal banking are delivered in posh surroundings by highly skilled employees. Low-end "financial" products, in contrast, are produced and delivered by computers and automatic teller machines. Only with the last competitive wave of 1988 did banks again focus on winning low-end customers through personal services. Government has also privatized public services, sometimes at high social cost, and it has reduced benefits to its workforce, not only by letting pay raises lag behind inflation, but, as we have seen, by relegating many jobs to "temporary" status and special contracts, without full benefits.

Privatization

Although privatization was ostensibly instituted to boost and modernize the economy, it has resulted in fewer efficiencies than intended, with much higher social costs, in products that are less safe, of lower quality, and less available, and, of most consequence for our study, the changes have resulted in fewer employment opportunities for the socially disadvantaged. The crises of savings and loans, banks, and insurance companies, as well as the experience of airlines and intercity buses in the 1980s suggest that deregulation and privatization, after a short period of intensified competition, may ultimately reduce competition. As fewer firms survive price wars, and as takeovers, mergers, and acquisitions rise, the concentration of ownership in these industries increases. The government has even sold off profitable public facilities. For example, in 1987, the government sold Conrail, the leading firm in freight transport, despite continuous profits since 1981. Service provision also falls as firms cut costs wherever possible. In commercial airlines, this has meant an increase in flight delays and cancellations, lost baggage, and difficulties in scheduling. In trucking and intercity bus service, it appears to have increased the accident rate.

In privatized industries, it has meant increased costs for and decreased access to services commonly thought to be public.[92]

A Comment on Public Policy

Global economic reordering and intensified competition have been followed by industrial change, a shift to the service sector, and a focus on paper profits. Public policymakers, while aiming vaguely to keep America competitive internationally, have neglected the long-term needs of manufacturing and shifted the burden of change to employees, those without employment, and ordinary citizens.

We do not mean to suggest that the problems of unemployment and poorly paid jobs would be solved by a return to mass manufacturing. There is no such evidence. Even where reinvestment in manufacturing has revived and where reindustrialization has occurred, the job structures are now more polarized than before.[93] Protected occupations in high-wage craftwork coexist with highly competitive, low-paid, and poorly regulated occupations, and with increasing numbers of part-time, temporary, or subcontracted jobs. In other cases there are fewer jobs needed to produce the same output.[94]

Federal policymakers remain mired in the past; they need to look to the future. Policies that emphasize trade retaliation will provide only marginal benefits for the poor. Programs that aim at improving the position of capital through tax initiatives, deregulation, and similar benefits are unlikely to build more or better jobs, but are likely to destroy job ladders. Supply-side excesses have exacerbated the problems of the poor by freeing business to seek higher returns by destroying jobs, consolidating enterprises, and making profits on currency and tax loopholes rather than by encouraging business to concentrate on the development of productive wealth. As a result, workers' incomes have been sacrificed for short-term capital gains.[95] In the long run, these policies, given the new global order, threaten to bring to American cities conditions reminiscent of the poverty of many Third-World nations.[96] The nation needs a strategy of economic planning that will build the necessary infrastructure, both human and physical, to meet the challenge of the next century.

Chapter 4

Separate Places: The Changing Shape of the American Metropolis

Cities and poor people living in them suffer particularly from the transformations that we detailed in Chapter 3. While rural poverty remains important, the shift of new jobs to the suburbs and sharp segregation of people of color into crowded, isolated neighborhoods have become defining characteristics of American society. The movement of middle-class African Americans and Latinos to suburbs since 1970 does not mask the alienation of those left behind.[1] As labor markets have become both more capricious and more demanding, few good full-time jobs have opened for unskilled men and women, white or minority. As the economy has shifted to services and as occupations have bifurcated even in manufacturing, possibilities for higher wages or promotion to better jobs have appeared for some, but steadily diminished for others.

City job losses and suburban growth not only leave urban economies stranded, but given the failures of national urban policy, they also leave public services without sufficient tax support, so that cities and their suburbs are driven still farther apart. Government jobs, one of the last redoubts for minority employment, have been cut and downgraded. A cycle of ever-worsening economic and public service conditions for minority city residents has set in.

Racial segregation has nearly always been a dominant characteristic of American cities. In the last thirty years it has become in many ways more rather than less pronounced. As is suggested by the data on hypersegregation we presented near the end of Chapter 2, the vast proportion of social and economic interaction of cities takes place only among whites, or among people of color, without any crossing of racial lines.[2] The situation is most extreme for African Americans, where high proportions live in virtually single-race tracts. There are similar if less pronounced separations of Latinos, Asians, and others.[3] There is an aura of fear that leads to partitions between metropolitan lives. White adults travel by train or private auto, via what one might call "honky tubes," from city offices to suburban residences.[4] White suburban teenagers do not often visit the city; African-American city teenagers rarely venture into the suburbs, or even into unfamiliar parts of the city. Grafted on top of historical circumstances, economic differences, and ethnic affinities, the old plagues of ignorance and racism play a big part.

Prospects for improvement in the economies of central cities, minority job networks, and residential integration of metropolitan areas are not good. Recent trajectories, if followed, will lead to continued worsening of the situation for minority persons, for central cities, and especially for those who live in high-poverty neighborhoods.

Changing Regional Economies and City Systems

The aggregate rate of decline (or growth) in any city depends on luck, structure, and history. Places endowed with a healthy portion of industry that enjoys booming demand for its products do relatively well; places dominated by firms in declining industries do not.[5] Cities with aging streets, bridges, sewer lines, and water treatment plants must bear substantial repair costs—hence high taxes and perhaps relative disinterest from investors. Old cities with lagging industrial sectors may be hit doubly hard; steel towns in Pennsylvania or Ohio are the prototypes. These places have become economically weak. This weakness in turn thins the social and economic fabric that holds the community together, so that not only does poverty rise, but incentives for new economic growth may in turn be weakened. Gary, Indiana, and especially East St. Louis are sad examples.

As part of a broad regional trend, manufacturing plants have moved away from the biggest cities of the old industrial heartland to the South, the West, and abroad. These losses have been reinforced by the general, national decrease in need for labor in manufacturing and related blue-collar occupations, along with an increase in demand for white-collar and service-sector employees. These geographic and occupational changes are consequences of technological advances in manufacturing that have resulted from changes in the way corporations are organized internally to produce and transport their goods, introduce new technologies, and provide new services.[6]

In the 1970s, scholars writing about regional response to global integration focused on the rough evidence of declining employment and population in the Northeast and growth in the Southwest, which they called the "frostbelt-sunbelt" or "rustbelt-sunbelt" shift.[7] Since the mid-1970s, the decline of traditional domestic manufacturing has meant that many cities, heavily dependent on those industries, lost significant parts of their employment base. Those losses in turn led to outmigration, tax loss, reduced services, and increased poverty.

In 1950, more than 70 percent of all manufacturing jobs were concentrated in the metropolitan areas of the Northeast and Midwest.[8] As national industry was intensely reorganized, there was a dramatic shift in total employment. The South and West grew more than twice as fast as the Northeast and Midwest regions from 1970 to 1980. Then, from 1979 to 1986, em-

TABLE 4.1
Change in Employment, All Sectors and Manufacturing, by Region, 1979–86

Region	% of Total U.S. Manufacturing, 1986	% Change in Manufacturing Employment, 1979–86	% Change in All Employment, 1979–86
Northeast	23.2	−15.5	9.8
Middle Atlantic	15.8	−18.7	7.8
New England	7.4	−7.8	15.4
Midwest	28.7	−17.3	0.8
West North Central	6.8	−10.4	3.8
East North Central	21.9	−19.3	−0.4
South	31.2	−3.8	15.4
West South Central	7.9	−8.3	12.3
East South Central	7.0	−7.4	5.6
South Atlantic	16.3	0.4	20.8
West	16.9	1.7	15.4
Pacific	13.7	0.5	14.7
Mountain	3.2	7.4	17.5
U.S. Total	100.0	−10.2	10.2

Source: Adapted from John Kasarda, "Jobs, Migration and Emerging Urban Mismatches," in *Urban Change and Poverty*, ed. Michael G. H. McGeary and Laurence E. Lynn, 148–198.

ployment stagnated in the Midwest, grew slowly in the Northeast, and grew rapidly in the South, the West, and New England (see Table 4.1). In the older industrial regions of the country, employment in manufacturing declined rapidly in the 1980s. Fewer manufacturing jobs are now concentrated in the original industrial areas than in the rest of the United States, the turning point coming in the late 1970s.

As a result of these manufacturing declines, job displacement is a serious problem, much worse in some regions than others. It results in deep and persistent poverty. Although in the 1980s services accounted for an astounding 90 percent of all new jobs,[9] with the exception of a few major metropolitan regions, service-sector employment grew relatively slowly in the

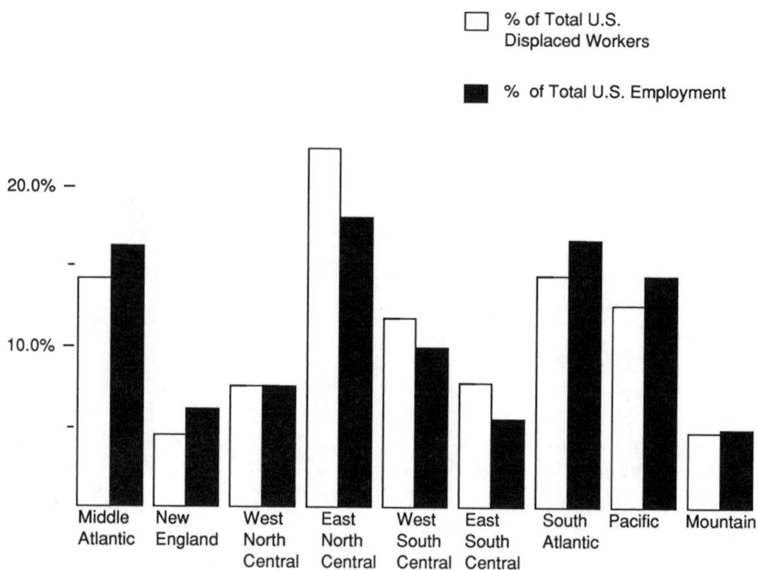

Figure 4.1. Percentage of U.S. Labor Force and Percentage of U.S. Displaced Workers, By Region, 1986. *Source:* Ann R. Markusen and Virginia Carlson, "Deindustrialization in the American Midwest: Causes and Responses," in *Deindustrialization and Regional Economic Transformation,* ed. Lloyd Rodwin and Hidehiko Sazanami (Boston: Unwin Hyman, 1989), Tables 2.1 and 2.2.

most severely affected job-loss areas—the Northeast and Midwest states. There, both manufacturing and service jobs are difficult to find, leaving many out of work.[10]

As Figure 4.1 shows, displaced workers in the mid-1980s were most highly concentrated in the eastern Midwest states (Michigan, Ohio, Indiana, Illinois, and Wisconsin). Despite accounting for only about 18 percent of the national workforce, this region accounted for 22 percent of displaced workers. Other manufacturing areas—the Middle Atlantic states (New York, New Jersey, and Pennsylvania) and the East South Central states (Mississippi, Alabama, Tennessee, and Kentucky)—

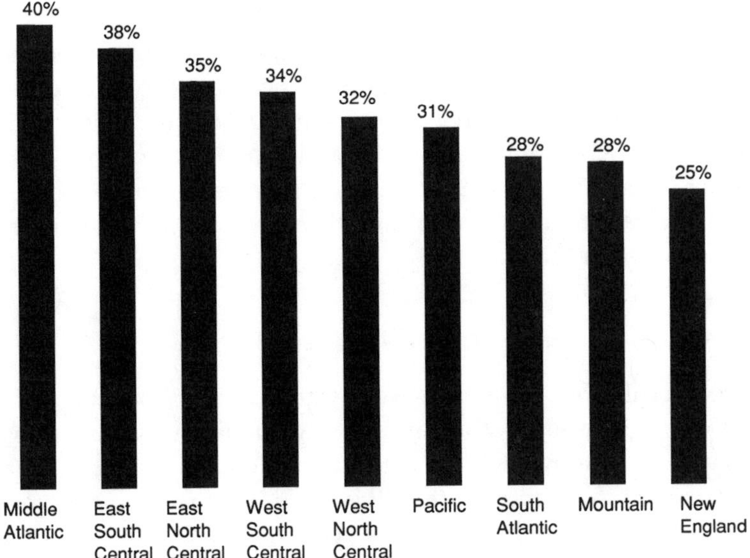

Figure 4.2. Persistent Worker Displacement Rates, by Region, 1986. *Source:* Ann R. Markusen and Virginia Carlson, "Deindustrialization in the American Midwest: Causes and Responses," in *Deindustrialization and Regional Economic Transformation*, ed. Lloyd Rodwin and Hidehiko Sazanami (Boston: Unwin Hyman, 1989), Table 2.3.

also had more than their share of displaced workers. All these states had heavy concentrations of lower-skilled minority workers.

Figure 4.2 shows that displaced workers in all regions, but especially in the old industrial areas, had great difficulty finding new jobs. For example, although the laid off timber, auto, and other workers of the Pacific Coast did better than their fellow displacees in the Northeast, still by 1986, 31 percent of them had no jobs. Forty percent of the displacees in the Middle Atlantic states had not found jobs.

The boom in the South and West and the decline of the Northeast and Midwest were initially attributed to the continued filling of the frontier, the seeking of better climate, a demographic shift to an older population, and corporate or military investment patterns.[11] No matter what the cause, this economic volatility most dramatically harmed African Americans and Latinos in the declining areas, since they had relatively less mobility than whites for both social and economic reasons. As a result, as manufacturing jobs moved, African Americans especially were stranded in communities that had no further demand for their talents.[12]

Urban Hierarchies

Theoretical and empirical work emphasizes how regional change is caused by the different functional roles that cities play in the international or national economic system.[13] As we have noted in Chapter 3, the division of labor results in a hierarchy of cities based on levels of economic specialization, with top cities dominated by higher-order administrative and coordinating functions.[14] Different city roles—that is, different positions in the urban hierarchy—result in varying kinds and degrees of economic growth.[15] Some cities are more vulnerable to recent economic changes.[16]

As the analysis in Chapter 3 suggests, top-ranked cities, the most "diversified, advanced service centers," appear to have benefited most. These cities are highly integrated into the international network of finance and management, and in them are concentrated the control functions of multinational and national corporations.[17] This control involves advanced services, which have grown at all levels of the hierarchy, especially in national economic capitals like New York, London, and Tokyo. There continues to be a very high concentration of the head offices of manufacturing firms in New York and Chicago, and, to a much lesser degree, in a half-dozen other cities.[18] Top cities also have high concentrations of investment banking, corporate law, management consulting, information processing, and other advanced business services, which are increasingly important in the economy. Although they have lost large numbers of jobs in traditional manufacturing, these few cities have rebuilt the foundations of their economies through the growth of advanced services. Corporate service activities give world cities a level of control over their destiny.[19] Thus, the rise of services and the internationalization of production have converged to benefit a few select places.[20] Even direct foreign investment has benefited those few cities in which banking, finance, and related corporate service activities are concentrated, especially the New York region, Chicago, the San Francisco Bay area, and Los Angeles.[21]

Yet even in these relatively well-off cities, the numbers of poor people are enormous, and their misery is increasing. Those laid off are not the same ones who get the new good jobs; many of those who do replace their jobs do so at lower pay. Both of these groups are added to those previously without work or with low wages. If anything, the separation that serves as the main theme of this book is most evident where large, poor, segregated ghettos and barrios sit side by side with booming financial centers.

Farther down the urban hierarchy, international competition and corporate restructuring have combined with inappropriate public policy to severely disrupt the economies of cities formerly based on manufacturing.[22] This disruption results from more than the faltering and decline of the industries themselves. Even in those places where plants continue in operation, officers and their staffs involved in planning, administration, and financial activities move to corporate headquarters (in other, fewer cities). These moves, which began during the 1960s and 1970s and continued through the accelerated takeovers and mergers in the 1980s, meant that manufacturing cities "lost what little involvement they may have had in the planning, administration, or research and development functions of their industry."[23] These cities were left extremely vulnerable to shifts in market conditions, because there was little likelihood of immediate growth in other sectors as traditional manufacturing declined—hence the name "rustbelt."

At the bottom of the hierarchy, the cities most likely to be hurt by economic change are those with narrow economic specialization. Each of these cities is highly imbedded with an associated set of businesses, each in a particular complex of industries (such as Detroit—automobiles, Rochester—scientific and office equipment, Akron—tires).[24] Even some metropolitan regions with historically large numbers of national corporate headquarters and divisional head offices, such as Cleveland and Milwaukee, have barely managed to offset production job losses in manufacturing by adding new employment in advanced services or corporate offices.[25]

Statistics on Milwaukee, for example, show a loss of 60,000 manufacturing jobs in two decades. The official unemployment rate in 1991 among African Americans—in spite of the fact that Milwaukee has one of the nation's most robust, revitalizing economies—was 20.1 percent, not counting people who have given up looking for work or those who are subemployed. The white unemployment rate was only 3.8 percent. As Alderman Michael McGee, who started a militant black militia in Milwaukee sums it up, "Things are not booming in the Black Community. The only new construction is churches, the No. 1 employer is drugs."[26]

Regional Change

The rise of some cities as opposed to others is also related to the business climate provided by local governments and community groups. Businesses tend to avoid cities that are perceived by business leaders to have antigrowth climates—characterized by high taxes, strict site regulations, and strong labor unions.[27] The recent movement of firms back to the Northeast (previously with very strong unions and high taxes) can be seen as the result of a process of rearrangement of the local political environment, which includes a weakening of prolabor and proneighborhood institutions.[28]

Industry in the 1970s preferred Southern and Western cities because labor was weak there. Southern and Western states offer a labor force inhibited by right-to-work legislation, which helps firms avoid unionization of new industrial plants and service industries.[29] Additionally, the presence of large immigrant and minority populations, often weakly attached to local politics and therefore relatively defenseless, may have further weakened the opportunities for labor organization. As Edward Bergman said:

> It's very hard to find a Southern city that's not doing well. . . . [Population and industry] trends that have accelerated since the early 1970s have brought much of the nation's urban prosperity to the South. . . . While smokestack industries have been declining in the Northeast and Middle West, manufacturers have been drawn to the South by the area's relatively low wages and anti-union attitudes.[30]

We caution against too much regional specification of industrial and employment change. As a counterexample, take the case of Los Angeles. As Edward Soja and his colleagues have shown, there one recognizes four familiar, strong elements of the urban economy: the "sunbelt" city of booming high-tech manufacture; the "control" city with a growing, high-finance "downtown"; the "rustbelt" city of declining heavy manufacturing (in autos and airplanes); the "Third-World" city of sweatshops with immigrant Asian and Latino workers.[31]

As the case of Los Angeles suggests, political and policy analysts in any particular city should look closely at local industrial structure, not just regional averages and trends. Nevertheless, there are justifiable regional generalizations. Regional economic decline is reflected not only in lost jobs and high unemployment, but in underemployment as well.[32] In 1980, underemployment rates ranged from almost 16 percent for Midwest metropolitan areas to over 20 percent in the metropolitan areas of the South.[33] The composition of underemployment varies sharply among regions, reflecting variations in the economic base. Rates in the Northeast industrial and Midwest metropolitan areas are lower than in the South and West. This variation is explained by differences in intermittent employment and in high levels of full-time, full-year employed workers with less than poverty-level wages. The boom-time reflected in low unemployment in the South and West may be good for business, but it can be hard on workers.

Geographic Wage Variations

Recent growth and projections of future employment suggest that the trends toward increased inequality of pay and growing numbers of low-wage jobs will continue. Manufacturing has steadily decreased its share of total employment in cities, while the share of service-sector employment has risen. In the 1960s, manufacturing accounted for nearly one-third of total metropolitan employment, but already by the late 1970s it employed hardly one-fifth of workers in large urban areas. The declines in central cities began earlier and have been much more severe. Finance, insurance, real estate, retail, and construction became relatively more important to the economic base of large metropolitan areas.

As noted in Chapter 3, the Bureau of Labor Statistics estimates that demand will increase disproportionately for low-wage workers. Cashiers, registered nurses, janitors, truck drivers, waitresses and waiters, wholesale trade salespersons, nursing aides and orderlies, retail sales personnel, accountants and auditors, and kindergarten and elementary teachers are among the growing occupations. Unfortunately, among this varied group of potential workers—using today's pay as a standard—only registered nurses, wholesale clerks, and accountants will earn more than the average weekly wage.[34]

Increased income inequality and low-wage job growth are pronounced throughout the Midwest states and in most of the largest cities of the country. In the Northeast and Midwest states, employment growth in the 1980s was almost exclusively low-wage. In the Midwest from 1979 to 1986 the number of low-wage, year-round, full-time jobs increased by 43 percent, high-wage jobs increased by 6 percent, and mid-wage jobs declined by 0.3 percent. In 1979, 80 percent of all jobs were mid-wage; that proportion fell to 76 percent by 1986.[35]

Inequality also appears to be greater in cities with higher rank in the urban hierarchy. This does not contradict our finding that world cities, or "control centers," are doing better economically than other cities. Indeed, part of the success of these top-ranked cities is their ability to internalize the world economy by shifting some workers into Third-World competition. One study found, for example, that the larger the population of the metropolitan area, the lower the incomes of families at the 10th and 25th income percentiles and the higher the incomes of families at the 75th and 90th percentiles. It should be no surprise, then, that the level of inequality for larger metropolitan areas by more general measures is also higher.[36] The poor are found in seas of wealth, where many are stranded permanently from any opportunity to earn even a modest living.

An explanation for the greater inequality found in larger cities lies in the high concentration of internationally linked services. There is an emerging dual class structure, a connection between the creation of a bifurcated occupational structure and the needs of international business. The upper tier of the labor market includes the managers, lawyers, and accountants who work in the control and coordination centers of global corporations and related business services, as well as professionals in health, education, and other costly personal services. The bottom tier has the collective function of supplying cleaners, servants, delivery persons, and other menial workers who serve the needs of the upper tier.[37] Below this level we find a large pool of underskilled persons who are poor whether they work or not. A large portion of the periphery of the service sector are casual workers who have only marginal attachments to work and fall into welfare, petty crime, or other survival modes.

The Suburbanization of Manufacturing and Service Jobs

The growth of suburbs is a long-standing process, and it has often been led by industrial moves. Business firms move when they expand operations, run out of space, or leave the city in search of cheaper land or construction costs. They leave to get away from unions or generally high-priced labor, to avoid regulations, or to get better access to transportation. They move to seek out clusters of particular kinds of potential employees, expand production, or cut costs. In a sense, of course, suburbanization is simply one aspect of urban growth.

Residential suburbanization has often accompanied moves of business and industry. In the boom after the Second World War housing took the lead; the entire national economy revolved around federal expenditures for public highways and subsidies for private houses. Long-term home mortgage lending, for example, was almost negligible prior to New Deal legislation (about $30 billion in 1930). Following changes in banking laws, subsidies, and public insurance, it exploded in 1950 to dominate the reorganized industry ($260 billion in 1965 and $590 billion in 1975).[38] The boom centered on the manufacturing of autos, steel, rubber, and cement, as well as on real estate and building materials.[39] For nearly three decades this growth of suburbs, fueled by general metropolitan growth as the farms and countryside were emptied, was contingent in multiple ways on healthy and growing central-city economies and on a slowly evolving division of labor.

Since about 1975, three changes have eroded this symbiosis. First, overall growth of metropolitan regions has slowed, no longer fueled either by farmers leaving an industrializing agriculture or by migration out of the South.[40] The U.S. population has become almost entirely urban. Half the country lives in metropolitan areas with more than a million residents. Approximately one quarter of the people reside in the seven largest metropolitan areas. Metropolitan growth is now due either to (low) domestic population increase or to international migration—to New York, Miami, San Francisco, Houston, and Los Angeles, in particular. Differential growth results from movement among the metropolitan areas, as in the case of the migration of American whites to the sunbelt. Second, in an opposed trajectory, the separation of urban and suburban activities has been accelerated by economic forces originating in the operations of the global economy. In spite of the fact that metropolitan growth has slowed, suburban activities have continued to expand rapidly. Third, racial and ethnic characteristics of the labor force, which have always been tied to metropolitan geography, now stand out as principal geographic features, defining both city neighborhoods and suburbs.

As we move the focus of our discussion to relatively technical topics of spatial-economic change, it is important to remember that not only jobs are at stake. Poverty and suburbanization are equally about social and political life. Florence Shapiro is the mayor of Plano, Texas, one of the many Dallas–Fort Worth suburbs that boomed in the 1980s. She says people moved to Plano before the jobs moved there, "to raise their children with others who enjoyed the same life style and the same values. . . . They wanted good schools and they didn't want to worry about crime." Actually, the connections between residential life and work are very close, as we shall see. David Ellwood points to the importance to workers (and future workers) of living near good schools and "people who work and can share information about jobs." At the other extreme of the metropolis, far from the suburbs, he says, "Living in the ghetto is detrimental not just because there are no jobs down the street, but because there are no people down the street with jobs."[41]

Office Work

Service and administrative jobs in metropolitan areas have been suburbanizing for a long time, predating the current period of economic restructuring. Ever since the introduction of office computer applications in the 1950s, standardized high-volume office tasks have been consolidated and moved in search of lower rents and labor costs. Many of these tasks—such as data entry—have made well-documented moves to the suburbs, where land is cheaper, transport is convenient, and clerical employees will work for low wages.[42] Office functions have been divided according to the amount of contact required with people or organizations outside the firm. Those activities that require fewer contacts are more likely to be relocated to suburban locations.[43]

The spatial division of office work greatly increased in the 1960s. Growing firms faced new administrative and technical needs, often related to their expanding spheres of operations, which strained the land and labor skills available at low cost in the central city. The increasingly international framework of competition put great pressure on firms to cut costs.

In recent years, we have seen an acceleration in this movement toward suburban sites.[44] In the five years between 1977 and 1982, for example, suburban jobs in services nearly doubled—four times the growth of service jobs in central cities. Suburban jobs in the administrative end of manufacturing firms increased by almost a quarter, compared to near stagnation in central cities.[45] Production jobs in manufacturing firms declined in both locations. Many inner-city firms closed, stranding a large pool of labor in the neighborhoods nearest the factories, especially workers whose living alternatives are restricted by discrimination.

The increasing tendency of service employers to locate in the suburbs is reflected also in the magnitude of office construction. By 1988, suburban office markets had grown to take up 59 percent of the nation's office space. Each year, nearly three-quarters of the one hundred million square feet of newly rented office space is in the suburbs.[46] In essence, jobs are moving to the white, nonunion periphery, leaving minority, less-educated city dwellers behind.

Land Costs, Production Costs, and Location

Most explanations of suburban economic growth emphasize the importance of changes in the balance of production costs between the central city and the suburbs. Explanations largely focus on the decisions of individual firms—or even groups of firms as industrial sectors. The most commonly accepted version of this argument emphasizes the dramatic reductions in cost of inputs such as transportation and rent, even wages, as firms move from central cities to the suburbs. These differences were brought about by heavy investments in the national highway system and by massive subsidies and guarantees for housing finance. In many respects, this suburb-building splurge was the defining characteristic of the boom that in the last chapter we called the "American Century."

"Urban ecological" researchers point out some of the factors, in addition to federally financed highways and subsidized suburban housing expansion, that have made metropolitan reorganization possible. According to economists Thomas Stanback and Richard Knight, it is natural for cities to expand because of affluence, access to automobiles, highway construction, expansion of air transport, and "institutional arrangements which have permitted firms to settle more readily [and] efficiently" in suburbs.[47]

Increased accessibility gives firms a chance to take advantage of lower taxes and land costs, easier access to other metropolitan areas, and improved recruiting of professionals and managers who prefer (and can afford) suburban living.[48] The savings in time offered by the comprehensive air-transport network expands the reach of markets, further encouraging a greater spatial division of labor.[49] Recent developments in communications technologies will extend this influence even further. Technical needs that are said to push airports farther away from cities also facilitate suburban growth as they stimulate new activities around them.

Two innovations attributed in part to the improvement of the highway system and massive automobile ownership are the suburban office park and shopping mall. Firms move to enjoy "good access to the highway system, attractive surroundings, and the mutual benefit . . . of increased prestige that accrues from proximity to [one another]."[50] Both of these development forms have posed severe challenges and competition to older employment and shopping districts in the central city.

In order to explain more concretely the form taken by suburban development, theorists have created typologies of the locational patterns associated with various industrial sectors and subsectors. A standard approach is to divide the metropolitan economy into local and export sectors. The local (or residentiary) sector produces and sells goods for local consumption, but exports nothing (office-cleaning and school-teaching are good examples). The export sector provides goods and services for markets outside of the local economy or for nonresidents (for example, steel manufacturing or the hotel industry).[51] Different growth processes affect the locational patterns of these two groups. In the export sector, as in manufacturing in general, headquarters and administrative offices tend to locate centrally, while production, research and development, warehousing, and regional sales offices decentralize to industrial parks and office parks, just as they also disperse internationally. As export-sector firms expand to operate on a national or multinational level, they increase their own internal division of labor. Routine functions tend to become more footloose, decentralizing to cheaper locations; administrative and research functions centralize to take advantage of infrastructure and agglomeration economies.[52] In the case of the local (nonexport) sector, business locational patterns are much more dependent on the maturity of the local economy. As a metropolis develops, local functional differentiation increases and firms serving the needs of residents decentralize.[53]

Although the neat dichotomy presented above has a certain appeal, in reality the location decisions of firms in various industrial sectors are more complex and differentiated, reflecting political struggles, institutional decisions, and other factors. The social characteristics of the labor force often over-ride other area-cost considerations. International factors, such as extremely intense competition from producers at new sites, are increasingly relevant. Narrow personal influences, such as the wishes of managers about the location of their housing, as well as broad political decisions, such as the pattern of defense contracts, are also influential.[54] The earlier importance of the transport costs of getting material inputs to the factory and the product to market—the location factors seen as most influential by observers through the 1960s—has faded as service- and high technology-based industries have grown in importance.[55] As we will see, these locational forces work to lock large segments of the African-American and Latino workforce out of the competition for new jobs. As costs rise for operating in the central city versus the suburbs and as needs of industry change in other ways to favor suburbs, urban decline follows as a consequence of global economic change.

Even in cities where costs of land and labor have not risen, firms have moved toward the suburbs (Oakland, California, and Newark, New Jersey, are good examples). Most evidence supports the view in these and similar cases that movement has been planned by administrative offices to take advantage of the available pool of relatively well-educated, low-wage white housewives in the suburbs.[56] They become competitors with

African-American and Latino men and women in the city. The pattern becomes self-reinforcing as mutually isolated minority-city and white-suburb residents become still further separated socially, so that employers more readily denigrate and fear minority, inner-city job applicants.

Evidence from surveys in Chicago and Washington, D.C., is particularly disturbing in this respect. In Chicago, suburban factory employers "consider race an important factor in hiring decisions and view inner-city workers, particularly black men, as unstable, uncooperative, dishonest and uneducated."[57] In both Chicago and Washington, D.C., African-American and white applicants were sent to apply for low-skill jobs in hotels, restaurants, retail stores, offices, and construction and manufacturing firms. Although in 70 percent of the cases there was no difference in treatment, in 20 percent whites were treated favorably, strongly suggesting, according to researcher Margery Turner, "that discrimination remains a major problem nationwide."[58] As we will see below, this overt discrimination against job applicants of color is added on top of the disadvantage imposed by long commutes from the ghetto to suburban workplaces.[59]

When we shift our focus to urban areas overall, suburbanization can be seen as part of the entire process of urbanization, in which the city as a whole is the site organized to facilitate most social and economic relations. We must thus acknowledge the importance of the historical development, examine the social relations among groups involved in city building as well as the urban economy, and understand how the physical form of the city reflects social relations.[60]

The form and type of the city depend heavily on its early boom period of construction (think of Chicago skyscrapers or Los Angeles freeways).[61] The spatial forms of cities have historically reflected the technology, division of labor, and form of business organization prevalent during their formative period of growth.[62] Suburbanization is thus a logical response: it allows not only growth, but escape from the obsolete. Like the forms of cities, suburban patterns vary depending on location and period.[63] Not just the physical form, but social class relations and the division of labor and politics also differ. These things, one might say, get built in, so that our cities are literally "museums of the past and [of] past social relations."[64] In this social sense, too, cities become outmoded, so that it is easier to build not only infrastructure, but also social relations anew, in new regions or in the suburbs. The leftover property and people in the cities thus decline in value. These losses must be absorbed by someone in some way—hence city fiscal crises, poverty, and decay.

In the process of suburbanization, as in all city building in market-run societies, the real estate market organizes the creation of the built environment. The need for certain uses alone is not enough to generate the appropriate built environment; the market for real estate must funnel investment. This happens in waves and is self-reinforcing: investments in hot areas attract other investors, while cold areas stagnate. Inner cities are redlined by banks against mortgage loans and greenlined by insurance companies against fire policies. Inner cities are poor investments because they are not considered immediately profitable and because there are future profits to be made if real estate prices can be further depressed. The creation of enterprise zones and similar policies to promote development will not shift this negative image of inner-city areas, but will only reinforce the stagnation. Privileged areas benefit from development of infrastructure encouraged under tax laws. The location and pricing of transit lines, rates set by public utilities, and extension of highways are usually biased against central cities. Tax laws and credit institutions that affect housing construction and affordability favor suburbs.

In summary, changes in the composition and organization of the national economy have led to further separation in economic, social, racial, and political patterns in metropolitan areas. Rapidly growing industries and firms are most often located at the urban fringe, while traditional city employers (mainly in basic industry, but also in government) are shrinking or shutting down and moving to the outskirts, or beyond. In exceptional cases, a few cities are growing as advanced service centers. A few labor-intensive industries, such as textiles and apparel, prefer the city, where they can take advantage of large concentrations of immigrants as low-wage employees. Firms in these sectors need no incentives other than the dilapidated conditions of many older industrial areas, low rents, and cheap labor. These cases are not the general trend, and they also eventually reinforce stagnation.

The Changing Location of Residences

As anyone who has ever bought a house or rented an apartment knows, the neighborhood matters. People with a lot of choice, those with resources and good incomes, move *in*—that is, they pick areas (usually suburban areas) with amenities, accessible to their needs, and often in the expectation of making money on a housing investment. Those with less choice, but some, with jobs and incomes that are low but rising, may move *out*—that is, they may escape declining neighborhoods, those with poor services or unsafe streets. The poor usually have little choice at all about where they live.

Observers of the American scene know, however, it is not just wealth, income, and social mobility, but race and ethnicity, too, that are essential forces in the physics of neighborhood change. These forces even introduce bias into our language: the word "neighborhood" now connotes a place in the city, not in the suburbs. People unable to move freely because of poverty, language limitations, or discrimination are severely restricted in their attempts to accommodate their living spaces to the changing industrial structure of the metropolitan economy.

Occupational status is a key explanatory variable. As cities change, neighborhoods become differentiated even along occupational lines. Workers in white-ethnic, blue-collar neighborhoods are among the most spatially constrained by the cost and accessibility of urban transportation. Neighborhoods thus reinforce, or reproduce, the different social strata of urban society.[65]

Neighborhood location and characteristics are also driven by the more direct interests of businesses in the real estate market. Great threats to low-income areas are posed by organizations and institutions that see the neighborhoods as real estate from which money is to be made. The threat is greatest to poor residents of poor areas, since they have the fewest options in terms of relocation.[66] The success of neighborhood defense depends inversely on the strategic value of the neighborhood in the urban area and on internal pressures for real estate property, but directly on the power and status of the residents in the larger political economy. Ironically, residents most dependent on their neighborhoods for daily local services, who might therefore want most strongly to protect the home turf, often have the least power and fewest services.

Given an ongoing process of acculturation and socioeconomic mobility,[67] relative income is an important predictor of location for white ethnic minorities. As people move up the economic ladder, they leave central-city neighborhoods for upgraded, often suburban areas. Levels of ethnic segregation decline in the course of this movement, paralleling the rise in income.[68] This "American Dream" pattern presents a dilemma for policymakers and sociologists alike. No one wants to deprive lower-income people of the opportunity to move up or out, but it is this movement that appears to some to condemn their former communities to perpetual poverty and eventually to halt the relocation cycle.[69]

The relationship among ethnic and racial groups in city and suburban neighborhoods varies as the metropolis matures and the society becomes more complex and heterogeneous. In most theories of metropolitan change, this maturation process involves an increase in household incomes. In the course of growth, inner-city zones are seen to "turn over" and move toward "higher and better uses" through a process much like ecological succession in nature. As this happens, residents of central areas are pushed to residential rings farther out.[70] This mode of analysis has been applied successfully to explain the location of white ethnic groups, predicting patterns that reflect people's tendency to live in areas with others with similar occupations, incomes, lifestyles, and ethnicity.[71]

Together these observations and findings provide a reasonably sound basis for an accurate description and explanation of metropolitan residential form—once the basic determinants of industrial growth are given. It becomes fairly clear why poor neighborhoods are where they are, and the obstacles to improvement stand out, at one level or another. In one basic way, however, these observations (and the "urban ecology" models on which they are based) fail miserably.[72] They do not account for the persistence of segregation, poverty, and inner-city location for African-American workers and their households. This failure points out the need to deal with race explicitly.

Suburbanization

Immediately after the Second World War, large-scale suburban house building and highway construction began, and there has been a massive exodus of people from the city ever since, accompanying the movement of industry. In some metropolitan areas, the outpouring was so quick that central cities lost population even during the 1950s and 1960s. Since then, the shift to the suburbs has continued. In 1960, central cities accounted for more than half the population of the country's metropolitan areas; by 1980 much of the basic shift had taken place, and central cities accounted for about 40 percent of the metro-

TABLE 4.2
City and Suburban Population, by Race, 1960–89 (in Thousands)

	White and Other Persons			African-American Persons		
	1960	1975	1989	1960	1975	1989
Metropolitan	114,193	124,652	165,767	15,824	18,006	25,402
Central city	45,342	46,837	57,912	12,439	13,858	17,211
Suburbs	68,852	77,815	107,854	3,384	4,148	8,191
Nonmetropolitan	63,306	62,123	49,894	6,525	6,083	4,930
Total population	177,499	186,775	215,661	22,349	24,089	30,332

Source: Bureau of the Census, *Current Population Survey, Money Income and Poverty Status in the United States*, P-60, various years.

politan population. That percentage remains constant into the 1990s, as new, smaller "metropolitan areas" make up for the relative losses from giant central cities.[73]

This movement formed what has become today's mainstream America—two-adult, white, middle-class families with higher incomes are very likely to live in the suburbs. (Ninety-four percent of the suburban population is white.) The shift outward has been massive, but it has not been generalized. Twenty-three percent of the central-city population is African-American[74] and 11 percent is Hispanic. Before we turn our focus to the minority groups left behind, we examine their patterns of suburbanization.

Relative to whites, African Americans have suburbanized very slowly and very little since the Second World War. In 1989, although they constituted 13 percent of the metropolitan population, they accounted for only 7 percent of suburbanites. Twenty-seven percent of all African Americans lived in suburbs, but 57 percent resided in central cities.[75] Although the African-American suburban population increased 23 percent between 1960 and 1975 and nearly doubled from then until 1989, the number was still only 2.7 million people. (The overall contrasts appear in Table 4.2.)

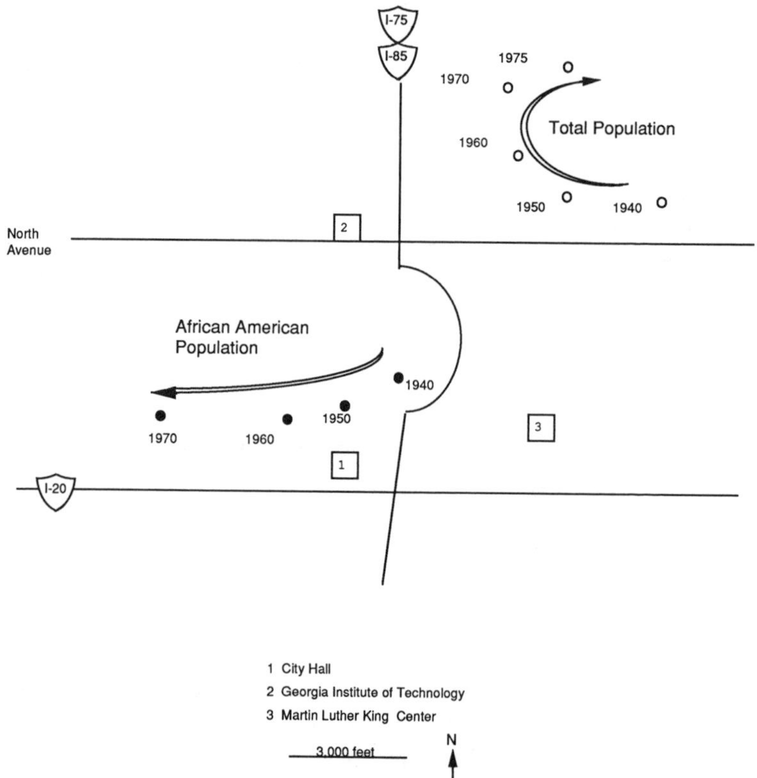

Figure 4.3. Movement of Residential Population Centers, Atlanta, by Race, 1940–75. *Source:* Adapted from Barclay G. Jones, "Applications of Centrographic Techniques to the Study of Urban Phenomena: Atlanta, Georgia, 1940–1975," *Economic Geography* 56, 3 (July 1990), 201–222, Table 4 and Figure 4.

Segregation

The measurement of residential segregation is a complex statistical task. There are problems of spatial aggregation and boundary definition, and there are risks of assigning district or neighborhood average characteristics to streets, blocks, or individual residents or families. As a consequence, even careful and reputable statisticians differ in their assessments. One thing is clear, however: in the entire postwar period, suburbanization has been a racially biased affair, whether by intention or not, and minorities have been left behind.[76] Figure 4.3, which depicts residential change for the metropolis of Atlanta, shows striking differences in the movement from year to year of the "average" location of Atlanta's African-American and white populations from 1940 to 1975. The two arrows show that while residents in general moved northeast to the suburbs, African-American residents moved west, staying close to downtown. Further analysis shows that while the white population dispersed, living each year more distant on average from downtown, the African-American population became more concentrated. Census data suggest these trends continue. Similar diagrams confirm parallel discrepant movement for many metropolitan areas and intercensal periods.

Residential assignment correlates very highly with race.[77] Even when income differences do not serve to keep white and African-American neighborhoods separate, formal and informal racial restrictions do. Various informal methods operate through the real estate profession, powerful informal networks, individually imposed rental restrictions, and fear.[78] Formal restrictions exist, too. Large-lot zoning operates to exclude households without enough wealth or income, as do zoning restrictions against rental housing, prohibition of industrial housing (including mobile homes), and a variety of other limitations. Through the high correlation of race with income and wealth, these limitations restrict the movement of minority households. Historically, lease covenants and other legal restrictions directly excluded minority owners or renters; even the Federal Housing Administration prohibited integrated housing developments in the suburbs. Much of the blame for the exacerbation of housing segregation belongs to the government.[79]

Studies of African-American suburbanization support the conclusion that discrimination still plays a strong role even against those who do move out of the city. Suburban movers are steered into selected neighborhoods and resegregated. They pay higher prices for inferior housing and poorer services than do whites of comparable income levels. In effect, for many the move to the suburbs just transfers the segregation to a new location.[80]

An overwhelming percentage of Hispanics—92 percent—lived in metropolitan areas in 1989. They comprised 10 percent of metropolitan residents, 7 percent of the suburban population, and 14 percent of the central city. Forty percent lived in suburbs; just over half of all Hispanics lived in central cities. The segregation of Puerto Ricans provides convincing evidence of the power of racial discrimination. While most Hispanics have traditionally followed the predictions of the ecological model, assimilating culturally and spatially when they have higher incomes, Puerto Ricans have not. They stay highly segregated even when they have high incomes. Although this could conceivably be because Puerto Ricans, from a multiracial culture, are less averse to settling near African Americans,[81] it is much more likely to be because whites discriminate against Puerto Ricans, especially those with dark skins.

Although the landmark housing legislation of the 1960s altered patterns of housing discrimination by outlawing the most blatant methods of exclusion, segregation remains pervasive in the United States. In spite of improvements, other than Native Americans, African Americans remain the most spatially isolated minority group. On the average, African-American isolation—a measure of the number of people who would have to move their residence to equalize the spatial distribution—is 2.5 times as high as the isolation of Latinos and 10 times higher than for Asians.

African Americans were somewhat less isolated (statistically speaking) in metropolitan areas with relatively few African Americans and in generally rapidly growing, small or middle-sized cities of the South and West. There is no evidence that large African-American ghettos in the North became less isolated from the mainstream in the 1970s; there is some evidence that their isolation increased. Aggregate national measures, meant to indicate the degree to which whites attempt to avoid members of minority groups, reveal some leveling in the segregation of African Americans (and Latinos). More detailed analysis of disaggregated data, however, makes it clear that there was little improvement, if any, in the cities of the Northeast, where the majority of urban African Americans live. These cities show relatively little change over the decade.

On the whole, Latinos became more segregated from whites in the 1970s, but still less than African Americans. Segregation was worst in the Northeast, where overall slow growth combined with large rates of immigration and white flight to produce a significant rise in the proportion of the population that was Latino. It was in these communities—Paterson, New Jersey, for example—that segregation of Latinos increased most. It also increased in large cities with heavy migration, such as Los Angeles and Anaheim, California.

Asians, due partly to their relatively few numbers, are much less physically isolated and have higher likelihoods of contact with whites. We do find the greatest levels of segregation in the cities having the largest Asian concentrations, yet even in these cities, Asians are much less concentrated. In spite of high Asian immigration and population growth, segregation measures declined in every metropolitan area studied, with the exception of San Jose. In most areas, Asian immigrants formed no particular community and settled in a dispersed pattern.

Displacement

Central-city residents have not just been left behind by upwardly mobile suburbanites. They also face displacement pressures from private-market gentrifiers, semipublic agencies like hospitals or universities intent on expansion, and public agencies building highways or implementing urban renewal. Remaining residents frequently also face higher rents from increase in the value of their neighborhood real estate, which may now be seen as potential development property.

The poor are the most likely group to be displaced, and their moves often result in overcrowding and poor housing.[82] Since they are poorer and often constrained by discrimination in the housing market, the costs these households bear for displacement are high. In 1979 researchers estimated that in the nation 1.5 to 2.5 million people (4 percent of movers) were displaced each year.[83] A 1985 study estimates that 40,000 to 100,000 people were involuntarily displaced each year in New York City alone.[84]

In notable areas of a few cities, first-time home buyers who are well off (gentrifiers) have moved to central neighborhoods. The small magnitude of this phenomenon should, however, be kept in mind: while its effect may be significant in specific areas of cities, and in a few special cities, the moves constituted less than one percent of the new national housing stock in 1982. Gentrified neighborhoods are concentrated in older "control" cities with high land values, such as New York, Boston, San Francisco, and Washington, D.C.[85] Evidence indicates that most gentrifiers are not suburbanites moving back to the central city but, rather, people already renting in the central city.[86]

A more focused threat is sometimes still posed (as it was in much greater volume in the city-expansion years of the 1960s) by massive urban infrastructure or development projects such as the razing of San Francisco's Western Addition (the Fillmore district), which eliminated an entire large residential population of African Americans to make way for real estate development and other neighborhood "improvements."[87] Highway projects have wiped out whole neighborhoods.[88]

Although comprehensive evidence is more difficult to collect, it seems that pressure of changes in real estate markets, from specific threats and general value increase, leads to further segregation of marginal groups. Poor people in minority groups are being pushed farther away from the opportunity to own homes or to live where they can more easily become participants in the larger socioeconomic system.

To summarize: overall, the restructuring of metropolitan residential areas whitened the already white suburbs and further concentrated African Americans and Latinos in darker-skinned-central city areas; wealth and income went to the suburbs and poverty was crowded in the city. African-American and Latino suburbanization has been much slower and more partial than the white dispersal, and it has ended in most cases in resegregation in the suburbs. These geographic changes have had enormous consequences for politics and public finance at all levels in America by isolating not only rich and poor, but dark-skinned people from light. Suburbanization has provided a principal mechanism for sorting out winners and losers, for assigning to different groups extra benefits and costs of restructuring of the economy. Not only do some winners find their way (fairly or not) to higher pay, but once there, they solidify their gains by separation. It is clear from income and wealth statistics (see Chapter 2) that the allocation of bonuses and deficits is biased against people of color (as against women), but it is now clear as well that the production of bias is aided and abetted by the process of geographic separation.

Poverty and Place

The joint effect of the movement of households and the movement of jobs takes us back to the starting point of this book—separation of work, residence, and economic, social, and political life. Now we focus on the high joblessness and poverty among persons of color who live in crowded central-city neighborhoods. In this section we show schematically how the global, national, and metropolitan changes discussed above have not only enforced but actually increased the isolation of poor African Americans in city ghettos. We begin by briefly analyzing the employment conditions of central cities.

The manufacturing job losses in old industrial cities during the 1970s and early 1980s led from high to very high unemployment rates for African Americans living there. As sociologist John Kasarda has shown using information from the Bureau of Labor Statistics, the situation grew dramatically worse for African-American men compared to white men.[89] In Detroit, for example, although the unemployment rate fell from 19 to 16 percent for white men from 1980 to 1985, it remained at catastrophic levels (around 30 percent) for African-American men. Although absolute levels were lower, trends toward increasing racial disparity were greater in Chicago. Elsewhere the situation worsened, too, but not so severely. For women the unemployment situation was better, even in the central cities of the industrial Northeast: between 1980 and 1985, women have generally seen their unemployment rates fall. The glaring exceptions for the biggest cities were African-American women in Chicago and Detroit, who had extremely high 1985 unemployment rates (23 percent and 31 percent, respectively).

The problems of central-city youth are also severe. Between 1969 and 1985, the unemployment rate for young white men in the cities rose from 7.3 to 13.5 percent. In addition, the proportion of young discouraged workers grew from 4.5 to 6.1 percent. As the industrial economy suffered difficulties, young men in the cities paid the price. For African-American young men, the price was higher still: their unemployment rates nearly trebled, from 13.0 to 37.1 percent, and the proportion of discouraged workers grew from 8.2 to 14.1 percent. Regionally, youth unemployment was worst in the Midwest and the Northeast, paralleling the situation for adult workers.

Table 4.3 reveals some astounding statistics. Each figure is the summation of two percentages: the percentage unem-

TABLE 4.3
Percentage of Central-City Men Not at Work, by Race and Age, 1969–85

	White			African-American		
	1969	1980	1985	1969	1980	1985
All regions						
Ages 16–24	11.8	17.3	19.6	21.2	42.7	51.2
25–64	7.4	15	16.6	13.7	29.5	35
Northeast						
Ages 16–24	14.3	22	26.1	24.2	53	68
25–64	8.5	18.1	19.8	15.5	30.2	32.1
Midwest						
Ages 16–24	10.2	17.3	26.2	23.5	59.9	NA
25–64	6.5	16.4	18.6	12.9	35.1	45.6
South						
Ages 16–24	10	17.1	12.6	15.4	28.9	43.5
25–64	6	12.6	14.1	12	26.4	31
West						
Ages 16–24	14	13.1	16.8	25.7	NA	38.9
25–64	8.8	13.7	14.9	14.1	24.1	29.1

Source: Adapted from John Kasarda, "Jobs, Migration and Emerging Urban Mismatches," in *Urban Change and Poverty*, ed. Michael G. H. McGeary and Laurence E. Lynn, 148–198.

ployed and the percentage neither in school nor in the labor force. In Midwestern central cities in 1969, for example, 1.4 percent of white men aged 25–64 were unemployed, and another 5.1 percent were neither in school nor in the labor force, which, when summed, reveal that 6.5 percent were "out of work." Perhaps this statistic, and the accompanying 1969 Midwest statistic of 10.2 percent for younger men out of work, should be taken as "norms," in the sense that they are measures of the most satisfactory employment situations we can document in real life in large, modern, industrial cities in the United States. (The employment situations for the same groups in the same year in the South were about the same.)

Against these "normal" statistics for participation in the workforce, how did things change in a decade and a half? How do young workers, and particularly young African-American workers, fare in the central cities? For all but two of thirty-seven categories of change in Table 4.3, we find that the situation worsened over time—in many cases, dramatically. By 1985, 26 percent of young white men in the Midwest were out of work. The best situation in 1985 for young African-American men was in the West, where 39 percent were out of work; in the Northeast the central-city out-of-work figure for African-American young men reached an incredible 68 percent.

More inclusive levels of underemployment, including involuntary part-time and very low wage work, also increased between 1970 and 1982, especially among young adults and those with low levels of education. Racial polarization also accelerated in central-city labor markets, as the absolute gap in underemployment between African Americans and whites increased substantially.

Three principal arguments are put forth by students of these situations to explain the extraordinarily high rates of unemployment and underemployment for African-American men in central cities: (1) there is severe discrimination in hiring; (2) educational shortcomings preclude employment in the growing service sector; and (3) the physical distance separating the ghetto and the suburb keeps city workers isolated from areas with multiplying jobs.

Discrimination

As we have argued above, the overall process of urban and metropolitan development has become a means of social and economic separation. Just as the suburb has been the avenue for advancement, the central city has become the receptacle for those with few chances. Poor, poorly educated African Americans especially are trapped semipermanently, other ethnic groups temporarily, it seems, and they all have limited job opportunities. Although it still provides special opportunities for some, for these groups the central-city location only adds to the economic, social, and individual inadequacies and constraints they already face.

It is difficult to say where the process begins, as the chicken-egg circle of residential and employment segregation, poor education, and inadequate services is mutually reinforcing. As sociologist Stephen Steinberg has written: "The first thing that needs to be said is that the very existence of a ghetto underclass is evidence of institutionalized racism. Ultimately, the ghetto underclass is the stepchild of slavery itself, linked to the present by patterns of racial segregation and inequality that are still found in all major institutions, including ghetto schools."[90]

This residential entrapment situates workers so they are likely to be pushed into job markets that take advantage of these constraints and the workers' limitations, including but not limited to lack of easy access. In a process of labor-force segmentation, vulnerable groups must accept work either at less pay or under poorer conditions than they would be expected to in a unified labor market. In the case of African-American workers, there is evidence that with the exception of college graduates, most are unable to penetrate higher-wage occupations, no matter how conducive their qualifications or location. Racially based wage differentials have increased in cities for all groups.[91] As we have noted earlier in this chapter, surveys in 1990 and 1991 show that suburban employers still discriminate severely against job applicants with darker skins.

Similar findings have been reported for Central American and Southeast Asian immigrants to central cities. The large-scale immigration of poor people from Third-World countries since 1965 has fed a process of growth of low-wage industries. Several studies have documented the persistence of the segmentation of immigrant workers into these low wage jobs.[92] Minorities are told that, if they expect employment at wages comparable to whites, their expectations are too high.[93] Even city growth in the sunbelt does not lower the barriers that channel minority workers into low wage jobs.[94]

It would be unreasonable to contend that employment, wage, and poverty differentials are entirely functions of race, ethnicity, and discrimination. All analysts agree that other factors enter in important and influential ways, if not directly then at least as intermediate and related causes. One of these factors is education.

Education Mismatch

As employment in manufacturing declined, especially in cities, it grew rapidly in services throughout the country. For example, although in 1953 jobs in white-collar service sectors employed fewer than 19 percent of all workers in New York, Philadelphia, Boston, Baltimore, and St. Louis, by 1985 this sector comprised the largest single source of jobs, employing 48 percent of the workers in these cities. Not only manufacturing, but other sectors of employment in these Northeast and Midwest central cities declined drastically, almost without exception; and they declined far more than services increased, so that total employment fell nearly 7 percent. In cities with much smaller African-American populations in other regions of the country—Atlanta, Houston, Denver, and San Francisco—the service sector has also grown, although less rapidly.[95]

As we have pointed out earlier, it is generally understood that jobs in white-collar, service, information-processing industries require higher levels of education than the manual labor jobs that have been displaced in the central city. In support of such arguments, researchers point to the fact that in the nine cities mentioned in the preceding paragraph, central-city jobs for those with at least some higher education increased overall from 1959 to 1985 by more than 1.5 million in total, but nearly a half-million jobs were lost for those without high school diplomas. Even more drastically skewed changes have taken place in Northeastern and Midwestern cities.[96]

Observers frequently assume lack of education precludes the chance of employment in white-collar jobs. This differential—a decrease in jobs that do not require much education and an increase in jobs that do—is presumed then to account for the rising unemployment rates of African-American workers, especially men. It is true that more than 445,000 African-American men of working age living in central cities in the Northeast (some 43 percent) did not hold high school diplomas in 1985.

In spite of this circumstantial evidence, we believe it is unreasonable to claim that the high school education requirements of the jobs in growing sectors explain the increasing unemployment of African Americans. After all, nearly 945,000 white men (29 percent of all white men in these central cities) did not have diplomas. Looking at residents of all central cities in the entire country, we find that 39 percent of African-American men and 25 percent of white men did not hold high school diplomas in 1985. These differences may be evidence of serious racial bias in the provision of education, past or present, but they are insufficient to explain the large differences in unemployment rates.

When we examine more appropriate and detailed evidence for explaining unemployment differentials by race, the conclusions must change. We find, for example, that the 1985 unemployment rate for African-American workers in central cities with no high school diplomas was nearly double the rate for whites without diplomas; among these less uneducated African-American workers, 27.3 percent were unemployed, compared to 15.5 percent for whites. What, then, causes the differentials? As Norman Fainstein argues, measures of educational attainment of workers tell us something about the characteristics of the employees, but nothing about the jobs. It would help to know what jobs the employed but unschooled whites perform. What needs to be determined is whether or not these two factors (characteristics of workers and job requirements) actually match, whether "uneducated" workers disproportionately occupy certain occupational or industrial categories.[97] In

New York City, for example, the greatest incidence of jobs requiring low skills is found in "business services," which happens to be the fastest-growing employment sector in the city and a center of African-American employment.[98] In the end, although all attribute great influence to education for getting good jobs and moving ahead, other barriers, including racial discrimination, play a hefty role.[99] We turn now to the final set of arguments about the reasons for such high rates of unemployment in the ghetto.

Spatial Lock

Many analysts argue that lack of access explains the low employment figures for African Americans in big cities. When the Kerner Commission reported in 1968, they coined the term "spatial mismatch" to refer to the physical separation between jobs in the distant suburbs and potential workers who were residents of the ghetto.[100] The argument, widely referred to as the "spatial-mismatch hypothesis," rests on several (now familiar) points: that jobs with low educational requirements are disappearing with the decline of traditional manufacturing industries, especially in the city; that central-city minority residents have been particularly dependent on these (declining) industries for work; that these city residents lack access to suburban jobs for want of automobiles and adequate public transport; and, finally, that minority workers are unskilled and therefore poorly matched with high-skill jobs in the service and high-tech sectors, which are available close to home in the central business district.[101]

The difficulty that central-city minority workers have finding and commuting to suburban jobs has been a controversial issue among scholars and policymakers, but there has been agreement on basic facts. One undoubted cause of isolation is poor access to means of transportation. If cars, buses, subways, or trains are not available to take workers to their jobs, then arguments about isolation from jobs are moot. Dependence on an auto for an outward commute is increasing, corresponding inversely to a decrease in the proportion of trips made from cities to suburban jobs by public transit. Between 1970 and 1980, while the number of urban-suburban commuters rose by 25 percent, the number making this trip by public transit fell by nearly a third. The proportion of trips by transit fell by more than half, from 10.9 to 4.7 percent of all work trips from the central city to the ring over the same time period.[102] Surveys indicate that this decline in transit use was not by choice: three-quarters of these reverse commuters failed to use transit because it was not available or was not conveniently accessible.[103] Studies show that distance from the ghetto is correlated negatively with African-American employment, thereby reinforcing the claim that transit dependency is a problem.

Automobile ownership data help explain why most suburban jobs are beyond the reach of African-American city residents, and they apply to other groups as well. In 1980, close to two out of five African-American city households lacked access to an automobile. In contrast, fewer than one in five white city households faced this problem, and virtually no suburbanites did. And while whites are becoming less transit-dependent, African Americans are becoming more so. Women—especially African-American women—are the most transit-dependent of all.[104]

Regionally, important differences emerge in transit use. Cities of the Northeast have experienced simultaneously the greatest losses in central-city manufacturing and the largest declines in public transit use for the journey to work.[105] New jobs are either not accessible by transit or new workers prefer cars. In either case, transit-dependent workers lose out.[106]

In spite of the self-evident nature of many of these issues of transit dependency, a word of caution is necessary. Many analysts who have tried to pinpoint the effects of transit dependency have concluded that it is difficult and probably inappropriate to assign a significant proportion of high ghetto unemployment rates to lack of physical access.[107] There may be sufficient jobs near the ghetto, enough at least to even out the discrepancies between white and African-American unemployment rates for city residents. The persistent differences in these rates suggest something else may be the cause.

Yet various methods of access to suburban jobs appear not to help enough. Federally funded transit programs, for example, aimed specifically at improving bus service to suburban workplaces, gave "little evidence that many jobs were found."[108] Along a slightly different line, a study of African-American suburbanization in Cleveland, Detroit, and Philadelphia found that residence in the suburbs does not automatically solve the male employment problem. Likewise, studies of African-American teenage unemployment in Chicago suggest that accessibility, while not irrelevant, matters only slightly. Comparable African-American and white teenagers fare just as differently when they live next to each other as when they live in areas with dramatic differences in job accessibility.[109] These studies cast serious doubt on the notion that migration to areas of greater employment growth will overcome racial imbalance and racially focused poverty.

The total separateness of the ghetto and barrio from the rest of society is caused by a combination of physical, social, and political isolation. If we aim with a different gun, we may shoot closer to the target. The ghetto and the barrio are symptoms and results of problems. While the spatial-mismatch hypothesis raises important issues, the problem is not primarily a spatial one. The theory concludes that movement toward jobs would alleviate the problem. It bypasses the problem of discrimination, an issue relevant to both the central-city concentration of African Americans and their access to jobs no matter where they are located. And it bypasses the problem of lack of education and its connection to discrimination. By focusing almost exclusively on distance and accessibility, researchers using this approach arrive at a poor understanding of the problem and recommend misguided policy.

On the one hand, it would appear absurd to claim that physical isolation in the ghetto or barrio does not hamper residents' ability to search for and keep jobs. On the other, it would be equally absurd to plead for dispersal of the ghetto or barrio as a solution. "Dispersal" of the ghetto or the barrio does not really make sense: the ghetto and barrio represent problems, transmit inequality, and serve as proxies for many other social processes that seem aimed toward the creation and reinforcement of separate societies.[110] Those problems must be attacked; when they are resolved, physical distance will no longer be a problem.

The original question was: what significance for job search does ghetto residence have? If racism and discrimination are essential components of restriction from jobs, but their operation cannot be identified by researchers as occurring in overt discriminatory acts in sufficient magnitude to explain such high underemployment rates, then we should suspect that racism and discrimination *use* the ghetto and barrio to restrict employment; they are warehousing areas.

Students of labor market segmentation have long known that at the most basic level (irrespective of education and training) access to jobs depends strongly on personal contacts: plumbers' sons get into the union, others (including their daughters) do not. Word of mouth serves to fill many factory jobs, basic low-skilled jobs, and clerical jobs. The issue is not simply making contact, but knowing the language of the job, observing conventional work practices, and so forth. Even when there are programs of affirmative action, information must flow, personal contacts are influential, style matters.

Wilson stresses the importance of background supports for job seekers. In the ghetto not only are employee networks thin, but social support and role models are missing.[111] The ghetto and barrio provide only a hollowed-out social structure for informal job contact, conditioning, and training. Young men and women are, in effect, socialized under conditions of deprivation, where job-related associations are not primary—and sometimes are hardly evident.

These ideas have been tested for urban youth, those presumably most susceptible to the damage caused by the absence of such networks. By broadening the definition of accessibility beyond distance from jobs (from city to suburb) to include density of job-information networks in the city, researchers find that ghetto residence is, indeed, an inhibitor to job access. In a study of census data for the fifty largest metropolitan areas, Katherine O'Regan and John Quigley have observed that young people aged 16 to 19 are less likely to find jobs if they live in the ghetto.[112] Their conclusion is based on findings that while social networks provide youth with access to jobs, such networks are often missing in the ghetto. These social networks include the jobs parents and siblings have, the routes and modes they use to commute, the industries in which they work, and neighborhood contacts with other people who are not poor and not African-American. When these supports are unavailable, the young people are less likely to get jobs, and more likely to lose them. The problem is not spatial *mismatch*, but spatial *lock*.

The changes that have undone and refit the global and national economies have also reworked the shape of American cities. In contrast to an earlier period when urban and suburban growth, both of industries and population, were positively symbiotic, since about 1975 different components of the urban economy have grown and declined in ways that have mixed with neighborhood changes so as to greatly help suburban residents, but to deeply harm those left behind in the cities.

Regional economic boom and bust, differential rates of city growth and decline, and a racist-based suburbanization have contributed directly to generate the conditions that create poverty. To be sure, it is possible that on rare, recent occasions suburbanization may be accompanied by rapid growth of a healthy central city with plentiful jobs and improving neighborhood conditions. In some stagnating regional economies the costs and losses may be widely distributed. More frequently, however, suburban growth has been the flip side of the city's decline and decay, or of a city's division into separate zones of white corporate wealth and African-American, Latino, and immigrant Third-World–like poverty. White flight (and sometimes minority middle-class flight) has most often left impoverished residents economically stranded, socially separated, and physically locked in isolation, with little political power and few public resources.

Chapter 5

Rebuilding the American City

There is a potential cycle for change. It begins with the local problem of urban poverty and central-city decay, then moves to local public recognition, which generates a local response. That response is severely constrained and confounded by lack of resources and power. In the best of circumstances—and we will argue the case for this—the conflict between attempts to deal locally with the problems of poverty, on the one hand, and lack of resources, on the other, will lead to coalitions and pressures on Congress, the federal judiciary, the White House, and federal agencies. In the face of these pressures, Congress will pass better federal laws and offer more generous budgets, the executive branch will better regulate the national economy, and industry will develop a more progressive response to competition in the global economy. These changes, in turn, will lead not only to better conditions, such as stronger labor demand, more attention to education, and broad health care coverage, but will also provide the funds municipalities need to become better places in which to work and live.[1]

Changes of this sort will not happen automatically or easily. Even when reforms begin, desirable as they would be, major changes in either markets or policy are unlikely in the short run. Neither is any set of partial reforms likely to "solve the poverty problem." Cognizant of these severe limitations, in this chapter we aim to be practical, to search for means by which—at the least—the serious problems of urban poverty will get written prominently into the political agenda.

It is not enough to call for a return to generous, liberal federal policy. Neither our analysis and the recommendations we make nor the excellent and more detailed proposals of others will stimulate governmental generosity. The authors of such proposals have no access to the White House basement, where they might push good legislation through Congress, to remake the country in their (and our) better image.[2] Instead, we believe, better policy to minimize poverty will result only from new political forces, which are most likely to be rooted in the poverty of the central city. We believe, that is, that an urban political strategy is the most practical approach for attacking America's poverty problems.

The time is ripe for this plan. City governments are poor and weak, and although they would like to solve the poverty problem, they are unable. The federal government, so distant from urban poverty, is preoccupied with international economic and political affairs. But as the problems mount, city officials and community-based organizations will increase their pressures and try to form new political coalitions. As these problems threaten national productivity, new solutions will become more attractive to various national groups, such as industrial leaders who fear for their international competitive advantage. If these city-based coalitions can be formed, then inroads can be made to improve federal policies and transfer some real power to the cities, and a cycle of positive feedback can begin.

This argument will proceed, section by section, through this chapter. First, we review the history of federal-local relations in fighting poverty. We begin by pointing out that federal aid has drastically declined. Cities are short of resources and nearly powerless in the face of suburban disparities and economic pressures from big business. The situation has been made worse by the rivalries forced on cities by federal programs and their antineighborhood bias.[3]

In the second section, we provide a selection of proposals for sensible, efficient, and efficacious federal programs to solve the urban poverty crisis. We observe the various options for public policy. The major portion of this section is devoted to a review of proposals for better federal policy. It is well for the reader to recall that the national response to global economic pressures can vary: Japan, France, Germany, Italy, and the Scandinavian countries, for example, have adopted policies considerably different from those adopted in the United States. Even in Great Britain, intercity rivalry is less destructive, because national laws and budgets provide a common base for family and urban services.[4] In particular, countries make political choices among technical options to help guide capitalist development. The United States has chosen, partly by lack of plan, regressive policies that guide choice of technology and work arrangements in counterproductive directions. The country could, however, plan more progressively. Reforms could encourage the educating and strengthening of the workforce, from the bottom up. This would be in contrast to the current practice of dividing and further separating labor, destroying opportunity for those at the bottom.

In the third section of this chapter, we examine the potential for political support to implement governmental programs. We raise a troubling question: from where will political support come for these reforms? We briefly review four possibilities, but feel compelled to judge three of them unlikely. The fourth, which stresses the latent strength of grass-roots politics in cities, leads us to the last section, where we focus on strengthening the urban role in the quest for better policy. There we will turn briefly to the heart of the matter—how we may work collectively inside cities to gather political support to fight poverty.

We examine the possibilities for a renewed and revived municipal politics. We first observe that one way to attack the set of problems treated in this book (poverty, low productivity, social division, and urban decay) is through local, progressive experiments. Their success has been documented in several cities. Chicago, Hartford, and Cleveland are among the examples, along with the more widely discussed but smaller city experiments in Burlington, Santa Monica, and Berkeley. If these experiments were to be multiplied and extended, they could show the way to the needed reconstruction of urban America. The evidence suggests there is room for municipal maneuvering in spite of the dismal prospect of a continued negative federal policy toward global competition, and it also suggests what kinds of programs are most effective.

We are more optimistic, still. When enough local change takes place, and when more experiments arise from the economic demands and political pressure of impoverished ghetto populations of African Americans, Latinos, and recent immigrants, they will provide the stimulus for coalitions to fight for better national policies for raising productivity and improving the U.S. response to global challenges. Once there are better national policies, they will stimulate still better local reforms, and the cycle may reinforce positive change.

Federal Aid, Municipal Expectations, and Antipoverty Programs

We open this section on federal-urban relations with a brief response to conservative pronouncements on the problems of the poor and the central city.

A Note on Neoconservatism

The American city shows a pressing need for more adequate national-level policies. The core of the metropolis is failing. Central cities are falling apart physically, economically, and socially. Whole neighborhoods are decaying, the people in them are suffering, and social disorganization threatens entire cities. Far too many people are poor across the nation, not just in the cities and not only when out of work. Their numbers are not declining, even during what the indicators say are economic good times. A generation has reached adulthood in poverty, and the children of that generation are threatened with worse. The gulf between haves and have-nots in this country has never been greater, and political communication never worse.

Few can doubt that the United States needs a new approach to problems of poverty, nor can they doubt the needs of the central city. It is difficult, therefore, to accept conservatives' arguments that we should leave well enough alone. It is hard to believe their theories that the situation will get better by itself. The evidence of the 1980s casts great doubt that problems of poverty will be resolved or even seriously reduced by benefits trickling down from general prosperity.

The conservative argument has been much popularized, but it is false. Most troublesome for our work at this juncture is a tendency in much contemporary discussion to use rhetoric that at once trivializes systematic causes of poverty and magnifies the problems thought to derive from improper individual behavior.[5] To put this bias in context, we borrow ideas from political economist Albert Hirschman, who has examined the problem of rhetoric in a broader but closely related context.

The rise of the welfare state in the twentieth century, Hirschman asserts, can be seen as the third stage in a protracted zig-zag struggle over centuries for the "development of true economic and social citizenship."[6] The first stage was the back-and-forth struggle for civil rights of speech, thought, religion, and justice. The second stage involved the effort to win political rights by extending the vote; and the third stage was the broader struggle to expand social and economic rights, "recognizing that minimum standards of education, health, economic well-being, and security are basic to the life of a civilized person."[7] Arguments for and against these developments of modern society have used greatly exaggerated rhetoric: progressives extoll the advantages of expanded rights, while conservatives warn of dangers. At each stage there may be progress, followed by proposals that attempt to undo the most recent gains. We are now in a period when "reactionary rhetoric" is particularly prominent.

Rhetorical and ideological backlashes stem not simply from gloomy estimates of human capacity (as by Edmund Burke on the French revolution or Thomas Malthus on the utility of starvation for checking the growth of the English working class), or from fear by the privileged classes that derives from their being outnumbered by the common people. Support for reaction is also provided by theoretical predispositions of the social sciences, especially the myth of self-regulating economics, which allows free-market enthusiasts to denounce as strongly "perverse" any effects from progressive interferences with the "natural" laws of supply and demand. The argument that welfare is the cause of poverty is a prominent example of this sort of reactionary argument, neatly echoing centuries of similar reaction to various stages of progress.[8]

The ideological onslaught of the last twenty years against redistributive policies has been widely justified in terms of national economic policy. Although the most negative and racist accompaniments of this policy have been kept usually out of sight, the agendas of those who abuse the theories of free-market economists and other archconservative social scientists have sometimes been transparent. The theories lend themselves to this abuse, as is suggested by the quantity of "counterintuitive" reasoning to which we have been subjected. Simulation models are designed to show that "at times programs cause exactly the reverse of desired results," as would be the case, for example, if by providing good housing for the poor the City of Boston would attract impoverished migrants and therefore worsen its average housing conditions. It is claimed that "our efforts to deal with distress themselves increase distress." Conservatives argue that "we tried to provide more for the poor and produced more poor instead. We tried to remove the barriers to escape from poverty, and inadvertently built a trap."[9]

These expectations of counterintuitive, reversed, and inadvertent consequences of progressive social policy exist more in the flawed reasoning of the right-wing critics than in reality. Although unanticipated consequences do often result from public (and private) actions, it is important to recognize that, as Hirschman points out, "there is actually nothing certain about such perverse effects."[10] It is claimed by conservatives, to take but one example, that minimum-wage legislation dries up jobs for the poor by making labor too expensive. But there is in fact little such evidence, and it could be in theory that a higher legal floor to wages would have precisely the intended salutory influence, that is, higher minimums would have "a positive effect on labor productivity and consequently on employment."[11] As the terms of public debate have shifted so as to frame a more conservative and less compassionate view, reformers have more and more difficulty defending in public perfectly reasonable attempts (such as the legislation of a higher minimum wage) to improve basic conditions for the poor.

When such extreme rhetoric dominates, then good reform is the victim. What is more, throughout history, even legislation purportedly enacted on behalf of the poor has been intended very often by its authors (or has been manipulated by others) to the disadvantage of the poor, to control them.[12] It is in this sense, especially in areas such as the administration of Aid to Families with Dependent Children (welfare), that reactionary sentiment against the poor has been most powerful and most pernicious. Although welfare does provide significant assistance to the poor, nevertheless it would seem to be designed with hostility in mind. As David Ellwood writes: "Our welfare/income support system sometimes seems to be the worst of all worlds. It antagonizes, stigmatizes, isolates and humiliates. It discourages work rather than reinforcing and supporting it. It gives few aids or signals to point people toward self support. It offers only two real options: work all the time or be on welfare."[13]

This welfare system and its various counterparts (which we discuss below) leave American cities in much bleaker circumstances than most European cities, where the reversals in social policy are limited and more social services are offered. In the United States negligent federal government, in the guise of promoting states' rights and home rule and surrounding itself by claims that localities know best what they need, has used the pressures from a changed international economy to justify turning back decades of progress, to continuously shift power and privilege away from the cities and the poor to the better-off in the suburbs. In these circumstances, it should not be a surprise that cities do not have the capacities or the zeal to address adequately problems of poverty.

We have pervasive evidence that poverty has increased in the United States. That same evidence also suggests that prosperity for the majority of the population is itself threatened by the bad conditions that afflict the poor and that debilitate U.S. cities. A poorly educated, inattentive, fearful population reared in the cities is likely to be inefficient, even hostile as a workforce, counterproductive as a citizenry, and dependent. Trickle-down benefits and stricter social control (both conservative suggestions) cannot adequately solve the problem. U.S. jails now hold a higher proportion of the population than is the case for any other major country in the world, save the defunct Soviet Union and South Africa. Building more jails, increasing police budgets, and slamming down on civil rights is the wrong way to go.

In fact, in a whole series of directions U.S. policy has gone awry. Severe and persistent urban poverty is only one manifestation of a soured national project. The solution to problems of urban poverty will have to be accompanied by solutions to other national problems as well.

To see how conservative arguments are so deeply flawed, we must study the historical evolution of the interconnected activities of the national, state, and local governments in dealing with the economy, poor families, and cities in trouble. We begin by documenting the expansion of the federal role with regard to urban poverty since the early 1930s, when national programs first provided assistance to the poor. Although we focus for the most part on specifically urban programs, we wish to leave no doubt about the principal effect of such intervention at the national level. As the statistics presented in earlier chapters demonstrate, and contrary to what conservative theory claims, expansion of federal spending for transfer programs, from Social Security to welfare to health care, resulted in sizeable reductions in poverty.[14]

Federal Antipoverty Policies

There was a long period of progress in federal antipoverty programs. It can be plausibly argued that major social policies to prevent the growth of inequalities were first established even as long as a century ago. As Lester Thurow, dean of the MIT management school, reminds us, Congress established the Interstate Commerce Commission in the 1800s and passed laws against the great commercial trusts "to stop a growing concentration of wealth and to prevent that wealth from being used exploitatively."

> The railroads were not to be allowed to exploit their economic advantage over farmers and the oil trust was not to be allowed to exploit the urban consumer. Compulsory education for all was established to create an egalitarian distribution of human capital and more marketable skills in order to prevent large inequalities in earnings. In the 20th century inheritance taxes and progressive income taxes were adopted to lessen inequalities.[15]

When poverty spread more widely and threatened the stability of the entire economy, the government shifted the emphasis of its programs from general inequality and comprehensive regulation to the problems of persons with absolute need. The government's first efforts to provide national resources to fight poverty occurred in the Great Depression of the 1930s. As Thurow writes: "The rising inequalities of the Great Depression brought Social Security, unemployment insurance and eventually medical insurance for the elderly and the poor to prevent people from falling out of the middle class when confronting unemployment, illness, old age and other harsh facts of life."[16]

National programs were created (the Works Progress Administration, Aid to Families with Dependent Children, Social Security, unemployment insurance, the Civilian Conservation Corps, and others) with the express design of building a broad national safety net to support people, to hold them above poverty and dependency. Within this broad, protective arrangement, local efforts were supported and encouraged to relieve poverty through the provision of better economic opportunity. The federal government concentrated on programs to enhance individual (and therefore family) economic security. Local institutions retained the responsibility for improving the conditions of the places where poverty occurred. A great deal of discretion was left to local government.

The Social Security Act of 1935, which was the heart of the national effort, put into place the basic structure of the American welfare state: general relief for the so-called unemployables, funded by the localities and states; work relief for employables, paid by the federal government; social insurance providing pensions to the retired and temporary relief to the jobless; and categorical public assistance to needy blind, aged, and children.

The Works Progress Administration (WPA), also established as a work relief program in 1935, was designed to cope with a situation of massive unemployment, create national wealth, and provide self-respect through the provision of useful work. As it turned out, the WPA never employed more than 39 percent of the 8 to 11 million unemployed. Moreover, because of hostile management in localities, the make-work nature of the jobs, and the low pay, the morale of many WPA participants did not improve.

Even at the time, top policymakers realized that the American body politic had a very limited capacity to target resources specifically to the poor. As the saying went, "a program for the poor was a poor [politically vulnerable] program." This reluctance to help the "undeserving" poor was seen clearly in state and local responses to the general relief program. Especially hard hit were the millions of people migrating around the country searching for communities that would give them a chance. In fear of a drain on local resources, many states and cities erected residency requirements as barriers to prevent poor people from staying. California even introduced border checks (serving also as agriculture inspection stations) designed to keep out the riffraff from the Midwest and South. A number of cities introduced stringent vagrancy laws aimed at the drifting poor.

Local officials also minimized relief expenditures by telling almost everyone—including aging workers without skills, women with dependent children, and the temporarily disabled—that they were employable and thus not eligible for assistance. Similar problems of excessive local control plagued Depression-era categorical-assistance programs, particularly the portion concerned with aid to dependent children. Southern states and proponents of "states' rights" won provisions in welfare legislation, allowing them to apply prejudicial conditions to exclude recipients. State laws requiring property ownership or the absence of a criminal record permitted many local officials to discriminate against African-American or Mexican-American households.

Local governments were not eager to administer the welfare state, and they invested much energy in controlling its growth, even by denying benefits to the legally eligible. Despite this and other imperfections, the new programs made progress helping the poor. During the 1930s, some 46 million people, 35 percent of the population, received public aid or social insurance at one time or another. Public funds for these programs scarcely existed in 1929; by 1939 they had grown to $5 billion, 27 percent of government expenditures at all levels and 7 percent of the national income.[17] These constituted dramatic improvements in federal capacity to keep individuals functioning in the economy and society.

The essential components of the American welfare state stayed the same for the next three decades, until the civil rights movement brought attention once again to the large numbers of disenfranchised and poor people in the country. The urban riots and rebellions of the 1960s signaled a transition in the national role in fighting poverty. Lyndon Johnson's declaration of a War on Poverty in 1964, the Moynihan report in 1965 on African-American families, and the Kerner Commission's 1968 report on urban unrest were all high-profile government attempts to draw national attention to poverty and marshall national resources for addressing it. There was a move away from simply helping poor people, toward complementary efforts to alter poor communities.

Rising Expectations for Municipal Power

Faced with riots in Detroit, Washington, D.C., Los Angeles, and most other major cities, the federal government in the mid-1960s tried to focus attention on the problems of poor neighborhoods. Between 1965 and 1969, some 250 people were killed, 12,000 injured, and 83,000 arrested in disorders in dozens of cities. The government responded.[18]

The Kerner Commission (President Johnson's National Advisory Commission on Civil Disorders) investigated the circumstances underlying the African-American neighborhood riots of the 1960s. The commission concluded not only that "our nation is moving toward two societies, one black, one white—separate and unequal," but also that the "alternative will require a commitment to national action—compassionate, massive and sustained, backed by the resources of the most powerful and the richest nation on this earth. From every American it will require new attitudes, new understanding, and, above all, new will."[19] The commission called for an end to racial discrimination, and for aggressive federal action to fight unemployment and improve education, housing, and welfare policy at the neighborhood and city levels. The report called, for example, for better coordination of the hundreds of employment programs already funded at the local level, as well as the creation of new federal programs to provide a million new jobs in communities in both the public and private sectors.[20]

The favorite analogy of the period was to compare poor neighborhoods with colonized, dependent, Third-World nations.[21] This concept of the neighborhood as a locus for policymaking was embodied partially even in national legislation. For example, the Model Cities Law required the formation of neighborhood advisory boards for the allocation of federal funds. The Carter administration (a decade later) went even further in attempting to strengthen the role of neighborhoods by establishing a bureau to deal with neighborhood development and autonomy. The Department of Housing and Urban Development (HUD) produced nearly a hundred categorical programs designed specifically for neighborhood revitalization, preservation, economic development, and political and social empowerment.

The funding increases that accompanied these new and expanded activities were truly enormous. As a proportion of all federal outlays, urban program expenditures increased from about 2 percent in 1960 to almost 12 percent in the mid-1970s. In real terms, given a period of rapidly growing federal budgets overall, this represented a gigantic and unprecedented increase in federal transfer payments to cities and their needy residents. There was vast expansion in programs that were locally run (if often federally administered) for housing, health care, street and highway building and repair, employment and training, and other municipal services.[22] "In New York City federal aid rose from 110 million dollars in fiscal year 1961 to nearly 1.1 billion dollars or about one-sixth of total municipal revenue in 1970. . . . In the late 1970s, federal aid to the City approached 2.5 billion dollars annually or about one-fifth the municipal budget."[23]

One major consequence of this explosive growth in municipal activities was a parallel heightening of expectations. City governments or, as we shall see, even neighborhood groups and community organizations, would henceforth be expected to deliver goods and services to improve housing, take care of neighborhoods, and provide jobs. Previously weak local public offices, many of them historically hostile to the needs of the poor, were suddenly the great source. Even though most of the resources originated in federal budgets that provided financial aid to states and municipalities, the public image was of vastly expanded municipal capacity and competence.

This expansion of federal support for city programs manifested a second important characteristic. Federal policymakers hoped that by pulling in disenfranchised groups, they could foster the reconstruction of threatened political and social institutions. To do so, they aimed their efforts at neighborhoods rather than cities overall. The Community Action programs, with their mandate for "maximum feasible participation," serve as a good example. By galvanizing poor and minority political communities, the federal government hoped to increase the likelihood that locally administered programs would actually meet these groups' needs, and, as John Mollenkopf points out, the Democrats hoped to sustain their threatened national coalition.[24] The federal government hoped not only to appease minorities' demands for political participation, but also to increase the capacity of local governments as the cornerstones for addressing localized problems. Nicholas Lemann recalls that the

1960s really was not "a time of faith in big government," but in local affairs. "The War on Poverty looked for solutions to poverty that would be local and diffuse, and would circumvent state and local government and Congress. . . . Its planners hoped to build public support for it by achieving quick, visible successes."[25]

The increased federal effort in fact aimed at an even more narrow geographic target. In response to claims that big-city political machines practiced intentional bias, and to account for the obvious connections between race and poverty, national policymakers actually bypassed municipal government. A vast array of federal programs was organized to service poor neighborhoods, as though they could be insulated from legally constituted municipal authorities and from the growth and job dynamics of the metropolitan economy. Local governments now also faced neighborhood groups that were federally sponsored, "groups which insisted upon added redistributive service-delivery programs."[26] As Douglas Yates writes: "Community action was designed as a strategy for fighting city hall, the schools, the housing authority, and the police. It was designed . . . in Washington, D.C., to provide creative conflict—to shake up remote and sluggish [city] bureaucracies."[27]

In the end, the combination of struggles for more civil rights, expanded economic opportunities, and increased local authority, accompanied by vastly higher levels of federal financial support, led to the parts adding to less than the whole. As groups pushed simultaneously for rights, jobs, and more political power, there developed several difficulties.

All these programs operated under the general belief that elected municipal government was not trustworthy enough to deal effectively (or in some instances fairly) with the needs of depressed communities. From the outset an increase in political power was the central target of the neighborhood movement, so that the fight against poverty was lost in the shuffle. Neighborhood power is an imprecise concept to begin with, and the objectives of those who sought to promote it were unclear. Local businesses, residents, and other interests used the concept to justify narrow, particular pursuits. As Marilyn Landau writes:

> Upper-income residents used [neighborhood power] to oppose the location of airports, hospitals, and highways, which provided jobs for lower-income groups. Minorities and labor used the concept to compete for more equitable shares of development projects. Progressives used it to challenge federal support for corporate development of central business districts. In fact, neighborhood became a spatial metaphor for all manner of existing urban conflicts: ethnics vs. blacks; renters vs. landlords; small vs. large property owners.[28]

A variety of coalitions formed, sometimes making allies of neighborhoods and city hall, other times pitting city hall against neighborhoods that were allied with the federal government. Community organizations claimed neighborhood property rights to oppose eminent domain. City planners envisioned decentralized, neighborhood planning to oppose downtown interests. Economic planners sought "substantive alternatives to traditional commercial revitalization, as in Russell's industrial conversion plans for Detroit."[29]

In the end, both citywide and neighborhood programs and budgets expanded. Inroads were made against poverty and urban decay. But then disaster struck. First, there was programmatic ineptitude and failure. Most notably, the sub–city hall efforts were not successful. "Members of Congress, mayors, governors, and Cabinet secretaries" were angered, and "hundreds of separate anti-poverty organizations run largely by inexperienced people . . . practically guaranteed . . . failures."[30] These programs, in retrospect, transferred little power to poor people in neighborhoods, helped only minimally with economic development, and provided precious few votes for a reconstructed, liberal Democratic majority. The second and bigger force for undoing these attempts at urban improvement and poverty reduction, however, was systematic, and it drew its negative strength from the process of suburbanization of employment opportunities and solvent taxpayers, the increasing pressures of global economic challenges, and the big turnaround those changes engendered in federal politics.

The Federal Retreat

One important result of these energetic attempts to reduce poverty, assist cities and neighborhoods, and transform local politics (and rebuild the Democratic party coalition) was an increase in expectations. As the proliferation of programs, activities, and funds led to more involvement, it also created the perception that local government is obligated to take direct responsibility for alleviating poverty and other socioeconomic ills. It is then ironic but predictable that while local institutions were given the mantle of responsibility for solving problems, they were provided with no independent source of resources and no autonomous authority to deal with them. They were allowed no fundamental improvements in municipal organization, increase in taxing power, extension of boundary lines (to annex suburbs), or augmentation of regulatory powers vis-à-vis private corporations. As a consequence, once the political interest in Washington turned away from cities and the flow of federal resources started to run dry, city governments found themselves struggling.

Political developments and social achievements led indeed to high expectations, and then crashed. The Great Society that "bestowed so many programs upon urban areas was by the late 1970s pouring nearly sixty billion dollars a year into cities for . . . housing assistance and mass transit, job training, water projects and block grants of seemingly infinite variety."[31] Boston, for example, which got only $10,000 from the federal government in 1960, garnered $90 million in 1980. How could expectations not rise? Then, only six years later, federal transfers were cut back to $36 million.[32]

If there was ever a recipe for municipal disaster, this was it. The federal cutbacks actually had begun earlier. Ever since the Nixon–Ford administration (1968–76), there had been a progression of cutbacks in federal aid, an attempt to lower taxes, reduce the commitment to expanding civil rights for minorities and women, and slash the size and scope of Washington's transfer payments to poor people and places. The size of the reduction was so dramatic that it has been much publicized and well studied. We will mention only a few illustrative details.

Investment in national infrastructure dropped as a proportion of GNP by one quarter from 1975 to 1990. Investment in education fell 28 percent (compared to GNP) from 1980 to 1990. The Reagan budgets by 1985 reduced outright spending on unemployment programs by 17 percent, and cut Aid for Families with Dependent Children (AFDC) expenditures by 14 percent.[33] The administration also lumped twenty-nine categorical education grants targeted toward low-income students—which had increased from $1 billion dollars in 1965 to $3.4 billion in 1980—into one block grant, reduced the budget by 24 percent, and loosened the reporting requirements, thereby weakening the focus on the needs of poor children.[34] The administration successfully scaled back the Urban Development Action Grant (UDAG) program by two-thirds, from a high of $675 million in 1981 to only $216 million in 1988—an even more drastic cut when inflation is factored in—and then did away with the UDAG program altogether. Since the peak in the 1970s, federal aid for low- and moderate-income housing has been drastically cut. For example, in 1980 HUD's housing program budget was $55.7 billion; by 1987 this had been reduced to $15.2 billion. In 1980, social spending consumed 54.3 percent of all government spending; by 1986, this had been reduced to 47.6 percent of total government expenditures.[35] According to the Congressional Research Service, the federal government cut aid to states and localities by 23.5 percent between 1980 and 1985.[36]

To cut transfer payments, the Reagan administration moved consciously to shift responsibilities but not resources to local governments and the nonprofit sector for "local" problems. Accompanied by reduced federal taxation, this strategy ostensibly would allow localities the opportunity to fulfill voters' desires more directly and more efficiently, using, if they wished, expanded local resource bases. Local officials would do better, it was argued, with minimal federal intervention. In February 1989 Katherine Bishop reported:

> The only clinic providing routine health care to the bulk of [Oakland, California's] poor closed today, a victim of insufficient state reimbursement. . . . The closing leaves patients on public assistance without ready access to doctors just as a surge in the use of crack has brought a dramatic increase in problem pregnancies and an exceptional number of babies born prematurely and addicted to cocaine. . . . Those unable to find private care will be thrust upon the overtaxed resources of the county hospital, Highland General, whose emergency room, known locally as "the knife and gun club" because it must care for the victims of street fights that crack use has brought, is already stretched to the breaking point.[37]

Progress in fighting poverty since the 1930s has not been completely undone by any means, but the new trend is clear. The responsibility for dealing with serious urban poverty has indeed been transferred from the federal realm. Changes in regulatory control over the national economy have redistributed benefits from the poor and middle class to the rich. And cities have been cast adrift. This is a dismal situation, indeed, as observers now agree.

The Debate on National Policy

To prepare this section, we catalogued numerous proposals for more constructive national policies regarding urban poverty. Somewhat to our surprise, we found a solid core of agreement among scholars, politicians, and business leaders.[38] There is even a modicum of agreement between the liberal Kerner Commission and the conservative American Enterprise Institute. Each pays attention to the need for effort in the four areas that Gary Sandefur of the Institute for Research on Poverty thinks most important: employment, education, welfare, and health.[39] To the extent the agreement exists, it originates, we believe, in the widely accepted fear that the problems of poverty can no longer be confined to small, isolated areas, nor to pathologies normally thought to be restricted to the poor. If a community of poverty produces illness, poor education, negative attitudes, poor work habits, and low productivity, it is sure eventually to cause problems for the country as a whole. Inasmuch as urban poverty is closely associated with collapsing and devalued housing, streets, bridges, utility systems, and other components of infrastructure, it also symbolizes (and results from) a huge drag on productivity and industrial flexibility nationally. These problems go far beyond urban poverty, but they are closely connected.

In earlier chapters we have argued how changes in the economy and failures in policy generate poverty. Here we wish to point out how rising poverty generates problems throughout the economy and hampers the development of sound overall policy. To work, industrial policy and antipoverty policy must complement one another.

Antipoverty policy cannot function without an array of positive changes in several directions. In our view, improvements are required in three major areas: industrial policy, educational opportunities, and family support. Successful programs and policies exist in each group in the United States, although for some programs, examples are best borrowed from other countries.

Better U.S. policy would result not only in rehabilitated cities, more equal income distribution, and less poverty in the cities and elsewhere, but also in a reconstructed economy and society, which would compete more effectively overseas. Most of the proposals we discuss have already been debated widely, although, we add, they have not been taken seriously by the federal government. We make no claims of originality, and we leave the particulars of federal policy to public debate, which, as we write, rages in newspapers, journals, and at the margin of legislative bodies.

Industrial Policy

In the face of severe competition from lower-cost producers in other countries, American firms must respond. They have two remarkably different options. The first option is to lower costs by cutting wages, demanding harder work, reducing benefits, replacing skilled workers with machines that put them out of work, and, if that does not work, then taking funds out of U.S. production entirely, investing either in financial affairs or in overseas plants. As we saw in Chapter 3, this deindustrialization process is the option many—perhaps a majority of—American firms have chosen, and it results in depressed wages, unemployment, and reduced incomes.[40]

Industrial policy that allows or even encourages this sort of negative change on the part of firms or industries has turned out to be counterproductive. At best these sorts of industrial adaptations make firms more competitive in the short run. In the long run the firms are less likely to stay competitive. Without adequate pay and training, workers become less, not more productive. Without heavy investment in both social and productive infrastructure, such as schooling and the sort of technical equipment that requires highly qualified workers, American industry loses in nose-to-nose competition with foreign industry, even when foreign workers are better paid.

American industry has a second option: to encourage labor. A high and pressing demand for labor is the fundamental condition for reduction in poverty. Good labor policy must be emphasized, in particular, because there are contrary forces.[41]

High labor demand can be a problem for business in the short run, as it can raise wages and therefore production costs and put pressure on profits. Industrial policy must resolve this problem.

A growing demand for labor was of course one of the components of the rapid economic growth and decline in poverty during most of the early post–World War II period. The principal reason these thirty years can be celebrated as the American Century is that the standard of living rose rapidly while the incidence of poverty fell, especially in the 1960s and early 1970s. The strong demand for basic labor improved the distribution of income, supported families, and tended to reduce poverty.

The Democratic party claimed strong employment and wage growth as a political mainstay from 1960 on, and the Republican party since the second term of Ronald Reagan has claimed rapid employment growth (without wage growth) as a major achievement. No one who worries seriously about reducing poverty forgets that there must be growth of jobs that pay decent wages.[42] The problem is, there are as many ways to generate jobs as there are to run the economy. Consequently, analysts and politicians have great difficulty agreeing on how to stimulate the growth of well-paying jobs. They even have difficulties agreeing that it is possible to do so.[43]

The question is not whether the United States needs an industrial policy. As the editor of *Business Week* puts it, "Every country has an industrial policy, and the United States is no exception. The only question is whether we will choose to make it explicit and effective."[44] Put slightly differently, the question is: what kind of industrial policy is appropriate? Consider these individual actions: the Treasury devalues the dollar, Congress rewrites the tax code and raises the minimum wage, the Defense Department selects a technology or a contractor, the Federal Communications Commission establishes a competitive process for determining who will manufacture high-resolution television, and the Environmental Protection Agency establishes rules governing imports from Mexico. These elements of an unconscious, implicit industrial policy benefit some companies and industries and not others, redistribute the tax burden, tilt advantages of competition, and result in "billions of dollars of revenues and productivity lost or gained."[45] We must add to this the large distortions caused by transfer of productive energy from the domestic economy into a hugely bloated military budget.

Leading economists and industrialists have estimated that faulty industrial policy causes losses by American companies that amount to hundreds of billions of dollars annually: $6 billion from counterfeiting and more from patent violation, $9 billion from inappropriate export controls, $36 billion in underpaid U.S. taxes by Japanese companies, and $51 billion from the low U.S. savings rate. The same analysts add $60 billion for drug abuse, $100 billion for remedial education, and, finally, $300 billion in waste from the U.S. tort system.[46] According to Robert Eisner, past president of the American Economics Association, it may take $50 billion to replace and repair bridges and $26 billion to repair highways, with another $14 billion for environmental cleanup, to which we may add $9 billion for education funding, $4 billion for public housing, and $130 billion for other problems.[47] Summing these up, Robert Reich comes up with a separate estimate of the deficit in physical and human infrastructure, not counting pollution abatement, at $200 billion each year throughout the 1990s.[48] These are heavy business costs, to be borne by the nation.

There are alternatives to poor industrial policy. Although there are surely unavoidable ups and downs, experiences in various Western European countries and Japan demonstrate that a mixed-capitalist, social-democratic society can manage its economy to produce long-run growth (or at least stability) while basic services and benefits are provided. The key lies in a constant push to improve the quality of the labor force by increasing labor's commitment to the job, raising the level of benefits, and using enhanced skills to improve productivity. The increased skills must be accompanied by technological innovation and investment, and education must be designed to match the new possibilities.

Although in the current dismay over bad U.S. industrial policy most signs are negative, it is good to remember that positive policy is not unknown to the United States. Elements of industrial policy to improve the labor force have worked in the past. "Project U.S.A.," a study by the Cornell Graduate School of Management, notes that immediately following the Second World War, "The G.I. Bill of Rights . . . greatly broadened and deepened the intellectual capital of the nation. It created a new generation of homeowners and stakeholders in the society. And perhaps most significantly, it more than paid for itself through its contribution to the nation's economic growth and welfare."[49]

The G.I. Bill was "far-sighted, far-reaching, and effective" as a promoter of economic development, and it did not work alone. Other elements of an implicit national industrial policy complemented it. The 1956 Highway Act built 42,500 miles of freeways, and the Education Act that followed the launching of the Soviet space satellite *Sputnik* gave a boost to schools and universities in general. The federal government also stimulated the development of civilian technologies through sponsorship of military work in computer science and in other spinoffs from military research. Federal guidance and subsidies of transportation, higher education, and research led to the creation of an "invaluable base of structural and human capital for further industrial growth." The Rural Electrification Act offered low-interest loans that changed the structure of the American countryside and led to enormous gains in agricultural productivity. Numerous other federal policies focused on stabilizing farm incomes and production, resulting in giant productivity gains and cost efficiencies that put U.S. agriculture and much of the U.S. workforce in an enviable competitive position worldwide.[50]

All aspects of industrial policy are important to antipoverty efforts, but one in particular is more directly related to our quest to challenge the roots of urban decay. This is the rebuilding of physical infrastructure, which could reduce the intensity of geographically concentrated poverty by resuscitating the decayed capacities for production and life-support of older cities. We take transportation as an example. Until recently, backbone infrastructure like interstate transportation has typically been the responsibility of the government. Looking far back from the interstate highway system, we observe that the government gave high priority to a national railroad system in the nineteenth century because it seemed likely to catalyze economic development. One tangible aspect of "industrial policy" then was public subsidy, the land grants that allowed huge private real estate profits to railroad investors. The policy had results. In spite of robber baron thievery, the railroads stimulated iron and steel industry development, and that spilled over into other industries. The success was repeated almost a century later, with the interstate highways, suburban beneficiaries perhaps being the new robber barons. Looking ahead from the interstate system to the 1990s, however, we find very little evidence of conscious transportation policy. Once the interstate system was largely completed in the 1960s, the national government abandoned its leadership, neglecting to fund new developments and repairs and to lay plans to guide states and private investors. As "Project U.S.A." reports, in spite of great need, there is no conscious national planning, and failure is all the more shocking in the face of the mounting problems: "Realistic estimates indicate that the United States will at least have to double its . . . spending . . . to maintain . . . infrastructure over the next ten years. Moveover, this estimate does not include the resources for developing new high-tech infrastructure systems necessary to meet the needs of the 21st century."[51]

The specific magnitudes are daunting: the Interstate Highway system needs to repair 2,000 miles of roadway each year, and over 250,000 bridges (half of those in the country) must be extensively repaired or replaced. The current rate of highway decline will cost 3.6 percent in productivity by 1995, a loss of roughly $160 billion in GNP.[52] Much larger losses will be sustained unless there are huge investments in the cores of older metropolitan areas, which have antiquated sewer, water, and other utility systems, as well as heavy need for replacement or rehabilitation of buildings, streets, factories, and bridges. A program to mend and maintain would provide jobs. Without a national project for reinvestment, the costs to older cities will be overwhelming, and the city governments will be forced to choose one unproductive route or another: they can try to repair the city and leave the people to rot, or they can let the infrastructure decay, and prepare some of their population to be competitive in other places. This moves us to the second group of government policies, which is focused more directly on people.

Education Programs

Before we examine education directly, we want to consider general principles that should apply to all essential services to citizens (and, we believe, resident aliens). Probably the most important principle is that service provision should be "universal." That is, services should be offered regardless of the recipient's wealth, income, or other personal qualifiers. Services, in general, should not be available only to the poor. Eligibility should not be means-tested. One example of an important service that is not means-tested is comprehensive health care, notably not available in the United States, except in the strictly bounded example of participants in a large, comprehensive health-maintenance organization such as the Kaiser Plan. Another, that used to be available to large portions of the U.S. urban population but is not available to most central-city families now, is high-quality public education, which includes preschool and public colleges and universities. Such services provide support to families, children, and adults, working both directly and indirectly to improve the distribution of income and reduce poverty.

There is a crucial difference between services that are offered to and used by all citizens (such as public schools in the suburbs) and services that are offered only to the poor (such as city public hospitals). When there is a means test, so that no one with too much income or wealth can get the service, then the recipients are stigmatized, public effort is likely to be reduced, and the quality of service is probably inferior. Sometimes recipients or their relatives are even forced into poverty, as in the case of subsidized medical services available only after couples have used up their savings and even home-ownership investments. Look at the case of central-city public schools. Many upper-middle-class residents now find a better alternative. Their decision to send their children to private schools, in response to inadequate public schools, ends up stigmatizing public school students, leads to weakened public support and therefore reduced public school budgets, and ultimately results in inferior education for the poor.[53] Society is separated. The gulf increases. To suggest possibilities for better policy, we review briefly three proposals for central-city schools.

We begin by recalling that there is overwhelming national support for education as the target of efforts to improve social and economic equality. A May 1991 *Newsweek* poll indicated that over two-thirds of Americans, regardless of race, believe African Americans "should focus most of their energy on improving education."[54] The three proposals we examine—community schools, early education, and work-study—all move in this direction. Once again, as in the case of industrial and antipoverty policies, we see the mutual reinforcing capacity of investments in education and in community-building. Good schools can add to individual opportunity, and they can also build community. Not least of all, the school is important because it can contribute a set of intellectual resources to assist in community transformation. Teachers and administrators can become advocates for community involvement and provide the continuing presence necessary to bring about reform in individuals, families, and neighborhoods. In addition, schools now have a significant number of minority persons in leadership positions who can serve as role models, personal bridges from the isolated community to the outside world, and spokespersons.

Reforms in a number of cities have aimed to make the school an important part of the community. In Oakland, California, for example, the school district is profoundly redirecting its mission, to develop a community framework for education not just for the child, but for the entire family and community.[55] The troubled Chicago school district, for example, has focused on the community as the basic unit for reform, decentralizing the entire program to the neighborhood level in an effort to rebuild community. In smaller communities highly successful public schools involve families, community members, school staff, and students in making decisions.[56] These efforts represent positive use of the only significant governmental institution available to communities. Most city neighborhoods have no public institutions other than schools and fire stations. Libraries, playgrounds, and other neighborhood facilities are shut from budget cuts or were never reopened after the riots of the 1960s and 1970s.

Schools also provide a new means of delivering social and community services. A number of school districts, like those in Atlanta, Georgia, and Oakland, California, are already coordinating family social services, ranging from employment and training to drug abuse counseling. These schools can be a new platform for community revitalization. City school districts can also increase the length of the school year, adding an entire year to the average inner-city child's twelve years of education.

This could make an enormous difference in raising skill levels of minority students and increasing their competitive abilities.

Federal funding is needed to support such community schools. Community education grants would assist urban school districts to develop community delivery systems. These grants would assist school districts to develop longer school years and coordinate community service programs, ranging from recreation to employment and training, family planning, drug counseling, economic development, and related family and community services. School districts, local governments, and nonprofit agencies affiliated with local colleges would get comprehensive planning grants to design community-school plans. These districts would receive multiyear funding based on the plan, which would include the allocation of local taxes and partnerships with nonprofit, charitable, and private business groups. There are already some fledgling efforts in the U.S. Department of Education to move in these directions. Several competitive grant programs support community schools. We are suggesting that community-based and -supported education become a national effort sustained by substantial resources.

The second major program should be in early education. The evidence is overwhelming that the earlier children start school the sooner they will be in positions to learn and contribute. Early childhood education is a good investment for the total society. Findings from Headstart and similar programs suggest enormous potential in reducing school failure, providing safe and secure child care, gaining access to parents for their education and training, and facilitating early detection of potential health and related problems. Opportunities for poor children could be appreciably improved by high-quality early education and child care programs. More local employment opportunities lie here, too.

Our third recommendation for federal education policy is the creation of a linkage between schools and workplaces. In an effort to reduce the fragile connection between work and school for many disadvantaged young persons, a national work experience program should be developed to allow a consortium of firms in each city to design in-school, after-school, and cooperative education programs for youth. School work-experience programs would operate like college work-study programs. Students would be allowed to complete part-time work at certified nonprofit groups, government agencies, and business firms. The school district would match employer salary up to an amount established statewide. The federal government would match the funds of states in implementing these programs, which would be developed in conjunction with national business organizations such as the National Alliance of Business and various minority business associations. These business organizations would establish local partners for the program and develop business education councils in communities where they do not exist or need strengthening.

The work-experience scheme would allow for development of apprenticeships in small and emerging fields like computer technology and biotechnology. Participants would receive the minimum wage, allowing them to avoid other, less academically related jobs that take time from their studies. The scheme would be administered centrally; students would receive school credit and be evaluated by work supervisors and school counselors. Teachers participating in the program would be awarded fellowships, funded jointly by the government and industry, for summer experience with the students' employers. The teachers, as well, would gain experience in the business or industry into which they are sending their students. The business participants would gain a clearer picture of the student population. This program would forge new, stronger relationships among school, business, and community.

Such innovative programs require leadership even more than money, but they need both. A few programs are already in place. They need the added impetus of national recognition, networking, and support so that even more creative local options will be designed.

Family Support

The third group of government policies to be improved involve transfers—cash payments to broad classes of citizens. These transfers include monthly checks to the elderly and family support payments to parents with children, programs for dependent adults, and health care. As we saw in Chapter 2, such transfers improve the distribution of income and work directly to reduce poverty of whole classes of people.

It is important, once again, to note the crucial difference between these universal payments, which are not restricted to those in need, and means-tested payments (like welfare), which are. Social Security is a good example. With few exceptions, payments go to all elderly persons, regardless of need: no one is excluded for being too well-off. The payments that go to poor people of course provide proportionately much more assistance, but political support is nevertheless broad. This transfer program is lobbied for ferociously by many who are well-to-do, and it is opposed by almost no one.[57] There is no stigma attached to the receipt of the transfer. The efficiency of administration is high, because the bureaucracy requires minimal checking for rule compliance or guarding against fraud. Furthermore, what recipients do with their money, or how they behave in general, is their own business.

These principles are important when we consider our proposals for family support programs. Such policies are found to be generally sound and workable in almost all European nations, Australia, and Canada. Transfers are large enough to help, but small enough to avoid adding any incentive to have children. Given the unforeseen growth in the number of female-headed households in the United States—precisely the group that is headed most surely for persistent poverty—a move to provide support without stigma makes sense. The transfers can be reinforced considerably by strict enforcement of fathers' financial responsibility.

A family support program could be administered through the Earned Income Tax Credit, already on the books and functioning, if EITC were made more generous and modified to allow an additional tax writeoff for each minor dependent. Families could elect to receive the credit as a direct payment, a refund on their taxes, or a deduction against their withholding, using vehicles easily understood by all Americans. This would provide at least a supplement, better yet an alternative to welfare and poverty, helping families to cope quickly with unemployment and reducing many social costs.

Although limited family support programs have functioned since the mid-1960s and transfers have "reduced the extent of both poverty and income disparities,"[58] the welfare system is subject to widespread criticism. Reform proposals range from doing away with welfare altogether and replacing it with workfare, using welfare entirely as a short-term transitional program, lasting only one or two years, or undoing the conservative cuts and more, raising welfare support to a liveable level. There is some merit to many of these proposals, but we believe it would be better to merge the entire welfare system with Social Security, removing completely the idea of remediation. Coupled with broad family support, this administrative change would be salutory. Eligible participants would sign up for benefits in the same way they apply for Social Security disability benefits. Even here it is possible to avoid a stigmatizing means test. Because most employees, even young teenagers working odd jobs, contribute to Social Security, most eligible participants (or their spouses prior to divorce) would have made contributions, and this includes the vast majority of the poor. Various changes in the assignment of benefits to spouses and children would facilitate increased responsibility. Financing would be possible inside the system, with rather small modifications. For example, it has been estimated that by taxing all income from Social Security, raising the payroll tax ceiling by $10,000, and increasing the contributions of married persons by one-half percent, the increase in yield would be $700 billion per year (in 1991 terms).[59]

There presently exists no comprehensive family support program for dependent adults. Those who choose to register for health disability, handicap, drug addiction, or other causes could either be placed in a group setting, as current policy often provides, or remain with parents or relatives or in adult foster care. The care-giver would receive an allowance for providing the care, once again as either a supplementary Social Security or EITC benefit. A similar approach has been proposed for the homeless.[60] Adult care programs in many states have some of these features. We wish to encourage communal and family settings, without making half-way houses and group homes the only alternative.

These combined programs for family support would not cost much more than the current welfare system, and the funding base is already in place. It merely replaces the form of payment and reorganizes the administration.[61] Most important, however, is the chance to remove the counterproductive stigma of welfare.

A crucial complement to these family support programs is improved health care policy. More than 30 million Americans now have no health insurance, and many others are covered inadequately. It is estimated that as many as half the population in any given year are at one time or another without any coverage.[62] Notably, many who are in the largest group of new workers, part-timers, are intentionally hired so firms can avoid health insurance premiums. (Even the federal government uses this escape clause.) Without insurance, illness threatens and often leads to poverty.

There are ways to deal effectively with the problem of health care. We must either incorporate a minimum health premium for all workers, require a health plan for all employers and the self-employed, or establish a national health plan. There is a growing majority who believe that all Americans should be covered by basic and catastrophic health insurance. In the absence of a national care plan, this approach would operate as workers' compensation does now. Employers would have the option of providing coverage or paying into the state medical insurance pool fund. The self-employed would be required to file with their state tax forms and pay premiums with taxes. Those without jobs would have premiums paid from state and federal funds. Health care would be available to all, regardless of the source of the premium.

Final Comments

It would be unrealistic to ignore questions about programs and laws promoting affirmative action. Different in nature from the three groups of antipoverty policy we have just discussed, affirmative action is, most unfortunately, still an essential requirement in the United States. Where redress is required, especially where discrimination persists, there can be no substitute for rules that push in the direction of fairness. The women's movement and the civil rights movement keep pushing because women, on the one hand, and minority men, women, and children, on the other, still suffer from discrimination in housing, employment, and public institutions. We will not take space here to elaborate how we think affirmative actions should work, nor will we specify how they may overlap, be integrated with, or supplement policies for industry, education, or family support. Affirmative action, nevertheless, is part of the discussion that will have to continue until federal policies are reformed.[63]

The reader will observe that we have left out two other crucial policies that must be developed specifically with the very poor in mind. The first is a national emergency employment program. We simply propose a youth service corps.[64] We leave the discussion for elsewhere. The second group includes programs for personal rehabilitation, counseling, job placement services, drug treatment, and the like. These remedial programs are absolutely necessary, and we expect they will be forthcoming in cities, once there is positive action on national policies for industry, education, and family support.

Even if economists, political scientists, planners, and various policymakers can agree on the policies to reduce poverty, that agreement provides no guarantee the policies will be enacted. There remain big issues of implementation. Questions of political support are essential. So, before turning (in the last section of the chapter) to treat specific questions, we investigate four alternative arenas for potential political support.

Sources of Political Support

Who can make these federal changes happen? While Americans agree reforms are required, not only to fight poverty but also to reposition the United States as an effective overseas competitor, they do not agree on how to get there. We consider four approaches. The first two would be dictated from the top down, because they depend on the interests of either corporate America or the managers of the old Democratic party coalition. The second two depend on pressure from the bottom up, either from the new suburban constituencies or, more likely, from the central city itself. These four approaches are not mutually exclusive, and they might even be supportive.

Top Down (I)

Potential support for antipoverty and procity policies might come from the leadership of some of the country's largest corporations. At first thought this seems an unlikely corner of the political economy for the expression of such liberal sentiments. There is, in fact, considerable support for reform, and there is nothing unusual about this interest of business in finding ways to implement better federal policy. Instead, there is seen to be clear self-interest in shifting the rising costs of social expenditures from private, corporate accounts, to the government, and there is also great fear of the explosive growth of an unproductive workforce. This desire to shift from the direct accounts of the corporation to the indirect accounts of the government (to be paid through taxation or inflation) does not arise from corporate worry about either poverty or the difficulties of central cities. Instead, it comes from the pressure on corporations to cut their operating costs in the face of ever-rising costs of employee selection, training, health care, and retirement benefits. Even the largest of corporations are finding it difficult to train qualified workers from among the many who lack adequate basic education, or to tax their profits enough to meet the heavy costs of health care and retirement.

One of the more striking pieces of evidence of such interest on the part of big corporations was the public statement on corporate needs for health care made in 1985 by Joseph Califano, who had been Secretary of Health, Education, and Welfare in the Johnson administration. While working for the Chrysler Corporation, he stressed the importance of expanded federal programs for national health insurance, especially the provision of financing. After findings by Chrysler that 25 percent of its health costs were probably due to inefficiency and waste, and that caps on payments by Medicare and state plans were ineffective in reducing costs, Califano called on Congress "to create a national commission to develop health policy to cut costs without reducing care."[65] This represented a notable turnaround in an almost solid corporate wall of opposition to any increases in public efforts to improve (and especially to nationalize any aspects of) the provision of health care.

Along a different line, the negative effects on business of poor public education were stressed by the revelations that the

New York Telephone Company had great difficulty finding new employees. Between January and July 1987, writes Elizabeth Neuffer in the *New York Times*, "only 3,619 of 22,880 applicants have passed the examinations, intended to test skills including vocabulary, number relationships and problem-solving for jobs ranging from telephone operator to service representative."[66] Not only did the telephone company turn down 84 percent of its applicants for lack of rudimentary literacy and mathematical skills, but their bad experience is shared by brokerage houses, secretarial services, and other employers who find applicants without a strong background in grammar, spelling, and language. A leading bank that interviewed 500 applicants every week reported hiring only about 3 percent.[67]

These problems are by no means confined to New York. In the report to President Reagan from the Commission on National Productivity, chairperson and Hewlett Packard chief executive officer John Young and his coauthors laid great stress on the liabilities of a weak public educational system. They sounded a clear warning about corporate losses being caused by public schools that are inferior, when compared to those in Japan and other important international competitors.[68] The biggest problems are in inner-city schools, which many poor children attend. These schools suffer most from the scissors movement of budget-cutting and growing numbers of students in need of extra support.

Of course these interests by big business in such a liberal, even progressive agenda are greatly tempered by the realization that the proposed programs cost money, and that funding must one way or another be a draw-down on receipts otherwise available for profits and private reinvestment. There are, in fact, real conflicts between the broad national interests of corporations and their narrow industrial or company interests. Corporate officers are often hard-calculating people, who look at the bottom lines. What they see as most desirable is the possibility of shifting costs, having the responsibilities taken up by the general public, so that their corporate and personal taxes will increase less than proportionately.

These leaders know that in the long run they and their businesses will benefit from national cost-sharing and the relatively wide guarantees to higher productivity that are provided by better education, health, and other social programs, because they will be less expensive than the alternatives. There are ample statistics to show that teachers are cheaper than jailers, even without counting the increased productivity due to learning and positive attitudes. Economic regulations in the United States, however, do not encourage U.S. corporations to plan for the long run. And private cost reductions and enhanced business productivity need long-term plans. The hoped-for cost transfers, from corporations to the state, will be a difficult change, especially without the risk of higher taxes on profits. The lack of outright progress to move these programs ahead through political channels, in spite of the positive evidence, is explained in good part by this conundrum.

A second hesitation on the part of big business is its own historical connection with the Republican party, as well as its old antagonisms toward organized labor. Unfortunately, the connection with the Republicans lumps big business leaders in a political alliance with reactionary rather than progressive economic interests; they appear unsympathetic to technological and organizational innovation, xenophobic in their reactions to both U.S. investment overseas and foreign investment in the United States, and, worst of all for the case at hand, hostile to nearly all forms of public expenditure. We hope corporate leaders will not lie in the bed archconservatives have made, but we see that much of the political hostility toward increased public taxation and expenditure for education, training, health, and retirement comes from the negative politics of racism, sexism, selfishness, and fear that so dominated the Republican strategy in the 1980s. We also recognize that progressive interests among corporations and their leaders by no means represent the interests of all corporations or all corporate leaders. There are those businesses that expect to continue to benefit from the availability of an unskilled, defenseless, and poorly paid workforce.

We argue that these various business interests do seem likely to consider new approaches, but they seem very unlikely to provide either the initiative or the main political pressure for better policies.

Top Down (II)

The more widespread expectation is that innovation will come through new policies designed and implemented in Washington by a revived Democratic party. The leadership that survives the old base of the party is the favored candidate for setting up the new agenda. The old coalition that grew from the New Deal included unions and other working-class, ethnic whites in city neighborhoods or inner suburbs, as well as minorities, public employees, city administrators, and a variety of unaffiliated liberals. A political coalition of groups like these would lead to strong, clear proposals for federal solutions to the problems of poverty and the central city, of the sort we presented in the section above. Such a revival might build on energy put forth by both the women's movement and the environmental movement, whose interests are in many cases compatible with those of the old liberal coalition. This is far from an unreasonable approach, particularly given the presumption, among most political scientists, "that national, not local, governments have a better record of promoting social reform."[69] The White House is the obvious place to start, although prospects for a reformed Democratic party winning the presidency in the 1990s seem unlikely.

The technical possibilities of a liberal, top-down solution to the problems of poverty and urban decline must be balanced against a considerable quantity of negative political evidence.

Most obviously there is the failure of the Democrats, including the more liberal wing of the party, to capture the White House since the Carter victory in 1976. The last three Democratic presidential candidates failed: first Jimmy Carter in his reelection attempt, then Walter Mondale, and finally Michael Dukakis. Even in Congress, where Democratic majorities have been almost continuous since the 1960s, a liberal agenda is hardly at the forefront. Even the old liberal coalition has broken up. Apart from various social, economic, and political influences—like slow economic growth—leading to new allegiances, there have been physical forces separating old partners. Most important has been the massive suburban movement of the white working class.

Our argument is similar to the one regarding corporate support. To be sure, many of the interests that once made up a winning liberal coalition would welcome more constructive policy to fight poverty—even reforms that imposed costs. They would also support reconstruction of the central city. They would even be joined by some business partners from the old "growth coalition." But enough elements of the old coalition are unlikely to come together again, and without them, the Democratic leadership may not regain executive power. Perhaps a new source of pressure will help to push hard for the ample programs needed to reduce poverty and restructure cities.[70]

Bottom Up (I)

Recent studies of the evolution of the metropolis have speculated about changes in the suburban community. Observers note, for example, that even conservatives in Orange County (in the Los Angeles area) are intrigued with planning as a technique for controlling the real estate market and protecting settled areas against the pressures of metropolitan growth. Elsewhere, families and single women with children, as well as the elderly, having moved earlier to the suburbs, now frequently find themselves burdened by expensive houses and high taxes; the houses are difficult to convert to multiple units, hard to reach by bus, and distant from specialized services and the cultural diversity offered by towns and cities. Scholars have lately recognized a serious need for central city services and culture, transport, and flexibility, as the suburban population and its needs change.[71] "Suburbs," that is, areas outside the jurisdiction of the "central city," now include a good number of poor areas, as well as an increasing number of minority populations. The way these areas fit into the calculation may in the future be radically different from the fit in the past.

It would take a huge stretch of the imagination to figure that the base, or even a substantial part of the base, of a new urban political strength could be built on suburban unrest. Even if the national economic pie is smaller, the suburban slice is large and still bigger. Even if the costs of urban decay and poverty mount and drag on corporate productivity, the connection to reduced suburban incomes and well-being is complicated and not readily evident. It is, after all, still quite possible for suburbs to avoid not only most urban problems, but also the responsibility for them. Suburban taxes may be high, but so are many suburban incomes and services. Grid-lock may block suburban streets and highways, but at least most residents have cars and places they can afford to go. Environmental reform, the women's movement, and even parts of the civil rights movement—as well as a relatively detached sympathy for the problems of the poor residents of central cities—will surely drive numerous suburban constituents into support of antipoverty and procity reforms. But we should not expect the driving force for reform to come from suburban areas, and we should continue to worry about congressional drag from disinterested suburban representatives. This leaves us with one good option to lead the others.

Bottom Up (II)

It is of course to the central city itself that we turn to find the greatest support for national policies aimed at reducing poverty and improving conditions of living in the central city. We now lay out the patterns by which we think central cities, particularly city halls, can build coalitions to create national pressure for an improved federal agenda.

Rebuilding the American City

Cities and city governments can modify the process of political and economic modernization to move away from the separations we have observed. We look at three urban options. The first is municipal experimentation with progressive reform. We ask if innovation is possible, whether any is taking place, and what benefits local reforms may offer to the poor. The second option for municipalities would stretch this approach a bit, using local reforms to transform federal practice. Might specific reforms and reform movements strike responsive chords in the federal bureaucracy? Is it possible municipal reforms fit into federal lawmaking? Can these changes lead to reinforcement, support, and perhaps further reform? The third option is the building of national coalitions based on urban reform governments.

What is required in all three cases may be thought of as an increase in collective capacity. Collective capacity, not individual or area development, must be built as the vehicle to fight poverty. Local institutions are needed to serve as the political and social platform for confronting poverty. Local government is the best place to start since it has the dual virtues of being part of the national political structure and being politically closest to the community that requires assistance. From the family to the neighborhood, the city, the state, and the federal government, emphasis must be placed on building coalitions that connect across these lines. The most abundant evidence of that collective capacity, and the ability to "connect" new interests, arises from studies of municipal innovations.

Possibilities for Local Reform

In his book *The Progressive City*, Pierre Clavel demonstrates not only that many municipal governments have successfully experimented with reforms, but also that they have done so in spite of adverse regional, national, (and international) economic conditions. These municipal reformers have provided the conditions for their residents to get better housing and improved, more accessible public services. They have found ways to stimulate business to provide more and better paid jobs. Clavel and Nancy Kleniewski take the argument further, claiming "that local governments have more maneuvering space than is commonly assumed."[72] Edward Blakely examines local potential for economic action, similarly observing that "because of the major changes in the international economy, rather than in spite of them," localities can successfully pursue economic development. John Logan and Todd Swanstrom argue that "a great deal more discretion exists . . . than is commonly believed. Many cities have more options to forge . . . development and to allocate costs and benefits among social groups than they have been willing to consider."[73] Clavel and Wim Wiewel, in a 1991 review of progressive urban reforms, note that "by the 1970s and 1980s . . . cities had relatively more choices in what policies to attempt . . . as the federal government withdrew. . . . Localities were more free to design their own solutions to local problems, and they did so."[74]

When grass-roots, neighborhood-based political movements work with coalitions to get hold of the instruments of legitimate power, such as the mayor's office or the city council, four kinds of intensely local progress are possible: altering the agenda for public debate, relating closely to neighborhood groups for support and then nourishing them, pulling diverse members into a municipal coalition, and, finally, building a core of experts to manage reform in a way that responds to the base and to the coalition's diversity. These are not just theoretical prospects; they are activities and results that have been observed in practice.[75]

In Burlington, Vermont, for example, Mayor Bernard Sanders made much of his socialist preferences, giving the city a voice to dispute "the claims of businessmen and developers" in efforts to influence economic policy, leading to real gains for "city working class and antidevelopment interests." In Santa Monica, California, a coalition pushing for rent control gained the upper hand in debate. They set a construction moratorium at their first council meeting, established new task forces to review projects, and took control over the process of development.[76]

In Berkeley, radical coalitions, even without a majority on the city council, used the ample California initiative process to move ahead on proposals for rent control, reorganization of the police force, a takeover of utilities, and an ordinance for neighborhood protection, all of which would shift the emphasis of public policy to benefit the poor. These "brought out the vote . . . and dramatized popular support." In Burlington, Sanders gained support from neighborhood groups when he opposed the city planning board, which favored development projects and a new and threatening highway. In Boston, a Rainbow Coalition base that organized around mayoral challenger Mel King, to the left of newly elected Mayor Raymond Flynn, provided Flynn the leverage to undertake progressive reforms, including improved housing policies and new demands on developers in the form of "linkage" fees to provide funds for housing and social services. In Cleveland, Mayor Dennis Kuchinich and Planning Commissioner Norman Krumholz were backed by neighborhood interests when they disrupted the suburban-dominated metropolitan transportation committee, so as to garner a larger share of funds for inner-city, flexible transportation, and also when they sued the private utility company to keep down inner-city rates.[77]

Expanding politically to build a local coalition beyond neighborhood interests, what Clavel and Wiewel call "transcending the base," is more difficult. Although in Santa Monica, California, leaders of a progressive government were able to negotiate the interests of their rent-control coalition around broad, common goals with homeowners and developers, they were not confronted with the most serious problems of poverty and race.

Most divisive is the issue of race. In Cleveland and Boston, mayors stumbled on this difficult issue. In the first case, when race-baiting crept into populist reformer Kucinich's re-election campaign, it "destroyed his chances of uniting the city's black and white working class neighborhoods against the banks" and lost him the election. In the second case, Flynn has been attacked from his left for his tepid approach to problems of minorities. In Hartford, Connecticut, progressive city council president Nick Carbonne built inter-racial coalitions to control development and to demand jobs for city residents from developers and large employers.

In many cities a core of officials and managers has experimented and found ways to stay in office, move ahead with a progressive agenda, increase public participation, and incorporate the interests of their support groups. It is no small matter that management style was able to change to break down bureaucratic obstacles. It was a real achievement to modify city practice to fit better the "informal and often highly charged styles of street organizing," thus building solid connections between city hall and previously disenfranchised poor neighborhoods. More important, these changes went further, to bridge class and race lines and bring the bureaucrats themselves into contact with their constituency. Managers, planners, and other city officials testify that they find their vision of the world permanently changed, their viewpoint now originating not just in their own, relatively privileged neighborhoods, experiences, and official positions, but in the neighborhoods of people who are poor.

These kinds of municipal innovations are widespread. They demonstrate a store of unused economic leverage, a political strength of organized communities, and a source of new social ideas. As their numbers increase, and as they connect, they will form an important part of the attack on poverty.

Influencing Federal Policy

It is one thing to claim and give evidence that to improve conditions for the poor there is considerable latitude for municipal experimentation with progressive change. It is quite another, however, to envision local experimentation being supported from outside (by funding from improved federal policy, for example). We will provide some evidence that this kind of support exists in limited amounts. But first we must give a cautionary note.

An instance of the opposite of support—implacable national government hostility toward progressive municipal reform—comes in response to success from municipal reformers in Great Britain. There, local elections put left-wing members of the Labor party into dominant majorities on metropolitan councils in a number of counties, including London, Sheffield, Leeds, and the West Midlands. With widespread support they enacted a variety of reforms in areas of employment, housing, and public services.[78] Perhaps one of the most memorable reforms was the Greater London Council's provision of highly subsidized public transportation, which the leader of the council used for his commute to work. For the Thatcher government, these reforms were too much. In order to quash them, the government changed national laws and abolished not just the offending councils, but all in the country—like hitting a fly with a sledge hammer. The progressive local governments were put out of business.[79] It is good to remember, however, not only that the Thatcher government represented the extreme right-wing and that their anti-Labor municipal reorganization was an extreme gesture, but also that generally new practices do not disappear along with the outster of reformers. The ideas stay on in collective memories, and of course, until legislation or regulation changes back, they continue in practice, with considerable pressure from the beneficiaries.[80] In the case of U.S. cities, although reform may be more difficult initially than in Great Britain, once in place it may be harder to remove because of various constitutional limitations.[81]

More positive evidence comes from U.S. efforts to combat homelessness and provide affordable housing. Two cases, documented by housing consultant Emily Paradise Achtenberg, shows how local grievances can affect local politics. Proponents can mount statewide coalitions, which in turn move to challenge and change federal housing regulations and legislation. These federal changes in turn alter the environment for local programs. Local changes start the cycle again; if improvements are seen, then the cycle may move in progressive sweeps across the landscape.

The attractive Northgate-Greenfield Apartments in Burlington, Vermont, were built twenty years ago on the lakeshore. Three hundred thirty-six mostly poor families in these subsidized units were threatened at the end of the 1980s with decontrol and prohibitive rent increases, because the developer wanted to prepay his mortgage.[82] Tenants organized to stop the prepayment and got the city to back them. Because it involved the largest residential property in Vermont, the project attracted attention. So did the developer, who owned a half-dozen other projects and was visible because he was active in Vermont's ski industry. Tenants, activists, and politicians formed a task force eventually incorporated as Northgate Non-

Profit, which found a partner in the statewide equity-raising group called Housing Vermont, and which worked with Vermont Housing and Conservation, a statewide trust fund, and various other state and city agencies to get financing and issue tax-exempt bonds for affordable housing.

At the same time, these groups worked with others nationally to decide how to influence bill-writing and then how to use the federal Emergency Low Income Housing Preservation Act of 1987. This act provided a moratorium on conversion and allowed community (social) ownership, even though the bill was originally written to help subsidized developers get new federal money to stay in their projects as private owners. Later, reformers influenced the 1990 amendment.[83] The Burlington people also worked to get a rehabilitation grant from HUD. The pressures from the residents, the city, and the activists were too much. The developer decided to sell to the tenants and the community—and not just in Burlington. He sold all his projects. Northgate became the first prepayment housing project nationally "to be transferred to community-based non-profit sponsored ownership." Neighborhood and municipal initiative got results.

Another 500-unit project in Sommerville, Massachusetts, a working-class suburb of Boston, became eligible for prepayment in 1989. A majority of the tenants are poor and a third are elderly. The project represents a big portion (about 20 percent) of Sommerville's afffordable housing stock. Once again, reformers and residents found themselves initially very weak compared to a disinterested landlord, who thought tenants not worth bargaining with. By joining with other local forces and taking their case statewide (during Governor Dukakis' presidential campaign) and to HUD, the tenants won against three powerful New York development partners, including the developer of Battery Park City.

At the national level the political activities required to save 800 apartments hardly seem so eventful. Even should a highly unlikely success take place, the saving of all 360,000 housing units from decontrol, housing reformers would still be a long way from what is necessary to make a dent in the problem of urban poverty.[84] There remain all the rest of the housing problems, and then problems with jobs, incomes, education, and more. Although it would be a major achievement to guarantee decent and affordable housing for perhaps a million persons, even this would be insufficient.

These cases, nevertheless, provide instructive examples of how local interests and actions can lead to modified federal programs, providing a new base for local action. In order to make the Burlington and Sommerville cases national, reformers participated in meetings of officials from various cities, in conferences of developers, housing specialists, and advocacy activists, and in negotiating sessions and lobbying efforts in Washington. This is how groups connect, how they change legislation, how coalitions get built and then move ahead with their agenda. The success of progressive forces in saving housing in spite of a hostile administration in Washington is encouraging.

There are numerous other examples of special efforts in housing, local economic development, and welfare reform, in which local officials and reformers attempt to modify federal law and administrative practice. For many years these efforts were promoted and documented by the Conference on State and Local Progressive Policies, at which local politicians, administrators, planners, and activist reformers met annually. Information is now disseminated through various national newsletters, such as the *Planners Network,* and it is collected to influence federal policy through groups like the Institute for Policy Studies.

Efforts in these areas are extremely important, and they comprise the second element in a national strategy for attacking urban poverty, leading the way to design of better programs and keeping political constituencies interested and involved. But still, these scattered improvements in federal policy do not change the major policies.

Local Coalitions and National Political Change

Now we must be more speculative, because there is less experience. We will look at two questions. First, can coalitions and networks of localities work to shift the center of power from national to state and local levels? This, after all, is one of the stated purposes of reforms in federal-local relations pushed by the Nixon, Reagan, and Bush administrations, and it is one that should be taken seriously by progressive reformers. The greater the local power, in theory, the more resources will be allocated to pressing domestic priorities. Instead, given almost total federal power and very little local power, the federal budget expands almost crazily through taxation, tax expenditures, and inflationary bag-holding (such as the cost of the Gulf war and the savings-and-loan bailout), while school and city budgets suffer from taxpayer revolt. With an increase in local power, a strong but now missing domestic and minority representation of central-city voters, women, and people of color may form on all levels of national politics.

The second question is broader still. Can networks of municipal reform governments change the entire federal agenda? They would have to make the case that better policies will help not only cities (and poor people elsewhere), but will assist also in the reconstruction of national productivity and the regaining of international competitiveness.

On the first question, of shifting power to the cities, it is clear that some kinds of policies, particularly those that are geographically sensitive, ought to be under the control of municipalities, others not. Changes for better industrial policy, an educational policy worthy of the name, and the provision of basic family services ought to be enacted at the national level. Municipal authority, however, should exert more influence on the pattern of economic and physical development, on the redistributive effect of municipal services, and, especially, on the effort to support troubled neighborhoods. Municipal governments and affiliated community-based organizations will play an important role. They have greatest sensitivity to the nature of their problems, ability to involve residents in finding solutions, and capacity to deliver where aid is needed.

Simple geographic proximity raises the the possibility of effective voting blocks by poor people or minorities in local elections, and it facilitates their oppositional activity versus landlords, downtown businesses, or not too distant neighborhoods.[85] In spite of all the evidence of separation, we do not live in a world of total alienation, where the notion of social responsibility is discarded in the face of the most obvious need. Instead, we live in a real world, still influenced by social forces. At the municipal level the abstractions of the real estate market become inflated rents and homeless families, the esoterics of labor markets turn into jobless men, poorly paid women, and hungry children, and the mysteries of fiscal austerity translate into closed hospitals, unfunded half-way houses, and sidewalks filled with hopeless people. These bitter realities are not part of the America anyone wants, but they are unavoidable aspects of life at the local level. They are also the basis for rising demands for more municipal authority.

The distinct worsening of poverty in the 1980s has built up pressures from the disruption of urban life. Gerald Frug has coined the phrase "municipal liberation" to capture how an expansion of local political and economic power can be envisioned as a means of facilitating more widespread and higher levels of participation, as counterpart to the increasing alienation of modern corporate bureaucratic society.[86] Frug argues that there is an enormous potential for local action, even on matters of economic development, which is undermined by traditional assumptions of municipal incapacity and by a web of weakening legal-political constraints. Christopher and Hazel Gunn have called for communities to "reclaim capital" by undertaking democratic initiatives in economic development.[87] Providing considerable support for Frug's political and legal theories, these political economists point out that there are ways for communities to gain financial resources, to build assets, and even to constrain the free actions of corporations.

We support these ideas because they suggest that the separation and polarization associated with poverty in cities may be countered. Rising demands will lead to new ways of building more effective municipal power. These ideas have not yet spread widely, but in some big cities progressive municipal politics have moved in these directions. The most prominent example is Chicago, where Mayor Harold Washington took a coalition of neighborhood groups into office and challenged the interests of suburbs and downtown business by involving many who had been disenfranchised. Washington built solid political support in the country's most separated African-American community and used it brilliantly to build a coalition with other progressive neighborhood forces.[88]

Two efforts in Chicago deserve our attention. The first is that the city itself established an economic development policy that refused simply to respond to external, corporate stimuli. In Ann Markusen's words, they chose instead to "build on the basics" by working inside the city to transform the floundering steel industry, by working with existing small manufacturers to maintain or increase employment and improve productivity, and by making demands on corporations already in place.[89] Noting changes in the global economy, the city government worked to cut deals directly with foreign corporations. They also worked to provide jobs for city residents and to direct municipal purchases toward city producers and suppliers. The city even sued Playskool when it shut down a plant, forcing employees out of work in apparent violation of a contract involving an earlier city loan.[90]

Second, the city worked intensely with neighborhood groups to turn the focus of public assistance away from subsidies to large, downtown businesses. Robert Mier, the city's commissioner of economic development (and later assistant to the mayor for all economic affairs), was able to build on his earlier founding of the Center for Urban Economic Development, which provides assistance to grass-roots and neighborhood groups. Other members of Washington's central group also came from the neighborhoods. Mier's chief assistant, Robert Giloth, had been a neighborhood organizer and a builder of coalitions. He and Ann Shlay document one of the more unusual fights, over a world's fair.[91]

Financial interests wanted the fair, arguably as a means of channeling large city subsidies into renewal of a railroad yard area adjacent to downtown, to facilitate inexpensive and profitable real estate expansion. There was of course interest by local businesses in the profits to be made from the brief boom the fair would provide. The neighborhoods, on the other hand, according to analysis by groups then working inside city hall, were convinced that benefits from the fair would be short-term and outweighed in the long run by city debt and higher taxes. In the new, more participatory style and content of Chicago politics, city hall needed only to proclaim neutrality. The neighborhoods won. In this and many similar decisions, over sports stadiums, street and highway investments, business taxes, and linkage fees, what was saved on the conventional subsidies to large businesses could be transferred into city budgets for housing, neighborhood improvement, public services, and the protection of existing jobs in small businesses throughout the city.[92] The coalition was fought by downtown business, but Mayor Washington held it together and enlisted a grudging cooperation. Thinking of the emerging national agreement about the importance of education, one of the saddest consequences of Harold Washington's tragic death is that his commanding authority is absent from the area where he next hoped to turn the city's power: school reform.

On the second question, that of forming national coalitions, we can say much less, but we can be equally hopeful, again illustrating our case with examples from Chicago. Harold

Washington had been in Congress. To be sure, as mayor his attention was mostly focused on the city, building his base, keeping the coalition together, staying in office, and strengthening real municipal power. But he left some time for larger affairs, and one of the objectives he shared with others was an attack on national politics through coalitions of city leaders. We think such a coalition becomes more likely as city changes continue.

Often, we admit, to the disappointment of many observers, African-American and Latino mayors have not moved progressively, instead simply reaping the fruits of office or working in traditional ways with the old political machines. But as competition for office increases and minority candidates vie against one another, the emergence of a progressive option seems more likely.[93] The 1990 election of Eliju Harris in Oakland, California, can be seen in this light, as the change appears to be taking the city in more progressive directions, to serve its poorer constituencies rather than simply its downtown boosters.

Where does this leave us? Cities, and especially the poor people who live in them, are beset with problems not of their own making. Hostile economic forces from the outside seem relentless, and political tendencies at the national level are unpromising. City governments and neighborhood groups have experimented successfully with reforms and have even managed to influence some federal policy for the better. But this leaves them well short of the capacity they need for cutting into persistent and debilitating poverty. Many will conclude that this is the end of the story. Maybe this is also the end of the American dream, and the country will begin a long decline with the destruction of its cities and the abandonment of its poor.

We are not so pessimistic. A few city leaders have found strength in adversity. They may find it possible to use this strength and key political positions to build multicity coalitions, adding to their numbers and their potential influence. These coalitions, we envision, would be based first on the interests of the poor, people of color, and the many others who still live and work in the cities. They might be joined by American corporations, the many who are threatened not only by external competition, but also by a weak domestic base for productivity growth. At some point they may turn around the trajectory of federal politics, command a revival of American generosity, and show that a dream for one is a dream for all.

Notes

Notes to Chapter 1

1. Cited in Walters, "Cities," p. 29.

2. John A. Bryne *et al.*, "Is the Boss Getting Paid Too Much?" *Business Week*, May 1, 1989, pp. 46–93. The survey covered 708 executives in 354 companies.

3. See Vietorisz, Goldsmith, and Mier, "Urban Poverty Strategies."

4. This view is epitomized by Banfield's, *Unheavenly City*, Gilder's, *Wealth and Poverty*, and Sowell's, *Conflict of Visions*.

5. The landmark studies were by anthropologist Oscar Lewis (*Five Families*), economist Everett Hagen (*Economics of Development*), psychologist David McClelland (*Achieving Society*), and political scientist Daniel Lerner (*Passing of Traditional Society*).

6. Rieder, *Carnarsie*, quoted in Edsall, "Race," p. 58. The ethnocentricity of such opinions, described in a study of a white ethnic Brooklyn neighborhood, was starkly revealed in the Howard Beach case, where a white mob chased an unknown innocent black man to his death. See other examples in Edsall, "Race."

7. See Valentine, *Culture and Poverty*; Leacock, *Culture of Poverty*; and Liebow, *Tally's Corner*.

8. The culture of poverty theory has been effectively attacked in the Third-World case as well, for example, by Hill (*Migrant Cocoa Farmers*), who celebrates the sharp market rationality of small farmers; Singer ("Towards a Political Economy"), who explains how broad economic and political circumstances limit the power of neighborhood organizations; and Perlman (*Myth of Marginality*), who buries the idea that Rio's slums are marginal to the society.

9. Wilson, *Annals*, pp. 182–192.

10. Mead, "Expectations and Welfare Work," pp. 249–250.

11. Ibid.

12. See Beckford, *Persistent Poverty*, for a view of the Third World.

13. For a similarly pessimistic interpretation, see Darity, "Racial Inequality."

14. We have paraphrased Marris, *Community Planning,* p. 119.
15. Ibid., p. 120.

Notes to Chapter 2

1. Galbraith, *Tenured Professor.*
2. Linda Greenhouse, "Rehnquist, in Rare Plea, Urges Raise for Judge," *New York Times,* Mar. 16, 1989, p. A16.
3. *New York Times,* Mar. 9, 1989, p. A31.
4. In 1989, 5 percent of households earned $90,000 or more; median household income was $28,906. In 1990 the joint median income was $33,045; for families it was $34,201, for individuals, $14,602 (U.S. Bureau of the Census, *Current Population Survey,* Annual Demographic File, Mar. 1990 [computer tape, 1991]). (A note on statistical sources: in this chapter, unless a specific citation is given, all income and population figures and percentages are calculated from the Annual Demographic File and the pertinent published volume of the U.S. Bureau of the Census, *Current Population Survey, Money Income and Poverty Status of the United States,* Series P-60 [Washington, D.C.: U.S. Government Printing Office, various years].)
5. See remarks by Representative Bernard Sanders in interview by Andrew Kopkind, "Bernie Sanders Does D.C.," *Nation,* June 3, 1991.
6. Rose, *American Profile Poster,* p. 9. See discussion of BLS standard below.
7. Twenty-nine percent are below $5,000.
8. Landis, "Future of America's Central Cities."
9. William J. Grinker, reported by Josh Barbanel, "How Despair is Engulfing a Generation in New York," *New York Times,* Apr. 2, 1989, p. 6E.
10. U.S. Bureau of the Census, *Demographic State of the Nation,* p. 3.
11. Greenstein and Barancik, *Drifting Apart,* pp. 8–9. Emphasis in original.
12. A note on U.S. Census definitions: A *family* is a group living together, related by marriage, adoption, or blood. A *household* (the subject of Figure 2.1) is all persons in the same dwelling unit.
13. Edmund Faltermayer, "Who Are the Rich?" *Fortune,* Dec. 17, 1990, p. 96, shows their share rising steadily from 7.3 percent in 1977 to 12.6 percent in 1990. Data are from the U.S. Congressional Budget Office estimates for 1990.
14. Mishel and Frankel, *State of Working America,* Tables 2.3, 9.6, and 9.7, pp. 50 and 260.

15. U.S. Joint Economic Committee, *Falling Behind*, Table 2, p. 4. Table 2 is from the U.S. Congressional Budget Office, which used *Current Population Survey* March 1980 and March 1990 pretax income. "Family" here includes people who live alone or with nonrelatives. Note that *Falling Behind*'s Table 2 is ambiguous: calculations using the dollar figures do not consistently yield the percentage changes.

16. Wealth statistics normally do not include the present value of pensions or Social Security. Wolff, "Wealth Holdings and Poverty Status in the U.S.," pp. 151–155, who has analyzed recent statistics in great detail, concludes that although pensions (thought of in terms of their net present value) add to the wealth disparity, Social Security benefits work in the other direction, for a net effect of zero.

17. More precisely, 2.7 percent. All wealth statistics come from Eargle, *Household Wealth*.

18. This majority constituted 91.3 percent of the population. The exact figures: the top group owned 27 percent, the next group 22 percent, and the majority 51 percent.

19. Eargle, *Household Wealth*, Table B.

20. The Gini coefficient, which varies from zero to one, measures the percent deviation from a uniform distribution, in which each household would receive the same income.

21. $6,380 in 1967, inflated to $20,952 in 1986.

22. We use the term "Latinos" except when making reference to statistics from the Census, which are collected for "Hispanics."

23. The exact census figures: $20,210, $35,980, $23,450.

24. 27.4 percent of Hispanic households fall into the bottom quintile of the national income distribution (Eargle, *Household Wealth*, Table H).

25. See U.S. Bureau of the Census, *Income and Poverty Status*, No. 154, for definitions.

26. The BLS stopped providing figures in 1981. See Rose, *American Profile Poster*, pp. 7–8.

27. Because income from welfare and especially Social Security is included, poverty rates are considerably reduced. In 1989, these transfers reduced the number of white poor people by 42 percent, African Americans by 20 percent, and Hispanics by 16 percent. For a discussion of how such detailed monetary measurements fit broader community understandings of who is "getting along" and who is not, see Vietorisz, Goldsmith, and Mier, "Urban Poverty Strategies."

28. The exact percentages are 34.3, 27.4, and 22.5. Urban statistics, which we will explore below, are more unbalanced by race and ethnicity.

29. 15.5 percent were poor.

30. 47.6 percent.

31. U.S. Bureau of the Census, *Income and Poverty Status,* No. 168, text, p. 2. All statistics are for 1989.

32. The same report cites a 1988 estimate of 735,000 Americans homeless on any given night. Although the U.S. Department of Housing and Urban Development claimed in 1987 that only 25,000 were homeless, the National Coalition on the Homeless may be closer to the truth in estimating 3 million persons. See Freeman and Hall, "Permanent Homelessness"; Dear and Wolch, *Landscapes of Despair;* Coates, *Street Is Not a Home.*

33. Wehler, *Childhood Hunger.* Data are from questionnaires of 2,335 families in seven sites in 1989 and 1990.

34. All data in this paragraph are for 1988, from the U.S. Public Health Service, *Health.*

35. 233 and 165 percent higher than white babies.

36. 210 and 150 percent.

37. U.S. Public Health Service, *Health,* p. 2.

38. Adding to statistical uncertainty, data on elderly Hispanics are available only since 1973.

39. Levitan and Shapiro, *Working but Poor,* Figure 2, p. 17.

40. Harrison and Gorham, "Black Wages." Annual wage levels are measured by standardizing part- and full-time earnings.

41. Burtless, *Future of Lousy Jobs,* p. 2; italics in original. In Chapters 3 and 4 we will discuss debates among statisticians and economists about the reasons for falling wages.

42. Sixty-eight percent of the wage-earning poor were white in 1989, 71 percent were aged 25–64. Of the full-time employed, 86 percent were white, 67 percent men, and 86 percent aged 25–64. Of the part-time employed, 31 percent were aged 18–24 and 67 percent were 25–64.

43. See letter by David Ellwood, Robert Greenstein, and Isaac Shapiro, *New York Times,* April 10, 1989.

44. Burtless, *Future of Lousy Jobs,* p. 15.

45. Source for women 20 years and older, U.S. Department of Labor, Bureau of Labor Statistics, *Employment and Earnings* 38, 4 (Apr. 1991).

46. Even the discouraged-worker category excludes many who would like to work, but do not try, such as women who have not seriously considered work because they have children but no possibility of child care.

47. Glickman, "Cities," Table 14.5.

48. Blackburn, Bloom, and Freeman, "Declining Economic Position," pp. 38–39. Emphasis in original.

49. Sheets, Nord, and Phelps, *Service Industries*, Table 4.3, p. 60.

50. Kasarda, "Urban Industrial Transition."

51. Sheets, Nord, and Phelps, *Service Industries*.

52. Boston, *Race*, 82–87, analyzes data from a detailed supplement on occupational mobility, training, experience, and job tenure in the January 1983 *Current Population Survey* of the U.S. Bureau of the Census.

53. Ibid., p. 133.

54. Sheets, Nord, and Phelps, *Service Industries*, Table 6.2, p. 83.

55. Falk and Lyson, *High Tech*, pp. 107–130.

56. Sheets, Nord, and Phelps, *Service Industries*, Table 3.6, p. 42; Falk and Lyson, *High Tech*, Table 5.1, p. 108.

57. Adams, Duncan, and Rogers, "Persistence of Urban Poverty," Table 5.3, pp. 90–91.

58. McGeary and Lynn, *Urban Change*, p. 8.

59. Hill and Bier, "Economic Restructuring," p. 136.

60. Jargowsky and Bane, "Ghetto Poverty," pp. 36–39.

61. Massey and Denton, "Hypersegregation," p. 389.

62. *Economist*, "Segregation and Stealth," Apr. 13, 1991, p. 31 (data from Knight-Ridder Newspapers).

63. Wilger, "Black-White Residential Segregation in 1980," Table 3.3.

64. Miller and Quigley, "Segregation," find as well that racial segregation is virtually independent of household type.

65. Michael McGee, Milwaukee alderman and founder of the Black Panther Militia, quoted in the *New York Times*, Mar. 19, 1991, p. A16.

66. Mincy, "Industrial Restructuring."

67. McGeary and Lynn, *Urban Change*, Table 1, p. 17.

68. Bane and Jargowsky, "Urban Poverty Areas," Table 5, p. 24.

69. Camilo José Vergara, "New York's New Ghettos," *Nation*, June 17, 1991, pp. 804–810. See also his "Big Apple Follies."

70. For 1969–78 data and discussion of the persistence of poverty, see Duncan, *Years of Poverty*. All other evidence in this section is from Adams, Duncan, and Rogers, "Persistence of Urban Poverty."

71. Adams, Duncan, and Rogers, "Persistence of Urban Poverty," Figure 4, p. 13. There is considerable corroborating evidence. See Salinas, "Subemployment and the Urban Underclass," for example. Her analysis of 1970–74 Continuous Work History Sample data from the

Department of Labor show that many subemployed adults (ages 25 to 55) were continuously subemployed between 1970 and 1974 (30 percent of white males, 43 percent of black males, 47 percent of white females, and 58 percent of black females). Since the period studied encompassed the peak of the 1971 business cycle, the data indicate that subemployment is not just a cyclical phenomenon.

Notes to Chapter 3

1. Vietorisz, "Global Information," argues that information technology actually undermines the basis of capitalism, which lies in the accumulation of "value."

2. Drennan, "New York Economy," pp. 25–26.

3. Hazel Henderson, author of *The Politics of the Solar Age*, quoted in "Experts Divided on Jobs in the 90s," *New York Times*, Apr. 16, 1989, pp. F1–F3.

4. The Gulf war was an extreme illustration of this argument: options were limited; the White House did not find a good alternative.

5. Botwinick, *Wage Differentials*, Chapter 8, discusses the difficulties introduced by these trends for organizing labor.

6. Where U.S. leading-edge technological dominance was once the rule (approximately 1945–70), it is now the exception. See Botwinick, *Wage Differentials*.

7. O'Connor, *Fiscal Crisis*, pp. 104–151; Radice, "Capital, Labor and the State."

8. Many small firms and some large ones (e.g., in textiles or electronics assembly) do not fit this pattern.

9. Thurow, "Regional Transformation," Table 8.2, p. 181. Data in the table are taken from OECD National Accounts.

10. Burns, "Urban Income Distribution"; Garofalo and Fogarty, "Hierarchy-Inequality Hypothesis"; Haworth, Long, and Rasmussen, "Income Distribution"; Hirsch, "Reexamination." For the case of New York, where most manufacturing was low-wage, see Drennan, "Local Economy"; and Bailey and Waldinger, "Division of Labor."

11. Stanback, *Service Economy*; Harrison and Bluestone, *Great U-Turn*.

12. The U.S. Supreme Court decision allowing a fish-packing plant to continue its plantation-like separation of low-paid Alaskan and Filipino workers from well-paid whites reminds us that not all manufacturing operations have accessible promotion ladders. See Linda Greenhouse, "Court Ruling," *New York Times*, June 6, 1989, pp. A1 and A24.

13. Bluestone and Harrison, *Deindustrialization of America*. They estimate that 22 million jobs were lost between 1969 and 1976.

14. Herz, "Worker Displacement," p. 3.

15. Ibid.

16. OTA, *Technology and Structural Unemployment*, Figure 1.6, p. 9.

17. Frank and Freeman, "Distributional Consequences," cited in Bluestone and Harrison, *Deindustrialization of America*, p. 45.

18. OTA, *Technology and Structural Unemployment*, Figure 1.6, p. 9.

19. Thurow, "Surge in Inequality."

20. Lawrence, *Can America Compete?* Table 2.5, p. 28.

21. Ibid., pp. 3–8, goes further, asserting that the high drop in Northeast and North-Central manufacturing employment is an unimportant statistical artifact resulting from the disproportionate weight of manufacturing in those regions.

22. Even one of the most vociferous enthusiasts of service-sector growth grants this point. See McKenzie, *Competing Visions*, pp. 44–45.

23. Burnstein, *Discrimination*.

24. Thurow, "Surge in Inequality"; Bluestone and Harrison, *Deindustrialization of America*.

25. Lawrence, *Can America Compete?*

26. Loveman and Tilly, "Good Jobs or Bad Jobs," p. 61. As they note, Thurow ("Surge in Inequality," p. 33) makes the same point by contrasting actual 1982 inequality with projections using the 1967 age-group distribution.

27. Harrison and Gorham ("Black Wages," figure 5) show that the proportion of young African-American men earning poverty wages rose from 18 to 34 percent.

28. The growth of services is often attributed to either the natural evolution of an advanced country or increased demand for services by dual-earner families and working singles with less time or more discretionary income. The first approach, the postindustrial view, assumes that services can continue to grow within the United States even without industrial production. See Walker, "Geographical Organization", and Cohen and Zysman, *Manufacturing Matters*, for critiques of this assumption. The second perspective is criticized by Harrison and Bluestone, *Great U-turn*, p. 74. On the other hand, in at least some cities (such as New York) service provision is the dominant export. See Drennan, "Local Economy"; *Econometric Model*.

29. Storper and Walker, *Capitalist Imperative*.

30. Unless otherwise noted, the discussion and statistics in this section, especially on oligopolies, competitive firms, and part-time work, are from Christopherson, "Emerging Patterns of Work."

31. Mollenkopf and Castells, *Dual City*.

32. The literature on labor market segmentation (LMS) is voluminous and contentious. Suffice it to say that employers may create barriers to entry so as to stabilize and control labor, while workers try to protect themselves against other (potential) workers and employers. For a particularly useful discussion see Assaad, "Structured Labour Markets."

33. Baran, "Technological Innovation and Deregulation."

34. Harrison and Bluestone, *Great U-Turn*.

35. See Baran, "Technological Innovation and Deregulation"; and Nelson, "Labor Demand," for discussions of how social characteristics of the potential labor force influence hiring practices and locational decisions.

36. Appelbaum, "Restructuring Work."

37. Gorz, *Economic Reason*.

38. U.S. Bureau of Labor Statistics, cited in Peter T. Kilborn, "The Work Week Grows," *New York Times*, June 3, 1990, pp. E1 and E3.

39. Solloway, "Labor and Health Policy," pp. 61–81.

40. Compared to only 25 percent in the service sector.

41. Hymer, *Multinational Corporation*. Chandler, *Visible Hand*, notes six levels of management.

42. Lipietz, "Imperialism," p. 100.

43. Bluestone and Harrison, *Deindustrialization of America*.

44. Fröbel, Heinrichs, and Kreye, *Division of Labor*; Hymer, *Multinational Corporation*.

45. Lall, *Economic Dislocation*; OTA, *Technology and Structural Unemployment*; Bluestone and Harrison, *Deindustrialization of America*.

46. Public scandals such as the Lockheed Corporation's million-dollar bribe of the Japanese prime minister only skim the surface. The intervention of International Telephone and Telegraph and U.S. agencies in toppling the elected government of Chile goes deeper. Perhaps still more significant are the explicit efforts by the International Monetary Fund to regulate the affairs of national economies in the interests of large banks and corporations. IMF strictures apply not only to Third-World debt-ridden countries, but they have been imposed on Great Britain as well.

47. Hymer, *Multinational Corporation*; Friedmann and Wolff, "World City Formation."

48. Jenkins, "Divisions"; Gordon, "Global Economy."

49. See Markusen, Hall, and Glasmeier, *High Tech America*; Scott and Storper, "Production"; Storper and Walker, *Capitalist Imperative*;

and others writing about territorial production complexes or industrial districts.

50. Scott, *Metropolis*.

51. Portes and Walton, *Labor, Class, and the International System*; Sassen, "Informal Economy."

52. As argued in Chapter 5. This is at least in part a consequence of conscious public policy. See Goldsmith, "Third World."

53. Storper and Walker, *Capitalist Imperative*; Fernández-Kelly, *For We Are Sold*.

54. Scott, *Metropolis*, pp. 210–211.

55. Williamson and Lindert, *American Inequality*.

56. Instead of an absolute decline, what appears to be occurring is qualitative change in the manner of manufacturing, involving greater intermediate service inputs between initial production and final sale. See Cohen and Zysman, *Manufacturing Matters*; and Walker, "Geographical Organization," pp. 377–408, for further critiques of the post-industrial model.

57. Maire, "Le chómage zéro, c'est possible," quoted in Gorz, *Economic Reason*, p. 6.

58. Freeman, Clark, and Soote, *Unemployment*.

59. Gorz, *Economic Reason*, p. 5.

60. Perez, "Structural Change"; Freeman, Clark, and Soete, *Unemployment*.

61. The comparison of Fujan and Gary was made by historian Bruce Cummings ("Archeology, Descent, Emergence: Japan in American Hegemony in the Twentieth Century," lecture for the Program on International Studies in Planning, Cornell University, May 3, 1991).

62. *Survey of Current Business* 71, 2 (Feb. 1991).

63. Harrison and Bluestone, *Great U-Turn*, Table 1.1, p. 9.

64. Such trading patterns among similar competitors had been predicted for some years and even recommended as policy for small developing countries. See Linder, *Trade and Transformation*; Hirsch, *Location of Industry*; and other works using Raymond Vernon's product-cycle theories. The composition of these trade patterns runs contrary to the expectations of conventional economics, which uses the theory of comparative advantage to predict trade of sophisticated, capital-intensive industrial goods from core countries in exchange for raw materials and labor-intensive goods from developing countries. See Shaikh, "Laws."

65. Harrison and Bluestone, *Great U-Turn*, p. 9.

66. Bluestone and Harrison, *Deindustrialization of America;* Piore and Sabel, *Second Industrial Divide.*

67. But note that half-capacity production in twin plants was also used as a conscious strategy to reduce union strength, strike threats, and related disruptions of production. See, for example, Bluestone and Harrison, *Deindustrialization of America,* Chapter 6.

68. Williamson, "Productivity"; Baumol et al., *Productivity.*

69. Evidence about productivity growth rates over shorter time periods, such as a single decade, must be treated with great caution, since data are highly sensitive to definitional and measurement error. Nevertheless, preliminary evidence is so dramatic that it leaves little doubt about the decline.

70. As Williamson, "Productivity," points out, increased productivity in other countries is in theory a blessing, because products are cheaper to import, benefiting consumers and producers. The problem is that in market societies benefits are not shared evenly.

71. Piore and Sabel, *Second Industrial Divide,* pp. 184–185.

72. Perna, "Shift from Manufacturing," pp. 32–33.

73. Wilson, "New Maquiladoras."

74. Kolko, *Restructuring the World Economy,* p. 215. Between 1969 and 1983, the value of items assembled abroad increased by almost 20 percent per year (OTA, *Technology and Structural Unemployment,* p. 32), thanks in part to fluctuating exchange rates. Daily foreign-exchange trading in the United States was less than $1 billion in 1969, and reached $23 billion by 1980 and $34 billion by 1983. Worldwide, daily foreign-exchange transactions doubled between 1979 and 1984, from $75 billion to $150 billion, and then rose to over $200 billion by 1986. In the United States, only 16 percent of this enormous volume of foreign exchange actually financed trade; the rest was used for speculative transactions. Kolko further estimates that 90 percent of worldwide currency exchanges are conducted by banks or other dealers.

75. Glickman, "Cities," p. 9, fn. 7; Bauer, "Foreign Investment," cited in Sassen-Koob, "Recomposition and Peripheralization."

76. Sassen-Koob, "Recomposition and Peripheralization," p. 93; Glickman and Woodward, *New Competitors.*

77. Sassen-Koob, "Recomposition and Peripheralization."

78. Piore and Sabel, *Second Industrial Divide.*

79. OPEC price increases permitted the largest oil companies of North America and Europe to raise profits 400 percent, increasing the pace and scale of capital circulation and the power of new centers in industrial countries (such as Houston and Dallas). The hefty rise in

gasoline prices extracted savings from even the poorest groups in America, savings that the oil companies could then use for financial services and international banking. See Tanzer, *International Oil*; and Sassen-Koob, "Recomposition and Peripheralization," p. 91.

80. The growth in world debt provides further illustration of the increasing interdependence of national economies. U.S. banks financed much of Third-World industrialization from the 1950s through the 1970s. They will never collect all the debts. Even absent the Soviet military counterbalance, the United States cannot force repayment. Many debtor countries are literally unable to pay: the higher their payments, the lower their domestic investments and rates of national economic growth in the future, endangering subsequent payments. De facto defaults are enormous—the stylish "debt swaps" are superficial in quantity. In fact, a huge loss in value has already gone onto the books of major U.S. banks. See Kolko, *Restructuring the World Economy*, pp. 73–77.

81. The ratio of gross and net public debt to GNP rose 31 and 44 percent, respectively, from 1982 until 1990, much more rapidly than in the other major industrial countries (OECD, "Analysis of Fiscal Policies," *Economic Outlook* 48 [Dec. 1990]: Table 34, p. 113. During past recoveries, the ratio of new consumer debt to net growth in disposable income was between 24 and 29 percent. In this last recovery, this ratio was 44 percent. Likewise, debt-to-equity ratios increased for business, as firms financed leveraged buyouts and takeovers with junk bonds and other high-interest loans. See Harrison and Bluestone, *Great U-Turn*, p. 150.

82. Harrison and Bluestone, *Great U-Turn*, p. 17.

83. Cohen et al., "Competitiveness"; Cohen and Zysman, *Manufacturing Matters*; Thurow and Tyson, "U.S. Trade Imbalance."

84. Judith H. Dobrzynski,"For Better or for Worse?" *Business Week*, Jan. 12, 1987, p. 38.

85. Harrison and Bluestone, *Great U-Turn*, p. 54.

86. Pat Choate, economist for TRW, quoted by Norman Jonas and Joan Berger, "Do All These Deals Help or Hurt the U.S. Economy?" *Business Week*, Nov. 24, 1986, p. 86.

87. Judith Dobrzynski, "More than Ever, It's Management for the Short Term," *Business Week*, Nov. 24, 1986, p. 93.

88. Unocal acquired a $4-billion debt to forestall a takeover (*Business Week*, Nov. 24, 1986, p. 86).

89. "Industry Cleans House," *Business Week*, Nov. 11, 1985, p. 33. Cited in Harrison and Bluestone, *Great U-Turn*, p. 55.

90. That is, taxing both corporate profits and dividend payments.

91. Bruce Nussbaum, "Deal Mania," *Business Week*, Nov. 24, 1986, pp. 74–76.

92. Harrison and Bluestone, *Great U-Turn*, p. 160, report airline difficulties, including alleged near-collisions.

93. Sassen, *Mobility*.

94. As in the above-mentioned case of modern steel manufacturing in Gary, Indiana.

95. See a candid assessment by a conservative political strategist (Philips, *Politics of Rich and Poor*).

96. The Reagan-Kemp Enterprize Zone bills can be interpreted this way. See Goldsmith, "Third World."

Notes to Chapter 4

1. In any case, few have moved: in 1960 African Americans made up 4.7 percent of the suburban population; in 1975, 5.1 percent, and in 1989, 7.1 percent.

2. Richard Sennett (*The Uses of Disorder: Personal Identity and City Life* [New York: Vintage, 1970] worried about tendencies in these directions years ago.

3. We must also mention Native Americans on reservations.

4. Martin Jaffe, "Viewpoint," *Planning Magazine*, 53 (Mar. 1989), p. 54, refers to Detroit's elevated building connections this way.

5. For a clear discussion of the importance of "export" industries, see Drennan, "Local Economy"; Jacobs, *Cities and the Wealth of Nations*.

6. Noyelle, "Advanced Services," pp. 143–164.

7. See the essays in Sawers and Tabb, *Sunbelt/Snowbelt*. For a description of this shift, see Weinstein and Firestine, *Regional Growth*.

8. Kasarda, "Jobs."

9. Thurow, "Regional Transformation," p. 180.

10. There are exceptions, like the New York region. See Drennan, "New York Economy."

11. Markusen, Hall, and Glasmeier, *High Tech America*; Stanback and Noyelle, *Cities in Transition*; Bergman, *Local Economies*.

12. Salinas, "Urban Growth," p. 261, suspects poor migrants to growing cities may displace workers already there. Phillips and Vidal, "Growth and Restructuring," p. 82, find that moves south or west actually *reduce* a worker's probability of upward mobility.

13. Mollenkopf, "Post Industrial Service City," builds on classical theories of hierarchies or systems of cities.

14. See Glickman, "Cities"; Rodriguez and Feagin, "Urban Specialization"; Stanback and Noyelle, *Cities in Transition*; Cohen, "Division of Labor."

15. Pred, *City Systems*.

16. Noyelle, "Advanced Services."

17. See Noyelle and Stanback, *Economic Transformation*. They also tend to have more technical innovation. The higher a city sits in the urban hierarchy, the younger are its industries. See Thompson, "National System of Cities."

18. Scott, *Metropolis*.

19. Cohen, "Division of Labor"; Noyelle, "Advanced Services."

20. See Friedmann and Wolff, "World City Formation"; Cohen, "Division of Labor"; Noyelle and Stanback, *Economic Transformation*. According to Stanback and Noyelle, there are only four national nodal cities in the United States—New York, Los Angeles, San Francisco, and Chicago.

21. Noyelle, "Advanced Services."

22. Some production centers, especially industrial-military locations such as San Diego and San Antonio, have benefited as military contracts have countered potential regional decline and provided the basis for future growth. See Glasmeier, Markusen, and Hall, *High Technology*; Markusen, *Gunbelt*.

23. Noyelle, "Advanced Services," p. 156.

24. San Jose suffers because of its specialization in electronics, but the case is analytically weak, since the city is part of the greater San Francisco metropolis.

25. Goldsmith, "Poverty and Profit"; Stanback and Noyelle, *Cities in Transition*.

26. *New York Times*, Mar. 19, 1991, p. A16.

27. Goodman, *Last Entrepreneurs*.

28. Harrison, "Regional Restructuring."

29. Mollenkopf, "Post Industrial Service City."

30. Edward Bergman, quoted in "The South Has Its Second Cities, and They Thrive," *New York Times*, Apr. 23, 1989. See also Glickman and Glasmeier, "International Economy."

31. The example comes from Soja, *Postmodern Geographics*, Chapter 8.

32. Sheets, Nord, and Phelps, *Service Industries*, p. 56.

33. Ibid., Table 4.5, p. 62. Labor market analysts point out that the federal government stopped measuring metropolitan *sub-area* underemployment after analysts observed how the statistics highlighted ter-

rible city labor market conditions. See William Spring, Bennett Harrison, and Thomas Vietorisz, "The Crises of the Underemployed," *New York Times Magazine*, Nov. 5, 1972, pp. 42–60; and Vietorisz, Harrison, and Mier, "Full Employment."

34. See Harrison and Bluestone, *Great U-Turn*; Thurow, "Regional Transformation," p. 180. The greatest relative concentrations of new jobs are in corporate, distributive, and nonprofit services, and in retail trade. Government employment has grown modestly.

35. Calculated from Harrison and Bluestone, *Great U-Turn*, Table A.2, 196ff. In the Northeast recovery, low-wage jobs were up by 28 percent, mid-wage up 8 percent, and high-wage up 38 percent.

36. Garofalo and Fogarty, "Hierarchy-Inequality Hypothesis."

37. Sassen-Koob, "Recomposition and Peripheralization"; Harrison and Bluestone, *Great U-Turn*; Gorz, *Economic Reason*.

38. Stone, "Housing."

39. Goldsmith and Jacobs, "Urban Policy."

40. The northward migration of African Americans ranks as one of the largest mass migrations in history. See Lemann, *Promised Land*.

41. Shapiro and Ellwood are quoted in Robert Suro, "Where Have All the Jobs Gone? Follow the Crab Grass," *New York Times*, Mar. 3, 1991, p. E5.

42. Tumminia, "Locational Factors"; Foley, "Suburbanization"; Hoos, *Automation*; Jones and Hall, "Office Suburbanization"; Daniels, "New Office."

43. See Goddard, *Office Location*, especially Chapter 5.

44. Nelson, "Labor Demand," presents a case study of this process in the San Francisco Bay Area.

45. Landis, "Central Cities," p. 8.

46. Ibid., Table 2, p. 11.

47. Stanback and Knight, *Suburbanization*, p. 24.

48. Ibid., p. 26.

49. This fact is highlighted in ibid.

50. Ibid., p. 39.

51. Goldsmith and Rothschild, "Regional Specialization." The partitioning between "export" and "residentiary" on basic and nonbasic activities is never entirely accurate, but for most analytical purposes it is satisfactory.

52. Stanback and Knight, *Suburbanization*, p. 14.

53. For an export-based econometric model of New York City and its region, see Drennan, *Econometric Model*.

54. See Markusen, *Gunbelt;* Saxenian, *Cheshire Cat's Grin.*

55. For a discussion of the applicability of location theory to high-tech industries, see Markusen, Hall, and Glasmeier, *High Tech America,* Chapter 8.

56. Nelson, "Labor Demand."

57. Turner and Fix, "Opportunities."

58. Ibid. In 7 percent of the cases the researchers found discrimination against whites.

59. Leonard, "Interaction," p. 19: "Residential segregation not only limits where blacks can live, it also influences where they work. Patterns of residential segregation are strongly reflected in patterns of employment segregation."

60. Walker, "Suburbanization." See also Gordon, "Capitalist Development"; and Ashton, "Urbanization."

61. See Gordon, "Capitalist Development"; Watkins, *Urban Economics;* and Harvey, *Limits to Capital.*

62. Watkins, *Urban Economics.*

63. Soja, "Economic Restructuring," develops a similar typology.

64. Walker, "Suburbanization," p. 406. See also Harvey, *Limits to Capital.*

65. See Scott, *Metropolis.*

66. Logan and Molotch, *Urban Fortunes.*

67. Massey, "Residential Segregation."

68. See Massey and Denton, "Hypersegregation"; Clark, "Residential Segregation."

69. This is an important component of W. J. Wilson's argument (*Truly Disadvantaged*).

70. The human (or urban) ecology school, including "social area analysis," analyzes racial and ethnic group location by socioeconomic status using an almost organic conception of cities, in which the dynamics of urban form are tied to processes that generate "efficient" or functional outcomes.

71. Berry and Kasarda, *Contemporary Urban Ecology,* discuss models of "factorial ecology."

72. Even most urban ecology proponents admit that the theory fails to explain why African Americans are located where they are and, more important, why they have not been able to move to other locations as rapidly as whites as their incomes rise.

73. See Drennan, "Local Economy."

74. U.S. Bureau of Census, *Current Population Survey,* cited in Grier and Grier, *Minorities,* Table 1, p. 6.

75. According to Grier and Grier, *Minorities*, the suburban figure for all other "nonwhite" racial groups combined is comparable.

76. Jackson, *Crabgrass Frontier*.

77. Massey and Denton, "Trends in Residential Segregation."

78. Rabin, "Metropolitan Decentralization," discusses some of these methods.

79. Tobin, "Divided Neighborhoods"; Goldsmith, "Ghetto."

80. Clay, "Black Suburbanization."

81. Massey, "Residential Segregation," pp. 329–330.

82. These conclusions were derived from measures of spatial isolation based on the isolation index. See ibid., p. 812. Changes in immigration laws, eliminating discriminatory national origins quotas, took effect in 1968. During the 1970s, 4.5 million legal immigrants and at least 2 million illegal immigrants entered the country. See also Schill and Nathan, *Revitalizing America's Cities*; and Logan and Molotch, *Urban Fortunes*.

83. Hartman, "Neighborhood Revitalization."

84. Marcuse, "Gentrification."

85. Although gentrified units are not actually new, just improved. See DeGiovanni, "Housing Market Activity."

86. A 1976 Census Bureau study found that 70 percent of central-city home buyers relocated from nearby; only 18 percent relocated from the suburbs. Cited in Babcock, *Unfairly Structured Cities*, p. 164.

87. Hartman, "Neighborhood Revitalization."

88. Babcock, *Unfairly Structured Cities*, p. 137; Caro, *Power Broker*.

89. The information in this section is from Kasarda, "Jobs," Table 14, p. 183; Table 16, p. 187.

90. Steinberg, "Underclass," pp. 47–48.

91. Lichter, "Racial Differences."

92. Freedman, "Urban Labor Markets."

93. See, for example, Bradbury and Browne, "Black Men"; Richard B. Freeman, "Create Jobs that Pay as Well as Crime," *New York Times*, July 20, 1986, p. F2.

94. Salinas, "Urban Growth."

95. Kasarda, "Jobs," Tables 9 and 10, pp. 170–171, 174–175.

96. Kasarda (ibid.) produces supporting statistics for New York, Philadelphia, Boston, Baltimore, St. Louis, Atlanta, Denver, and San Francisco. Only in Houston (in this sample) did the number of jobs increase substantially for those without high school diplomas.

97. Fainstein, "Underclass/Mismatch Hypothesis."

98. Sassen-Koob, "Global Cities." Likewise, a study by the Federal

Reserve Bank of New York concluded that changes in industrial composition cannot adequately explain African-American employment problems (Chall, "'Skills Mismatch'").

99. Schulman, "Discrimination"; Boston, *Race*.

100. Kerner Commission, *Report*, p. 278.

101. Fainstein, "Underclass/Mismatch Hypothesis," p. 432. As Fainstein notes, it is also argued that welfare dependency ties African Americans to home, so they have been unwilling to migrate to the Southwest where new jobs might be available.

102. Rabin, "Metropolitan Decentralization," p. 10.

103. Fulton, "Public Transportation."

104. Rabin, "Metropolitan Decentralization," Tables 5 and 10.

105. Ibid.

106. Leonard ("Interaction") shows that the farther away from the ghetto a firm locates, the fewer blacks it employs. He concludes that residential location, therefore, not only limits where blacks can live, but also where they can work.

107. Ibid., pp. 3–6. Mayer and Jencks, "Growing Up," review literally dozens of studies and conclude that "the 'spatial mismatch' hypothesis . . . fail[s] to match the evidence" (p. 1445). See also Ellwood, "Spatial Mismatch Hypothesis."

108. Meyer and Gomez-Ibanez, *Autos*, p. 231, cited in Leonard, "Interaction," p. 5.

109. Ellwood, "Spatial Mismatch Hypothesis."

110. These notions gave rise to the enormous controversy among researchers and policymakers when Kain and Persky first presented "Gilded Ghetto" in 1968. See also Goldsmith, "Ghetto."

111. Wilson, *Truly Disadvantaged*.

112. O'Regan and Quigley, "Labor Market Access."

Notes to Chapter 5

1. The recession of 1991 underscored the need for reform, as deficits threatened the finances of city and state governments.

2. For example, in the note added to the second edition of *The Truly Disadvantaged*, Wilson calls for nearly full social democracy. Although he recognizes its dependency on rapid economic growth, he eschews any discussion of the politics of implementation. Ellwood, in *Poor Support*, seems to envision his proposals for the welfare system enacted by fiat (he is, sensibly, we believe, explicitly cautious about expecting a return to high economic growth).

3. Kantor, "Case for a National Urban Policy."

4. Agnew, "Market Relations"; Boaden, *Urban Policy Making*; and Kantor, "Case for a National Urban Policy," p. 408.

5. See, for example, Phillips, *Politics of Rich and Poor*; and Stockman, *Triumph of Politics*, for evidence of the do-nothing, laissez-faire, benign-neglect approach toward problems of the poor that was so popular among conservatives of the Reagan administration.

6. The term is from T. H. Marshall's 1949 lecture, cited by Hirschman, *Rhetoric of Reaction*.

7. Ibid., p. 63.

8. Hirschmann, *Rhetoric of Reaction*.

9. Forrester, "Counter-intuitive Behavior of Social Systems"; Glazer, "Limits of Social Policy"; and Murray, *Losing Ground*, all quoted by Hirschman, *Rhetoric of Reaction*, Chapter 2. Hirschman (pp. 29–30) comments on Murray: "almost any idea that has not been around for awhile has a good chance of being mistaken for an original insight."

10. Hirschman, *Rhetoric of Reaction*, p. 30.

11. Ibid.

12. Piven and Cloward, *Regulating the Poor*. Note also the "we/they" dichotomy suggested in the quotation by Murray, just above.

13. Ellwood, *Poor Support*, p. 137.

14. Ellwood (ibid., p. 159) points out that the federal focus has moved from individuals, to communities, and back to individuals, but he and others also leave no doubt about the effectiveness of transfer payments.

15. Thurow, "Surge in Inequality," p. 36.

16. Ibid.

17. Patterson, *America's Struggle*, pp. 60–76.

18. Herbers, "Kerner Report," p. 20.

19. Kerner Commission, *Report*, pp. 221 and 1.

20. Ibid., p. 223.

21. Blauner, *Racial Oppression*; Goldsmith, "Ghetto."

22. Goldsmith and Derian, "Is There an Urban Policy." The increase from 1967 to 1978 was eightfold.

23. Brecher and Horton, *Setting Municipal Priorities*, p. 11.

24. Mollenkopf, *Contested City*.

25. Lemann, "Unfinished War," p. 38

26. Peterson, *City Limits*, pp. 212–213.

27. Yates, *Ungovernable City*, p. 51.

28. Landau, *Race, Poverty and the Cities*, p. 37.

29. Ibid.; see also Luria and Russell, *Rational Reindustrialization*.

30. Lemann, "Unfinished War," p. 38.

31. Walters, "Cities on Their Own," p. 29.

32. Now, to make matters worse, the limited resources available to cities are usually turned to other matters, such as competition for business growth (ibid., pp. 27–32).

33. Quigley and Rubinfeld, *American Domestic Priorities*, p. 97.

34. Ibid., pp. 127–128. This consolidation was done with the Educational Consolidation and Improvement Act of 1981.

35. U.S. Department of Commerce, Statistical Abstracts of the United States, 1989 edition.

36. Rymarowicz and Zimmerman, *Federal Tax*, cited by Gold, "State Fiscal Conditions," p. 298.

37. Palmer and Sawhill, *Reagan Experiment*, pp. 10–11. Katherine Bishop, *New York Times*, West Coast edition, Feb. 2, 1989.

38. Leading poverty scholars (Wilson, Ellwood, Moynihan, and Katz), business spokespersons, and others coming from various political directions, all agree that on this score policies advocated by Social Democrats (or Democratic Socialists?) are correct.

39. Sandefur, "Blacks, Hispanics, American Indians," pp. 57–68; see also Peterson, *New Urban Reality*, pp. 24–29

40. See the analysis of technology choice in Noble, *America by Design*.

41. Although we must admit we find no one who says explicitly that a high demand for workers is *not* an important requirement for an improved distribution of income and a reduction of poverty, there are many who avoid mentioning it.

42. In the debates on ghetto underdevelopment in the 1970s, otherwise differing analysts agreed on this point. See, e.g., the reviews by Goldsmith, "Ghetto"; and Harrison, "Ghetto."

43. Ellwood, *Poor Support*.

44. William Holstein, editor of *Business Week*, lecture at Cornell University, quoted in a project report to Alan McAdams by Bayer, Little, and Silver, "Project U.S.A.," p. 58.

45. Ibid., p. 56.

46. These figures are taken from the President's Commission on Industrial Competitiveness (*Global Competition*), the National Academy of Sciences, the Internal Revenue Service, economist Gary Jufbauer of Georgetown University, and Peter Huber of the Manhattan Institute, all cited in ibid., p. 56.

47. Eisner, "Real Deficits," p. 135.

48. Reich, "Real Economy." p. 51

49. Bayer, Little, and Silver, "Project U.S.A.," p. 56. Unless otherwise noted, this is the source for all the information on industrial policy.

50. Ibid., pp. 57–58, 61.

51. Ibid., p. 60

52. Ibid.

53. This is aside from the debates about the public funding of private schools. It is worth noting that considerable public aid to these (relatively privileged) private schools is already provided. Aside from books, health services, and other benefits, in New York State public school districts are required to pay for buses to transport private school children, and they must do this even when they do not bus their own students!

54. *Newsweek*, May 6, 1991, p. 31.

55. Working Seminar on Family and American Welfare Policy, *New Consensus*.

56. In Ithaca, N.Y., for example, the Alternative Community School, a member of the National Coalition of Essential Schools, is directed by an advisory board made up of parents, community members, school staff, and students.

57. The combination of Social Security taxes and payments is regressive—the rich pay lower proportional taxes but get higher absolute transfers.

58. Danziger, "Antipoverty Policy," quoted in Sandefur, "Blacks, Hispanics, American Indians," p. 67.

59. Reich, "Real Economy."

60. Rossi and Wright, "The Urban Homeless."

61. Father support requirements would tend to reduce public costs.

62. "Dan Rather Reports," CBS, June 24, 1991.

63. We note Wilson's caution and even Steinberg's grudging acknowledgment of the political liabilities of race-specific policies, but we find racial discrimination so thoroughly woven into the social fabric that we cannot see how programs of affirmative action can be avoided if fairness is to be achieved. The problem, as Wilson points out, is to make it work for the poor.

64. See, e.g., Goldsmith and Vietorisz, "Parallel Economy."

65. *New York Times*, May 6, 1985, p. 23.

66. *New York Times*, July 4, 1987, p. 29.

67. Ibid.

68. President's Commission on Industrial Competitiveness, *Global Competition*.

69. Kantor, "Case for a National Urban Policy," p. 412.

70. Mollenkopf, *Contested City*, gives a solid explanation for the collapes of urban growth coalitions.

71. Hayden, *Redesigning the American Dream*.

72. Clavel and Kleniewski, "Space for Progressive Local Policy," p. 221.

73. Blakely, *Planning Local Economic Development*, p. 50. Logan & Swanstrom, *Beyond the City Limits*, pp. 5–6.

74. We are indebted to Clavel and Wiewel for allowing us to read and quote from their draft "Introduction" to *Progressive City Government*. Unless otherwise noted, all the information and citations in this section are from Clavel and Wiewel, "Introduction," pp. 19–30.

75. The set of four we have constructed from a longer list in ibid.

76. Shearer, "In Search of Equal Partnerships."

77. Krumholz and Forester, *Making Equity Planning Work*.

78. Bennington, "Local Economic Strategies."

79. Livingstone, *If Voting Changed Anything*.

80. This is a point made by Clavel in various places. In the early 1990s British Prime Minister John Major decided to re-establish metropolitan councils.

81. Fainstein, "Economics, Politics, and Development Policy."

82. We are grateful to Achtenberg for allowing us to read and quote from an unpublished draft of "Preserving Expiring Use Projects," from which we have drawn all our information on Northgate, Clarendon Hill Towers, and conversion.

83. The Low Income Housing Preservation and Resident Homeownership Act of 1990.

84. Achtenberg judges it unlikely that even a majority of the threatened housing will be saved, because of the enormously high costs of paying off the windfall profits, which federal legislation still promises to the landlords.

85. See Davis, *Contested Ground*.

86. Frug, "City."

87. Gunn and Gunn, *Reclaiming Capital*.

88. See Mier, Moe, and Sherr, "Strategic Planning."

89. Markusen, "Steel and Southeast Chicago."

90. Giloth and Mier, "Spatial Change and Social Justice."

91. Shlay and Giloth, "Social Organization."

92. Information from our conversations with Robert Mier.

93. See Mier, Fitzgerald, and Randolph, "African-American Elected Officials."

Bibliography

Achtenberg, Emily P., "Preserving Expiring Use Projects: Strategies for Social Ownership and Permanent Affordability," Photocopy, unpublished MS, Cambridge, Mass., May 22, 1991.

Adams, Terry K., Greg J. Duncan and Willard L. Rogers. "The Persistence of Urban Poverty." In *Quiet Riots: Race and Poverty in the United States*, ed. Fred R. Harris and Roger W. Wilkins, 78–99. New York: Pantheon, 1988.

Agnew, J. A. "Market Relations and Locational Conflict in Cross-National Perspective." In *Urbanization and Conflict in Market Societies*, ed. K. R. Cox, 128–143. Chicago, Ill.: Maaroufa Press, 1978.

Appelbaum, E. "Restructuring Work: Temporary, Part-time and At-Home Employment." *In Computer Chips and Paper Clips: Technology and Women's Employment*, ed. Heidi Hartmann, Washington, D.C.: National Academy Press, 1986.

Ashton, Patrick J. "Urbanization and the Dynamics of Suburban Development under Capitalism." In *Marxism and the Metropolis: New Perspectives in Urban Political Economy*, ed. W. K. Tabb and L. Sawers, 54–81. New York: Oxford University Press, 1984.

Assaad, Ragui. "Structured Labour Markets: The Case of the Construction Sector in Egypt." Ph.D. diss., Cornell University, 1990.

Babcock, Blair. *Unfairly Structured Cities*. Oxford: Basil Blackwell, 1984.

Bailey, Thomas and Roger Waldinger. "The Changing Ethnic/Racial Division of Labor." In *Dual City: Restructuring New York*, ed. John Hull Mollenkopf and Manuel Castells, 43–78. New York: Russell Sage Foundation, 1991.

Bane, Mary Jo, and Paul Jargowsky, "Urban Poverty Areas: Basic Questions Concerning Prevalence, Growth, and Dynamics." Paper prepared for the Center for Health and Human Resource Policy, John F. Kennedy School of Government, Harvard University, Cambridge, Mass., Feb. 28, 1988.

Banfield, Edward C. *The Unheavenly City: The Nature and Future of Our Urban Crisis*. Boston: Little, Brown, 1968.

Baran, Barbara. "Technological Innovation and Deregulation: The Transformation of the Labor Process in the Insurance Industries." Working paper, Berkeley Roundtable on the International Economy, University of California, Berkeley, Calif., 1985.

Bauer, David. "The Question of Foreign Investment." *New York Affairs* 6, 2 (1982): 52–58.

Baumol, William J., et al. *Productivity and American Leadership: The Long View*. Cambridge, Mass.: MIT Press, 1989.

Bayer, Michael, Lynn Little, and Stephen Silver, eds. "Project U.S.A.: A Study of American Competitiveness and What Must Be Done to Restore It." Report prepared for the Graduate School of Management, Cornell University, Ithaca, N.Y., June 15, 1991.

Beckford, George. *Persistent Poverty: Underdevelopment in Plantation Economies*. New York: Oxford University Press, 1972.

Bennington, John. "Local Economic Strategies." *Local Economy* 1 (1986): 7–24.

Bergman, Edward, ed. *Local Economies in Transition*. Durham, N.C.: Duke University Press, 1986.

Berry, Brian J., and John D. Kasarda. *Contemporary Urban Ecology*. New York: Macmillan, 1977.

Blackburn, McKinley L., David E. Bloom and Richard B. Freeman. "The Declining Economic Position of Less Skilled American Men." In *A Future of Lousy Jobs: The Changing Structure of U.S. Wages*, ed. Gary Burtless, 31–67. Washington, D.C.: Brookings Institution, 1990.

Blakely, Edward J. *Planning Local Economic Development: Theory and Practice*. Newbury Park, Calif.: Sage, 1989.

Blauner, Robert. *Racial Oppression in America*. New York: Harper and Row, 1972.

Bluestone, Barry, and Bennett Harrison. *The Deindustrialization of America: Plant Closings, Community Abandonment, and the Dismantling of Basic Industry*. New York: Basic Books, 1982.

Boaden, N. *Urban Policy Making*. Cambridge, U.K.: Cambridge University Press, 1971.

Boston, Thomas. *Race, Class, and Conservatism*. Boston: Allen and Unwin, 1988.

Botwinick, Howard J. *Wage Differentials and the Competition of Capitals*. Princeton, N.J.: Princeton University Press, 1992.

Bradbury, Katherine L., and Lynne E. Browne. "Black Men in the Labor Market." *New England Economic Review* 18 (Mar./Apr. 1986): 32–42.

Brecher, Charles, and Raymond D. Horton, eds. *Setting Municipal Priorities, 1990*. New York: New York University Press, 1989.

Burns, L. "The Urban Income Distribution." *Regional Science and Urban Economics* 5 (1975): 465–485.

Burnstein, Paul. *Discrimination, Jobs, and Politics*. Chicago: University of Chicago Press, 1985.

Burtless, Gary, ed. *A Future of Lousy Jobs: The Changing Structure of U.S. Wages*. Washington, D.C.: Brookings Institution, 1990.

Caro, Robert. *The Power Broker*. New York: Knopf, 1974.

Chall, Daniel. "New York City's 'Skills Mismatch.'" *Federal Reserve Bank of New York Quarterly Review* 10 (Spring 1985): 20–27.

Chandler, Alfred. *The Visible Hand: The Managerial Revolution in American Business*. Cambridge, Mass.: Belknap Press, 1977.

Christopherson, Susan. "Emerging Patterns of Work in the U.S." Paper presented to the OECD Working Group on Technological Change and Human Resources, Columbia University, New York, N.Y., Sept. 1988.

Clark, W. A. V. "Residential Segregation in American Cities: A Review and Interpretation." *Population Research and Policy Review* 5 (1986): 95–127.

Clavel, Pierre. *The Progressive City*. New Brunswick, N.J.: Rutgers University Press, 1986.

Clavel, Pierre, and Nancy Kleniewski. "Space for Progressive Local Policy: Examples from the United States and the United Kingdom." In *Beyond the City Limits: Urban Policy and Economic Restructuring in Comparative Perspective*, ed. John R. Logan and Todd Swanstrom, 199–234. Philadelphia, Pa.: Temple University Press, 1990.

Clavel, Pierre, and Wim Wiewel. *Harold Washington and the Neighborhoods: Progressive City Government in Chicago, 1983–1987*. New Brunswick, N.J.: Rutgers University Press, 1991.

Clay, Phillip L. "The Process of Black Suburbanization," *Urban Affairs Quarterly* 14, 6 (1979): 405–424.

Coates, Robert C. *A Street Is Not a Home*. Buffalo: Prometheus Books, 1990.

Cohen, Robert B. "The New International Division of Labor, Multinational Corporations and Urban Hierarchy." In *Urbanization and Urban Planning in Capitalist Society*, ed. Michael Dear and Allen J. Scott, 287–315. London: Methuen, 1981.

Cohen, Stephen, D. Teece, L. Tyson, and J. Zysman. "Competitiveness." Working paper no. 8, Berkeley Roundtable on International Competitiveness, Berkeley, Calif., 1985.

Cohen, Stephen, and John Zysman. *Manufacturing Matters: The Myth of the Post Industrial Economy*. New York: Basic Books, 1987.

Council of Economic Advisors. *Economic Report of the President, 1991*. Washington, D.C.: U.S. Government Printing Office, 1991.

Daniels, Peter W. "New Office in the Suburbs." In *Suburban Growth: Geographical Process at the Edge of the Western City*, ed. J. E. Johnson, 177–200. Chicester: Wiley, 1974.

Danziger, Sheldon H. "Antipoverty Policy and Welfare Reform." Paper presented at the Rockefeller Foundation Conference on Welfare Reform, Williamsburg, Va., Feb. 16–18, 1988.

Darity, William A. "Racial Inequality in the Managerial Age: An Alternative Vision to the NRC Report." *American Economic Review* 80, 2 (1990): 247–251.

Davis, John Emmeus. *Contested Ground: Collective Action and the Urban Neighborhood*. Ithaca, N.Y.: Cornell University Press, 1991.

Dear, Michael, and Jennifer Wolch. *Landscapes of Despair: From Deinstitutionalization to Homelessness*. Princeton, N.J.: Princeton University Press, 1987.

DeGiovanni, Frank. "Patterns of Change in Housing Market Activity in Revitalizing Neighborhoods." *Journal of the American Planning Association* 49 (Winter 1983): 22–39.

Drennan, Matthew P. "The Decline and Rise of the New York Economy." In *Dual City: Restructuring New York*, ed. John Hull Mollenkopf and Manuel Castells, 25–41. New York: Russell Sage Foundation, 1991.

———. *An Econometric Model of the New York City Region*. New York: New York University Press, 1985.

———. "The Local Economy." In *Setting Municipal Priorities, 1990*, ed. Charles Brecher and Raymond D. Horton, 27–49. New York: New York University Press, 1989.

Duncan, Greg J. *Years of Poverty, Years of Plenty: The Changing Economic Fortunes of American Workers and Families*. Ann Arbor, Mich.: Survey Research Center, Institute for Social Research, University of Michigan, 1984.

Eargle, Judith. *Household Wealth and Asset Ownership, 1988*. Current Population Reports, Household Economic Studies, Series P-70, No. 22. Washington, D.C.: U.S. Department of Commerce, Bureau of the Census, 1990.

Edsall, Thomas Byrne. "Race." *Atlantic Monthly* 267, 5 (1991): 53–86.

Eisner, Robert. "Our Real Deficits." *Journal of the American Planning Association* 57, 2 (1991): 131–135.

Ellwood, David. *Poor Support: Poverty in the American Family*. New York: Basic Books, 1988.

———. "The Spatial Mismatch Hypothesis: Are There Teenage Jobs Missing in the Ghetto?" In *The Black Youth Employment Crisis*, ed. R. Freeman and H. Holzer, 147–190. Chicago: University of Chicago Press, 1986.

Fainstein, Norman I. "The Underclass/Mismatch Hypothesis as an Explanation for Black Economic Deprivation." *Politics and Society* 15, 4 (1986–87): 403–451.

Fainstein, Susan S. "Economics, Politics, and Development Policy: The Convergence of New York and London." In *Beyond the City Limits: Urban Policy and Economic Restructuring in Comparative Perspective*, ed. John R. Logan and Todd Swanstrom, 119–149. Philadelphia, Pa.: Temple University Press, 1990.

Falk, William W., and Thomas A. Lyson. *High Tech, Low Tech, No Tech: Recent Industrial and Occupational Change in the South*. Albany, N.Y.: State University of New York Press, 1988.

Farley, Reynolds, and Steven Schecterman. "The Social and Economic Status of Blacks: Does It Vary by Size of Metropolis?" Photocopy, Population Studies Center, University of Michigan, Ann Arbor, Mich., June 1990.

Fernández-Kelly, Maria Patricia. *For We Are Sold, I and My People: Women and Industry in Mexico's Frontier*. Albany, N.Y.: State University of New York Press, 1983.

Foley, Donald. "The Suburbanization of Administrative Offices in the San Francisco Bay Area." Research report no. 10, Real Estate Research Program, Berkeley, Calif., 1957.

Frank, Robert, and Richard Freeman. "The Distributional Consequences of Direct Foreign Investment." In *The Impact of International Trade and Investment on Employment: A Conference of the U.S. Department of Labor*, ed. William Dewald, 153–176. Washington, D.C.: U.S. Government Printing Office, 1978.

Freedman, Marcia. "Urban Labor Markets and Ethnicity: Segments and Shelters Reexamined." In *Urban Ethnicity in the United States: New Immigrants and Old Minorities*, ed. L. Maldonado and J. Moore, 145–165. Urban Affairs Annual Reviews, vol. 29. Beverly Hills, Calif.: Sage, 1985.

Freeman, Christopher, John Clark, and Luc Soete. *Unemployment and Technical Innovation: A Study of Long Waves and Economic Development*. Westport, Conn.: Greenwood Press, 1982.

Freeman, R. B., and B. Hall. "Permanent Homelessness in America?" *Population Research and Policy Review* 6, 1 (1987): 3–27.

Friedmann, John, and Goetz Wolff. "World City Formation: An Agenda for Research and Action." *International Journal of Urban and Regional Research* 6 (1982): 309–344.

Fröbel, Folker, Jurgen Heinrichs, and Otto Kreye. *The New International Division of Labor: Structural Unemployment in Industrialized Countries and Industrialization in Developing Countries.* Cambridge: Cambridge University Press, 1980.

Frug, Gerald. "The City as a Legal Concept." *Harvard Law Review* 93, 6 (1980): 1059–1154.

Fulton, P. "Public Transportation: Solving the Commuting Problem?" *Transportation Research Record* 928 (1983): 3.

Galbraith, John Kenneth. *A Tenured Professor: A Novel.* Boston, Mass.: Houghton Mifflin, 1990.

Garofalo, Gaspar, and Michael S. Fogarty. "Urban Income Distribution: The Urban Hierarchy-Inequality Hypothesis." *Review of Economics and Statistics* 61, 3 (1979): 381–388.

Gilder, George. *Wealth and Poverty.* New York: Basic Books, 1981.

Giloth, Robert P., and Robert Mier. "Spatial Change and Social Justice: Alternative Economic Development in Chicago." *Economic Restructuring and Political Response,* ed. Robert A. Beauregard 181–208. Urban Affairs Annual Reviews, vol. 34. Beverly Hills, Calif.: Sage, 1989.

Glickman, Norman J. "Cities and the International Division of Labor." Working paper no. 31, Lyndon B. Johnson School of Public Affairs, University of Texas, Austin, Tex., 1985.

Glickman, Norman J., and Amy K. Glasmeier. "The International Economy and the American South." In *Deindustrialization and Regional Economic Transformation: The Experience of the United States,* ed. Lloyd Rodwin and Hidehiko Sazanami, 60–80. Boston, Mass.: Unwin Hyman, 1989.

Glickman, Norman J., and Douglas P. Woodward. *The New Competitors: How Foreign Investors Are Changing the U.S. Economy.* New York: Basic Books, 1989.

Goddard, J. B. *Office Location in Urban and Regional Development.* London: Oxford University Press, 1975.

Gold, Steven D. "State Fiscal Conditions." In *Urban Change and Poverty,* ed. Michael G. H. McGeary and Laurence E. Lynn, 284–307. Washington, D.C.: National Academy Press, 1988.

Goldsmith, William W. "Bringing the Third World Home: Enterprise Zones." *Working Papers Magazine* 9, 2 (1982): 24–30.

———. "The Ghetto as a Resource for Black America." *Journal of the American Institute of Planners* 40, 1 (1974): 17–30.

———. "Poverty and Profit in Urban Growth and Decline." In *Race, Poverty and the Urban Underclass*, ed. Clement Cottingham, 35–59. Lexington, Mass.: Heath, 1982.

Goldsmith, William W., and Michael Derian. "Is There an Urban Policy?" *Journal of Regional Science* 19, 1 (1979): 93–198.

Goldsmith, William W., and Harvey Jacobs. "The Improbability of Urban Policy: The Case of the United States." *Journal of the American Planning Association* 48, 1 (1982): 53–66.

Goldsmith, William W., and Mario Rothschild. "The Effect of Regional Specialization on Local Economic Activity: A Study of Chile." *Papers of the Regional Science Association* 31 (1974): 183–201.

Goldsmith, William W., and Thomas Vietorisz. "Operation Bootstrap, Industrial Autonomy, and a Parallel Economy for Puerto Rico." *International Regional Science Review* 4, 1 (1979): 1–22.

Goodman, Robert. *The Last Entrepreneurs: America's Regional Wars for Jobs and Dollars*. New York: Simon and Schuster, 1979.

Gordon, David M. "Capitalist Development and the History of American Cities." In *Marxism and the Metropolis: New Perspectives in Urban Political Economy*, ed. W. K. Tabb and L. Sawers, 21–53. New York: Oxford University Press, 1984.

———. "The Global Economy: New Edifice or Crumbling Foundation?" *New Left Review* (Apr. 1988): 24–64.

Gorz, Andre. *Critique of Economic Reason*. Trans. Gillian Handyside and Chris Turner. New York: Verso, 1989.

Greenstein, Robert, and Scott Barancik. *Drifting Apart: New Findings on Growing Income Disparities Between the Rich, the Poor, and the Middle Class*. Washington, D.C.: Center on Budget and Policy Priorities, 1990.

Grier, Eunice, and George Grier. *Minorities in Suburbia: A Mid-1980's Update*. Washington, D.C.: Urban Institute, 1988.

Gunn, Christopher, and Hazel Dayton Gunn. *Reclaiming Capital: Democratic Initiatives and Community Development*. Ithaca, N.Y.: Cornell University Press, 1991.

Hagen, Everett Einar. *Economics of Development*. Homewood, Ill.: Irwin, 1986.

Harrison, Bennett. "Ghetto Economic Development: A Survey." *Journal of Economic Literature* 12 (1974).

———. "Regional Restructuring and 'Good Business Climate': The Economic Transformation of New England since World War II." In *Sunbelt/Snowbelt: Urban Development and Regional Restructuring*, ed. Larry Sawers and William K. Tabb, 48–96. New York: Oxford University Press, 1984.

Harrison, Bennett, and Barry Bluestone. *The Great U-Turn: Corporate Restructuring and the Polarizing of America*. New York: Basic Books, 1988.

Harrison, Bennett, and Lucy Gorham. "What Happened to Black Wages in the 1980s: Family Incomes, Individual Earnings, and the Growth of the African American Middle Class." Working paper no. 90– 1, Carnegie Mellon University School of Urban and Public Affairs, Pittsburgh, Pa., 1990.

Hartman, Chester. "Comment on 'Neighborhood Revitalization and Displacement: A Review of the Evidence.'" *Journal of the American Planning Association* 45 (October 1979): 488–491.

Harvey, David. *The Limits to Capital*. Chicago: University of Chicago Press, 1982.

Haworth, C. T., J. Long, and D. Rasmussen. "Income Distribution, City Size, and Urban Growth." *Urban Studies* 15, 1 (1978): 1–7.

Hayden, Dolores. *Redesigning the American Dream: The Future of Housing, Work, and Family Life*. New York: W. W. Norton, 1984.

Henderson, Hazel. *The Politics of the Solar Age: Alternatives to Economics*. Garden City, N.Y.: Anchor Press/Doubleday, 1981.

Herbers, John. "The Kerner Report: A Journalist's View." In *Quiet Riots: Race and Poverty in the United States*, ed. Fred R. Harris and Roger W. Wilkins, 16–26. New York: Pantheon, 1988.

Herz, Diane E. "Worker Displacement Still Common in the Late 1980s." *Monthly Labor Review* 14, 5 (1991): 3–9.

Hill, Edward W., and Thomas Bier. "Economic Restructuring, Earnings, Occupations, and Housing Values in Cleveland." *Economic Development Quarterly* 3, 2 (1989): 123–144.

Hill, Polly. *The Migrant Cocoa Farmers of Southern Ghana: A Study in Rural Capitalism*. Cambridge, U.K.: Cambridge University Press, 1963.

Hirsch, B. "Income Distribution, City Size, and Urban Growth: A Reexamination." *Urban Studies* 19 (Feb. 1982): 71–74.

Hirsch, Seev. *Location of Industry and International Competitiveness*. Oxford: Clarendon Press, 1967.

Hirschman, Albert O. *The Rhetoric of Reaction*. Cambridge, Mass.: Harvard University Press, 1991.

Hoos, I. *Automation in the Office*. Washington, D.C.: Public Affairs Press, 1961.

Hymer, Stephen. *The Multinational Corporation: A Radical Approach*. Ed. Robert Cohen et al. Cambridge and New York: Cambridge University Press, 1979.

Jackson, Kenneth. *Crabgrass Frontier: The Suburbanization of the United States*. New York: Oxford University Press, 1985.

Jacobs, Jane. *Cities and the Wealth of Nations*. New York: Random House, 1984.

Jargowsky, Paul A., and Mary Jo Bane. "Ghetto Poverty: Basic Questions." In *Inner City Poverty in the United States*, ed. Laurence E. Lynn and G. H. McGeary. Washington, D.C.: National Academy Press, 1990.

Jaynes, Gerald D., and Robin M. Williams, Jr., eds. *A Common Destiny: Blacks in American Society*. Washington, D.C.: National Academy Press, 1989.

Jenkins, R. "Divisions over the International Division of Labor." *Capital and Class* 22 (Spring 1984): 28–57.

Jones, D., and R. Hall. "Office Suburbanization in the United States." *Town and Country Planning* 40 (1972): 470–473.

Kain, John F., and Joseph Persky. "Alternatives to the Gilded Ghetto." Discussion paper no. 21, Program on Regional and Urban Economics, Harvard University, Cambridge, Mass., 1968.

Kantor, Paul. "A Case for a National Urban Policy: Governmentalization of Economic Dependency." *Urban Affairs Quarterly* 26, 3 (1990): 394–415.

Kasarda, John. "Jobs, Migration and Emerging Urban Mismatches." In *Urban Change and Poverty*, ed. Michael G. H. McGeary and L. E. Lynn, Jr., 148–198. Washington, D.C.: National Academy Press, 1988.

———. "Urban Industrial Transition and the Underclass." *Annals of the American Academy of Political and Social Science* 501 (Jan. 1989): 26–47.

Kerner Commission. *Report of the National Advisory Commission on Civil Disorders*. New York: Dutton, 1968.

Kolko, Joyce. *Restructuring the World Economy*. New York: Pantheon, 1988.

Krumholz, Norman, and John Forester. *Making Equity Planning Work: Leadership in the Public Sector*. Philadelphia, Pa.: Temple University Press, 1990.

Lall, Betty, ed. "Economic Dislocation and Job Loss." New York: Extension and Public-Service Division, New York State School of Industrial Relations, Metropolitan District, Cornell University, 1985.

Landau, Madeline. *Race, Poverty and the Cities: Hyperinnovation in Complex Policy Systems*. Berkeley, Calif.: Institute for Governmental Studies, University of California, 1988.

Landis, John. "The Future of America's Central Cities." Working paper no. 486, Institute of Urban and Regional Development, Berkeley, Calif., 1988.

Lawrence, R. *Can America Compete?* Washington, D.C.: Brookings Institution, 1984.

Leacock, Eleanor Burke, ed. *The Culture of Poverty: A Critique*. New York: Simon and Schuster, 1971.

Lemann, Nicholas. *The Promised Land*. New York: Knopf, 1991.

———. "The Unfinished War." *Atlantic Monthly* (Jan. 1989): 37–56.

Leonard, Jonathan S. "The Interaction of Residential Segregation and Employment Discrimination." NBER working paper no. 1274, National Bureau of Economic Research, Cambridge, Mass., 1984.

Lerner, Daniel. *The Passing of Traditional Society*. New York: Free Press of Glencoe, 1958.

Levitan, Sar, and Isaac Shapiro. *Working but Poor: America's Contradictions*. Baltimore: Johns Hopkins University Press, 1987.

Lewis, Oscar. *Five Families: Mexican Case Studies in the Culture of Poverty*. New York: Basic Books, 1959.

Lichter, D. T. "Racial Differences in Underemployment in American Cities." *American Journal of Sociology* 93 (Jan. 1988): 771–792.

Liebow, Elliot. *Tally's Corner: A Study of Negro Street Corner Men*. Boston: Little, Brown, 1967.

Linder, Staffan. *An Essay on Trade and Transformation*. New York: Wiley, 1961.

Lipietz, Alain. "Imperialism or the Beast of the Apocalypse." *Capital and Class* 22 (Spring 1984): 81–109.

Livingstone, Ken. *If Voting Changed Anything, They'd Abolish It*. Glasgow: Fontana Paperbacks, 1987.

Logan, John, and Harvey Molotch. *Urban Fortunes: The Political Economy of Place*. Berkeley, Calif.: University of California Press, 1987.

Logan, John R., and Todd Swanstrom, eds. *Beyond the City Limits: Urban Policy and Economic Restructuring in Comparative Perspective*. Philadelphia, Pa.: Temple University Press, 1990.

Loveman, G. W., and Chris Tilly. "Good Jobs or Bad Jobs: What Does the Evidence Say?" *New England Economic Review* 20 (Jan./Feb. 1988): 46–65.

Luria, Dan, and Jack Russell. *Rational Reindustrialization: An Economic Development Agenda for Detroit*. Detroit, Mich.: Widgetripper Press, 1981.

Lynn, Laurence E., and G. H. McGeary. *Inner City Poverty in the United States*. Washington, D.C.: National Academy Press, 1990.

McClelland, David C. *The Achieving Society*. Princeton, N.J.: Van Nostrand, 1961.

McGeary, Michael G. H., and Laurence E. Lynn, eds. *Urban Change and Poverty*. Washington, D.C.: National Academy Press, 1988.

McKenzie, Richard. *Competing Visions: The Political Conflict over America's Economic Future*. Washington, D.C.: Cato Institute, 1985.

Maire, Edmond. "Le chómage zéro, c'est possible." *Alternatives économiques* 48 (June 1987).

Marcuse, Peter. "Gentrification, Abandonment, and Displacement: Connections, Causes, and Policy Responses in New York City." *Journal of Urban Contemporary Law* 28 (1985): 195–240.

Markusen, Ann. R. *The Rise of the Gunbelt: The Military Remapping of Industrial America*. New York: Oxford University Press, 1991.

———. "Steel and Southeast Chicago: Reasons and Opportunities for Industrial Renewal." Research report to the Mayor's Task Force on Steel and Southeast Chicago, Center for Urban Affairs and Policy Research, Northwestern University, Evanston, Ill., Nov. 1985.

Markusen, Ann R., and Virginia Carlson. "Deindustrialization in the American Midwest: Causes and Responses." In *Deindustrialization and Regional Economic Transformation*, ed. Lloyd Rodwin and Hidehiko Sazanami, 29–59. Boston: Unwin Hyman, 1989.

Markusen, Ann R., Peter Hall, and Amy Glasmeier. *High Tech America: The What, How, Where, and Why of the Sunrise Industries*. Boston: Allen and Unwin, 1986.

Marris, Peter. *Community Planning and Conceptions of Change*. London: Routledge and Kegan Paul, 1982.

Massey, Douglas. "Ethnic Residential Segregation: A Theoretical Synthesis and Empirical Review." *Sociology and Social Research* 69, 3 (1985): 315–350.

Massey, Douglas, and Nancy Denton. "Hypersegregation in U.S. Metropolitan Areas: Black and Hispanic Segregation along Five Dimensions." *Demography* 26, 3 (1989): 373–389.

———. "Trends in Residential Segregation of Blacks, Hispanics and Asians, 1970–1980." *American Sociological Review* 52, 6 (1987): 802–825.

Mayer, Susan, and Christopher Jencks. "Growing Up in Poor Neighborhoods: How Much Does It Matter." *Science* 242 (Mar. 17, 1989): 1441–1447.

Mead, Lawrence M. "Expectations and Welfare Work: WIN in New York State." *Polity* 23, 2 (Winter 1985): 224–252.

Meyer, John, and José Gómez-Ibáñez. *Autos, Transit and Cities*. Cambridge, Mass.: Harvard University Press, 1981.

Mier, Robert E., Joan Fitzgerald, and Lewis Randolph. "African-American Elected Officials and the Future of Progressive Political Movements." In *Economic Development Policy Formation: Experiences in the United States and the United Kingdom*, ed. David Fasenfest. New York: St. Martins Press, 1992.

Mier, Robert, K. J. Moe, and I. Sherr. "Strategic Planning and the Pursuit of Reform, Economic Development, and Equity." *Journal of the American Planning Association* 52 (1986): 299–309.

Miller, Vincent P., and John M. Quigley. "Segregation by Racial and Demographic Group: Evidence from the San Francisco Bay Area." *Urban Studies* 27, 1 (1990): 3–21.

Mincy, Ronald. "Industrial Restructuring, Dynamic Events and the Racial Composition of Concentrated Poverty." Paper prepared for the Social Science Research Council, New York, N.Y., Sept. 12, 1988.

Mishel, Lawrence, and David M. Frankel. *The State of Working America, 1990–1991*. Armonk, N.Y.: M. E. Sharp, 1991.

Mollenkopf, John H. *The Contested City*. Princeton, N.J.: Princeton University Press, 1983.

———. "Paths toward the Post Industrial Service City: The Northeast and the Southwest." In *Cities under Stress: The Fiscal Crises of Urban America*, ed. R. W. Burchell and D. Listokin, 77–112. New Brunswick: Center for Urban Policy Research, Rutgers, State University of New Jersey, 1981.

Mollenkopf, John H., and Manuel Castells, ed. *Dual City: Restructuring New York*. New York: Russell Sage Foundation, 1991.

Murray, Charles. *Losing Ground: American Social Policy*. New York: Basic Books, 1984.

Nelson, Kirstin. "Labor Demand, Labor Supply and the Suburbanization of Low-wage Office Work." In *Production, Work and Territory: The Geographical Anatomy of Industrial Capitalism*, ed. Allen J. Scott and Michael Storper, 149–171. Boston: Allen and Unwin, 1986.

Noble, David F. *America by Design: Science, Technology, and the Rise of Corporate Capitalism*. Oxford: Oxford University Press, 1977.

Noyelle, Thierry J. "Advanced Services in the System of Cities." In *Local Economies in Transition: Policy Realities and Development Potentials*, ed. Edward Bergman, 143–164. Durham, N.C.: Duke University Press, 1986.

Noyelle, Thierry J., and Thomas M. Stanback. *The Economic Transformation of American Cities*. Totowa, N.J.: Rowman and Allenheld, 1984.

O'Connor, James. *The Fiscal Crisis of the State.* New York: St. Martin's Press, 1973.

Office of Technology Assessment (OTA). *Technology and Structural Unemployment: Re-employing Displaced Adults.* Washington, D.C.: U.S. Government Printing Office, 1986.

O'Regan, Katherine M., and John M. Quigley. "Labor Market Access and the Labor Market Outcomes for Urban Youth." *Regional Science and Urban Economics* 21 (1991): 277–293.

Organisation for Economic Co-operation and Development (OECD). "Analysis of Fiscal Policies." *OECD Economic Outlook* 48 (1990): 113–116.

———. *OECD Economic Outlook: Historical Statistics 1960–1988.* Paris: OECD, 1989.

Palmer, John, and Isabel Sawhill. *The Reagan Experiment.* Washington, D.C.: Urban Institute Press, 1982.

Patterson, James T. *America's Struggle Against Poverty, 1900–1985.* Cambridge, Mass.: Harvard University Press, 1986.

Perez, Carlota. "Structural Change and Assimilation of New Technologies in the Economic and Social Systems." *Futures* 15, 5 (1983): 357–375.

Perlman, Janice E. *The Myth of Marginality: Urban Poverty and Politics in Rio de Janeiro.* Berkeley, Calif.: University of California Press, 1976.

Perna, Nicholas S. "The Shift from Manufacturing to Services: A Concerned View." *New England Economic Review* 9 (Jan./Feb. 1987): 30–38.

Peterson, Paul. *City Limits.* Chicago: University of Chicago Press, 1981.

Peterson, Paul E., ed. *The New Urban Reality.* Washington, D.C.: Brookings Institution, 1985.

Philips, Kevin. *The Politics of Rich and Poor.* New York: Random House, 1990.

Phillips, Robin S., and Avis C. Vidal. "The Growth and Restructuring of Metropolitan Economies: The Context for Economic Development Policy." *Journal of the American Planning Association* 49, 3 (1983): 291–306.

Piore, Michael, and Charles Sabel. *The Second Industrial Divide: Possibilities for Prosperity.* New York: Basic Books, 1984.

Piven, Francis, and Richard Cloward. *Regulating the Poor: The Functions of Public Welfare.* New York: Pantheon, 1971.

Portes, Alejandro, and John Walton. *Labor, Class, and the International System.* New York: Academic Press, 1981.

Pred, Alan. *City Systems in Advanced Economies*. New York: Wiley, 1977.

Quigley, John, and Daniel Rubinfeld. *American Domestic Priorities*. Berkeley, Calif.: University of California Press, 1985.

Rabin, Yale. "Metropolitan Decentralization, Transit Dependence, and the Employment Isolation of Central City Black Workers. Paper prepared for Symposium on the Role of Housing Mobility in Achieving Equal Opportunity for Minorities, Urban Institute, Washington, D.C., Apr. 21–22, 1988.

Radice, Hugo. "Capital, Labor and the State in the World Economy." Lecture presented at Cornell University, Ithaca, N.Y., Sept. 1987.

Reich, Robert B. "The Real Economy." *Atlantic Monthly* 267, 2 (1991): 35–52.

Rieder, Jonathan. *Carnarsie: The Jews and Italians of Brooklyn Against Liberalism*. Cambridge, Mass.: Harvard University Press, 1985.

Rodriguez, N. P., and J. R. Feagin. "Urban Specialization in the World System: An Investigation of Historical Cases." *Urban Affairs Quarterly* 22, 2 (1986): 187–220.

Rose, Stephen J. *The American Profile Poster: Who Owns What, Who Makes How Much, Who Works Where, and Who Lives with Whom*. New York: Pantheon, 1986.

Rossi, Peter H., and James D. Wright. "The Urban Homeless: A Portrait of Urban Dislocation." *Annals of the American Academy of Political and Social Sciences* 501 (1989): 132–142.

Rymarowicz, L., and D. Zimmerman. *The Effect of Federal Tax and Budget Policies in the 1980s on the State-Local Sector*. Washington, D.C.: Congressional Research Service, 1986.

Salinas, Patricia. "Subemployment and the Urban Underclass: A Policy Research Report." Paper distributed by Graduate Program in Community and Regional Planning, University of Texas, Austin, Tex., 1980.

———. "Urban Growth, Subemployment, and Mobility." In *Local Economies in Transition: Policy Realities and Development Potentials*, ed. E. M. Bergman, 248–270. Durham, N.C.: Duke University Press, 1986.

Sandefur, Gary D. "Blacks, Hispanics, American Indians, and Poverty—and What Worked." In *Quiet Riots: Race and Poverty in the United States*, ed. Fred R. Harris and Roger W. Wilkins, 46–74. New York: Pantheon, 1988.

Sassen, Saskia, "The Informal Economy." In *Dual City: Restructuring New York*, ed. John H. Mollenkopf and Manuel Castells, 79–102. New York: Russell Sage Foundation, 1991.

———. *The Mobility of Labor and Capital: A Study in International Investment and Labor Flow*. Cambridge and New York: Cambridge University Press, 1988.

Sassen-Koob, Saskia. "The New Labor Demand in Global Cities." In *Cities in Transformation: Class, Capital, and the State*, ed. Michael Smith, 139–171. Urban Affairs Annual Review, vol. 26. Beverly Hills, Calif.: Sage, 1984.

———. "Recomposition and Peripheralization at the Core." *Contemporary Marxism* 5 (1982): 88–100.

Sawers, Larry, and William Tabb, eds. *Sunbelt/Snowbelt: Urban Development and Regional Restructuring*. New York: Oxford University Press, 1984.

Saxenian, Anna Lee. "The Cheshire Cat's Grin: Innovation, Regional Development and the Cambridge Case." *Economy and Society* 18, 4 (Nov. 1989): 448–477.

Schill, Michael H., and Richard P. Nathan. *Revitalizing America's Cities: Neighborhood Reinvestment and Displacement*. Albany, N.Y.: State University of New York Press, 1983.

Schulman, S. "Discrimination, Human Capital, and Black-White Unemployment: Evidence from Cities." *Journal of Human Resources* 22, 3 (1987): 361–376.

Scott, Allen. *Metropolis: From the Division of Labor to Urban Form*. Berkeley, Calif.: University of California Press, 1988.

Scott, Allen J., and Michael Storper. "Production, Work, Territory: Contemporary Realities and Theoretical Tasks." In *Production, Work, and Territory: The Geographical Anatomy of Industrial Capitalism*, ed. Allen Scott and Michael Storper, 3–15. Boston: Allen and Unwin, 1986.

Shaikh, Anwar. "Laws of Production and Laws of Algebra: Humbug II." In *Growth, Profits and Property: Essays in the Revival of Political Economy*, ed. Edward J. Nell, 80–95. Cambridge: Cambridge University Press, 1980.

Shearer, Derek. "In Search of Equal Partnerships: Prospects for Progressive Urban Policy in the 1990s." In *Unequal Partnerships: The Political Economy of Urban Redevelopment in Postwar America*, ed. Gregory D. Squires, 289–307. New Brunswick, N.J.: Rutgers University Press, 1989.

Sheets, Robert, Stephen Nord, and John Phelps. *The Impact of Service Industries on Underemployment in Metropolitan Economies*. Lexington, Mass.: Lexington Books, 1987.

Shlay, Anne B., and Robert P. Giloth. "Social Organization of a Land

Based Elite: The Case of the Failed Chicago 1992 World's Fair." *Journal of Urban Affairs* 9, 4 (1986): 305–324.

Silvestri, Gary, and John Lukasiewicz. "Projections of Occupational Employment, 1988–2000." *Monthly Labor Review* 112, 11 (Nov. 1988): 42–65.

Singer, Paul T. *Economia Política da Urbanização* (Political Economy of Urbanization). Sáo Paulo: Editora Brasiliense, 1973.

Soja, Edward W. "Economic Restructuring and the Internationalization of the Los Angeles Region." In *The Capitalist City*, ed. P. E. Smith and J. R. Feagin, 178–198. New York: Basil Blackwell, 1987.

———. *Postmodern Geographies: The Reassertion of Space in Critical Social Theory*. London: Verso, 1987.

Solloway, Michele R. "Labor and Health Policy in the 1990s: Meeting the Challenge of a Changing Economy," Ph.D. thesis, University of California at Berkeley, 1991.

Sowell, Thomas. *A Conflict of Visions*. New York: W. Morrow, 1987.

Stanback, Thomas. *Understanding the Service Economy: Employment, Productivity, Location*. Baltimore: Johns Hopkins University Press, 1979.

Stanback, Thomas M., and Richard Knight. *Suburbanization and the City*. New York: Allanheld, Osmun, 1976.

Stanback, Thomas, and Thierry Noyelle. *Cities in Transition*. Totowa, N.J.: Rowman and Allanheld, 1982.

Steinberg, Stephen. "The Underclass: A Case of Color Blindness." *New Politics* 11, 3 (1989): 142–166.

Stockman, David Allan. *The Triumph of Politics: How the Reagan Revolution Failed*. New York: Harper and Row, 1986.

Stone, Michael. "Housing and the American Economy: A Marxist Perspective." In *Urban and Regional Planning in an Age of Austerity*, ed. Pierre Clavel, John Forester, and William W. Goldsmith, 81–108. New York: Pergamon Press, 1980.

Storper, Michael, and Richard Walker. *The Capitalist Imperative: Territory, Technology and Industrial Growth*. Oxford: Basil Blackwell, 1989.

Tanzer, Michael. *The Political Economy of International Oil and the Underdeveloped Countries*. Boston: Beacon Press, 1969.

Thompson, Wilbur. "The National System of Cities as an Object of Public Policy." *Urban Studies* 9, 1 (1972): 99–116.

Thurow, Lester C. "Regional Transformation and the Service Activities." In *Deindustrialization and Regional Economic Transformation: The Experience of the United States*, ed. Lloyd Rodwin and Hidehiko Sazanami, 179–198. Boston: Unwin Hyman, 1989.

———. "Surge in Inequality." *Scientific American* 256, 5 (1987): 30–37.

Thurow, Lester C., and L. Tyson. "Adjusting the U.S. Trade Imbalance: A Black Hole in the World Economy." Working paper no. 24, Berkeley Roundtable on the International Economy, University of California, Berkeley, Calif., 1987.

Tobin, G. A., ed. "Divided Neighborhoods: Changing Patterns of Racial Segregation." *Urban Affairs Annual Review* 32. Newbury Park, Calif.: Sage Publications, 1987.

Tumminia, A. E. "Locational Factors for the Office Function of Industry." Masters' thesis, Columbia University, 1953.

Turner, Margery, and Michael Fix, "Opportunities Denied, Opportunities Diminished," Report from the Urban Institute, Washington, D.C., May 1991.

U.S. Congress. Joint Economic Committee. *Falling Behind: The Growing Income Gap in America*. Washington, D.C.: U.S. Government Printing Office, 1991.

———. House Committee on Ways and Means. *Overview of Entitlement Programs: Green Book, 1991*. Washington, D.C.: U.S. Government Printing Office, 1991.

———. House Select Committee on Children, Youth and Families. *Barriers and Opportunities for America's Young Black Men*. Hearing, 101st Cong., 1st sess., July 25, 1989. Washington, D.C.: U.S. Government Printing Office, 1989.

U.S. Department of Commerce. Bureau of the Census. *Current Population Survey*. Washington, D.C., 1990; computer tape, 1991.

———. *Current Population Survey, Money Income and Poverty Status in the United States*. Series P-60. Washington, D.C.: U.S. Government Printing Office [various years].

———. *Demographic State of the Nation*. Washington, D.C.: U.S. Government Printing Office, 1990.

———. *Statistical Abstracts of the United States*. Washington, D.C.: U.S. Government Printing Office, 1989.

U.S. Department of Labor. Bureau of Labor Statistics. *Employment and Earnings*, 38, 4 (Apr. 1991). Washington, D.C.: U.S. Government Printing Office.

U.S. President's Commission on Industrial Competitiveness. *Global Competition: The New Reality*. Washington, D.C.: U.S. Government Printing Office, 1985.

U.S. Public Health Service. *Health, United States*. Washington, D.C.: U.S. Government Printing Office, 1990.

Valentine, Charles A. *Culture and Poverty: Critique and Counter-Proposals*. Chicago, Ill.: University of Chicago Press, 1968.

Vergara, Camilo José. "Big Apple Follies." *Planning* 57, 7 (1991).

Vietorisz, Thomas. "Global Information," unpublished MS., Ithaca, N.Y., 1991.

Vietorisz, Thomas, William Goldsmith, and Robert Mier. "Urban Poverty Strategies: A Comparison of Latin America and the United States." School of Architecture and Urban Planning, University of California, Los Angeles, 1975.

Vietorisz, Thomas, Bennett Harrison, and Robert Mier. "Full Employment at Living Wages." *Annals of the American Academy of Political and Social Sciences* 418 (March 1975): 94–107.

Walker, Richard. "The Geographical Organization of Production Systems." *Environment and Planning: Society and Space* 6 (1988): 377–408.

———. "A Theory of Suburbanization: Capitalism and the Construction of Urban Space in the U.S." In *Urbanization and Urban Planning in a Capitalist Society*, ed. Michael Dear and A. J. Scott, 383–429. London: Methuen, 1981.

Walters, Jonathan. "Cities on Their Own." *Governing* 4, 7 (1991): 26–32.

Watkins, Alfred J. *The Practice of Urban Economics*. Sage Library of Social Research, vol. 107. Beverly Hills, Calif.: Sage, 1980.

Wehler, Cheryl. *Survey on Childhood Hunger*. Washington, D.C.: Food Research and Action Center, Community Childhood Hunger Identification Project, 1991.

Weinstein, Bernard L., and Robert E. Firestine. *Regional Growth and Decline in the United States: The Rise of the Sunbelt and the Decline of the Northeast*. New York: Praeger, 1978.

Wilger, Robert J. "Black-White Residential Segregation in 1980." Ph.D. diss., University of Michigan, 1988.

Williamson, Jeffrey G. "Productivity and American Leadership: A Review Article." *Journal of Economic Literature* 29, 1 (1991): 51–68.

Williamson, Jeffrey G., and Peter G. Lindert. *American Inequality: A Macroeconomic History*. New York: Academic Press, 1980.

Wilson, Patricia. "The New Maquiladoras: Flexible Manufacturing and Local Linkages. In *The Maquiladora Industry: Economic Solution or Problem*? ed. Khosrow Fatemi. New York: Praeger, 1990.

Wilson, William J. "The Underclass: Issues, Perspectives, and Public Policy." *The Annals of the American Academy of Political and Social Sciences* 501 (1989): 182–192.

———. *The Truly Disadvantaged: The Inner City, the Underclass, and Public Policy*. Chicago: University of Chicago Press, 1987.

Wolff, Edward N. "Wealth Holdings and Poverty Status in the U.S." *Review of Income and Wealth* 36, 2 (1990): 143–165.

Working Seminar on Family and American Welfare Policy. *The New Consensus on Family and Welfare*. Washington, D.C.: American Enterprise Institute for Public Policy Research, 1987.

Yates, Daniel. *The Ungovernable City*. Cambridge, Mass.: MIT Press, 1977.

Index